READING
MATTERS

ARMINLEAR

Library of Congress Control Number: 2022932531

ISBN (hardcover): 978-1-956450-20-0
(paperback): 978-1-956450-14-9
(eBook): 978-1-956450-15-6

 Armin Lear Press Inc
215 W Riverside Drive, #4362
Estes Park, CO 80517

READING
MATTERS

How Literature Influences Life

Janet Levine

For my grandchildren
Aza, Lee, Rilla
May their love of reading become lifelong treasure

CONTENTS

INTRODUCTION

Reading great literature can unlock your mind.

In *Reading Matters* we uncover how this process works by closely exploring the texts specifically chosen for this purpose, and their intellectual and artistic significance. We engage with the mind of an accomplished writer—in fiction through characters' minds, in nonfiction directly in the text. Something of what we are reading may touch us, fomenting change in our brain and perhaps change in our minds to a greater or lesser degree. Occasionally, we may experience a volcanic insight. We might find ourselves saying, "This blew my mind!"

Maybe the books we explore open our awareness to ideas we've never thought of—or to an experience we remember in some way. When the books jolt us into recalling those moments, usually subconsciously, a switch clicks on, and we see perceptions and assumptions that we've looked at before in a new light. This may occur in an instantaneous epiphany. Or it might be an epiphany that forms incrementally over time.

Somehow, somewhere in our consciousness, gossamer threads of memory of experiences, place and time reside primed to be triggered.

We all hold rich, inner worlds of associative thinking that are deeply part of ourselves. Worlds that in some way challenge and even change our assumptions.

These experiences—whether "ah-ha" moments or more gradual epiphanies—are what I aspire for us to experience in reading this book. The texts are chosen intentionally to challenge us to think, either to enhance our current thinking or to invite us to think in new ways about the major issues of the human condition into which they delve. These literary works—both timely and timeless and from across continents—explore consequential issues, one in each chapter, such as moral responsibility, possibilities of redemption, spiritual journeys, reality and illusion, our relationship to time and place, relationships in general, and governance of the state and self. Each chapter in this book explores one element of the human condition. We may know many of the texts, or some of the texts, or none. But we will be aware of the elements of the human condition presented in the texts. We may find in a book a new avenue for accessing literature and/or accessing philosophical ideas and psychological understandings inherent in the literature. By giving us the experience of engaging with great literature and the possibility of being changed by our reading, I hope to empower us to do the same with many pieces of literature.

This way of challenging and recalibrating our assumptions is especially relevant in the era we are living through. Reading great literature offers us an opportunity to examine what we truly think and believe and possibly to revise those assumptions. As we read, our assumptions are unconsciously mapped against the ideas in the text, allowing us to sense and perhaps re-evaluate those perspectives.

As we confront current, significant, challenging issues, predominant and troubling worldwide, many of us are experiencing an unmooring of our mores. We live in an era of shifting realities, such as "fake news" and "alternative facts," dramatically impacting our perception of reality. Literature can offer us a rudder to help us navigate this turmoil and uncertainty.

This deeper understanding for the reader arises because of how meaning springs from the syntax of the work being read and the way words cohere. The artistry found in the work of master writers lies in the craft of developing multi-layered texts—texts that can be read on a literal narrative level, a symbolic level (characters are symbols for events, impulses, emotions) and even a metaphysical level. For these writers, their skills are so proficient that they can be inspired by any original spark of an idea and express it in this multi-level fashion. Many authors describe how, in the moment of writing, they do not have to think at all but just let the words come. Later they may refine the words, but initially they simply let them flow. Their artistry lies in how they unite older ideas, and universal ideas, into previously unrelated new and original forms, so these ideas become not only relevant but also resonate in us, shifting our perceptions, refining our old ways of looking at the world and creating new directions.

Literature is one of the classic means for molding and modifying what I call our mind structure—the system of beliefs and assumptions that frame our outlook on experience, shaping our reality. We tend to inherit our mind structure passively from the world around us, especially as children, and as adults we may assume it cannot be changed. But mind structures are fluid. We can shape our mind structure as we choose if we do it consciously.

"Mind structure" is an omnibus term I created as a container of ideas, including the effects of literature on readers—effects I've studied and observed during many years of working with and teaching this material.

Our mind structure is the pattern of responses that forms the basis of how we experience reality. Our singular sense of reality is ours alone. Our mind structures underlie our behavior in all situations in which we find ourselves, including all groups we participate in large and small—our families, our schools, our local activities and sports groups, our work organizations, and our societal, political, national, and international affiliations.

Largely formed in childhood, our mind structure usually mirrors that of our parents' or perhaps not. In childhood, we absorb all the influences from the people and world around us like a sponge without thinking about them. That's just how our world is. Our brain accepts the input and forms assumptions that become our perceptions.

Our mind structure morphs into our belief system, and we cling to it as if it is the essence of ourselves. It is difficult to be aware that this is something we have control over, and not something that controls us.

However, as we grow older, have new and different experiences, and interact with other people, we may realize that they're looking at the same thing we are but thinking quite differently about it. This puzzles us and we may ask ourselves: Why is it that they say that? Or think that?

Mind structures are in fact malleable, impermanent, and both comforting and illusionary and as ephemeral as gossamer threads. Most changes to mind structures happen incrementally, while some can happen instantaneously. Inputs such as ideas—from many sources including reading books, watching plays and movies, attending lectures, interacting in conversations—may send tremors through our mind structure, and that can lead to shifts in our perceptions of how the world is. Cognition and innovative thinking can shake the threads and change our mind structure, perhaps even several times during our life span.

There is a biological basis for this mind structure change.

Neuroscientists have developed an understanding of how mind structures are constructed by the brain from a multiplicity of sensory inputs. However, the mechanism of the "ah-ha" or epiphanies associated with reading is not understood.[1]

Great literature—memorable, timeless literature—lays open the rich, inner worlds of an author's created characters. As we read great fiction, we know the characters as they often don't even know themselves. We conjure them according to our assumptions. Part of great literature is that the characters can surprise us, evolving into something other than who we imagined them to be and overturning those assumptions we've made. They can become part of our epiphany process, as their inner life is revealed, page by page, insight by insight.

This is the alchemy that great literature can materialize for us, the ability to access what is meaningful for the character, and an innovative manifestation on the author's part of what is universal in humanity.

People across time and place experience the same universal emotions. This is why we see the same well-loved texts remain relevant through the ages. They are enduring, well-reputed, and often used as classic examples of specific ideas and universal emotions. Similarly, people in different worlds can be touched by the same universal human emotions; reading books in translation can be equally formative. While the words themselves change, the emotions conveyed by the words carry the same emotional impact.

For instance, in the Western tradition, if we think back to the ancient playwrights and philosophers who wrote significant works like Sophocles' tragedy *Antigone,* or visionary creations like Plato's *The Republic*, these works and others delve into emotions of revenge, love, hate, sadness, tenderness, brutality, joy, trauma, terror, betrayal, and on and on, all of them universal emotions. People then, over two thousand years ago, heard or read the words of those writers in Ancient Greek.

We read them now in many languages. The technology of expressing human experience in many eras, such as the Elizabethan theater of Shakespeare and more modern plays like Pirandello's *Six Characters in Search of an Author,* may change. Still, a great truism is that the human condition never does.

I have chosen various texts I find insightful and powerful and through which epiphanies occurred for me, my students, and undoubtedly hundreds of thousands of readers around the world.

Even though different readers may identify with other characters, we will recognize characteristics and personality traits in all the characters in these chosen texts: their powers and weaknesses, successes and failures, gifts and foibles. Their narratives highlight the boundaries and territory of their mind structures and the landscapes of their inner worlds. They create an opening for us to perhaps experience a change in our mind structure through our recognition of them. Hopefully, through our reading, we may experience the spark plug of literature driving mind structure changes.

Chapter One spotlights moral responsibility in two books, *The Drowned and The Saved* by Primo Levi and *The Reader* by Bernhard Schlink. At times in our lives, outer circumstances beyond our control shape our mind structure. How would any of us act in situations posing exigent moral dilemmas? The chapter introduces ideas on the sins of commission and omission. Specifically, it explores how post-Nazi Germans grapple with their history and possible thought paths for us as we grapple with our history.

Chapter Two explores redemption, tolerance, adaptability, and acceptance in *Disgrace* by J.M. Coetzee. We follow the trajectory of Professor David Lurie's redemptive journey from egocentric philanderer and exploiter to some sense of self-awareness of the chaos he has caused in the lives of those closest to him. David's journey involves black and white South Africans struggling to accommodate their mind structure to living in post-apartheid South Africa.

Chapter Three illuminates inner journeys in *Siddhartha* by Hermann Hesse and *Shambhala: The Sacred Path of the Warrior* by Chögyam Trungpa. We can follow the description of experiential journeys on being and becoming and some essential insights on East Asian mind structures. They include concepts related to understanding aspects of our inner life, and of meditation and meditation practices. The texts also serve as an introduction to Buddhism and concepts of wisdom and compassion that form a cultural mind structure.

Chapter Four invites a journey into perception, reality, and illusion as presented in *Hamlet* by William Shakespeare. This play highlights essential understandings of Western mind structures such as individualism and resolute acceptance of Life's changing circumstances. *Hamlet* richly expresses ideas on existence: being and becoming; death; reality and illusion.

Chapter Five winds through *Einstein's Dreams* by Alan Lightman and *The Four Quartets* by T. S. Eliot. Undoubtedly, we all have questions about what role time plays in our lives and by inference our mind structures. These two authors tackle questions such as: What is time? What is our place in time? Is timelessness a feasible concept? Do memory and history help us understand time? What is the relationship between human existence and time? Does spirituality add to an understanding of time?

Chapter Six delves into associative thinking, memory, and loss as they arise in *To The Lighthouse* by Virginia Woolf. Woolf evokes her childhood memories to weave a fictional masterpiece of time passing. She presents the interiority of her characters' streams of consciousness. These passages raise questions on the reliability of memory, the power of associative thinking and assumptions, and how reality may be only present in each passing moment.

Chapter Seven focuses on the individual self and societal collectivism in *The Republic* by Plato; and in complementary texts to *The Republic*, Leo Tolstoy's novella *The Death of Ivan Ilyich*, and an Andrew Sullivan essay. These texts demonstrate the formation of mind structures in both how we can model and build an ideal society, a "city on the hill." In Plato's model, we find ideas on becoming both an enlightened ruler (governance of the state) and a master of the inner self. Plato's idealistic proposals, and practices, advocate progress toward a perfected society. In these troubled times, when we do not know what to think of the political situation worldwide, reading *The Republic* may help us be better informed of the processes at work in these situations, view them from a different perspective, from a shift in our mind structure.

Chapter Eight captures a sense of place as presented in three brief extracts from *The River of Grass* by Margery Stoneman Douglas; *The Road from Coorain* by Jill Ker Conway; *Inside Apartheid* by Janet Levine. Discernable in each is the subconscious process of the authors' associative thinking. Subtle undercurrents demonstrate how a sense of place, even a place that one loves dearly, is never only a stand-alone facet of memory. It is impacted and surrounded by many other mind structure inputs.

The mind structure of magical realism is presented by Gabriel García Márquez. His writing offers an alternative mind structure to a sense of place. When trying to fathom the concept of reality, Márquez creates a mind structure he calls "magical realism."

In the chapters, I have used excerpts from the books being studied; I encourage you to read the books in their entirety. I taught much of the material in this book for twenty-five years at Milton Academy, an independent school in Massachusetts. This book introduces the material to others.

I am humbled by and indebted to all the authors present here and countless others who have been my lifelong companions, both literary masters and philosophical-psychological guides, and whose works continue to amaze, delight, and encourage me to believe that we can all strive to be awakened versions of ourselves.

I write simply because I have knowledge and experience in these matters, and I want to share them in the hope of enriching your life.

Let's begin our adventure together.

1

FACETS OF MORAL RESPONSIBILITY

In both *The Drowned and the Saved* by Primo Levi and *The Reader* by Bernhard Schlink, the texts discussed in this chapter, a central motif revolves around the principle of moral responsibility. This term encompasses a multi-faceted array of responses on aspects of human empathy. While the designation "moral responsibility" may carry the solemnity of a universal principle, many facets of this principle exist, as many possibilities as there are humans on earth.

Levi shares his firsthand experience of the Nazi Holocaust and considers several aspects of acts of commission and omission. Schlink, a novelist, writes of the experiences of two characters caught in the aftermath of Nazi horror. They become entangled in a lifelong web of empathy and antipathy, sharing a complex moral tale woven from several strands of these facets of moral responsibility.

Essentially, the idea of moral responsibility presupposes that we are disposed, in varying socio-political and individual circumstances, to show empathy toward our fellow humans and all life on this planet. This disposition is evident in natural crises caused by fire, floods, famine, and so on, and those that are manmade, such as political upheavals that affect millions.

To a greater or lesser extent, it is common for the principle of moral responsibility to be embedded in our mind structure. As described in the Introduction, "mind structure" is an omnibus term I created as a conceptual container for the pattern of responses that forms the basis of how we experience reality. Moral responsibility is one element of that perceived reality.

We are all, at times, trapped in outer circumstances beyond our control. How we respond to those situations shapes or changes aspects of our mind structures. In some circumstances, our sense of moral responsibility, reinforced by the actions of others, can impact the collective mind structure of a stratum of society or even an entire nation.

Although both texts we explore in this chapter are rooted in the same horrific reality of Nazi Germany and its aftermath, they are written with different aims and carry different viewpoints. As we explore them, they offer many possible thought paths for us to ponder, maybe even to shift assumptions of our understanding of this empathic principle.

Levi, born in Italy and a survivor of Auschwitz, one of the largest Nazi concentration camps, writes several essays from a late-in-life perspective. He uses the form of narrative nonfiction in *The Drowned and the Saved*, pulling back his lens of memory to include some philosophical distance in his reflections. The reminiscences of his time both as a Nazi concentration camp victim and as a lifelong chronicler of Nazi hubris, outrage, and horror give us direct access to his mind structure, which evolves from his earlier works of righteous anger to this more measured response.

The Reader, a novel by Bernhardt Schlink, born in Germany in the decade after the Holocaust, examines the after-effects of the Nazi horror but essentially sets that macrocosm of chaos and destruction aside to concentrate on a multilayered, microcosmic depiction of two individuals, Michael, and Hanna. This fictional account gives us access to the mind structure of the character, Michael, and through his eyes, to that of the other protagonist, Hanna. Michael internalizes thoughts and emotions—so deeply—that they are not readily accessible even to himself. We only ever glimpse aspects of Hanna's mind from Michael's point of view. We need to be deft in discerning an understanding of Michael's belief system to uncover the complicated aspects of his empathy towards Hanna.

The texts demonstrate the responses of a nonfiction writer, Levi, and two fictional characters, Michael, and Hanna, to situations posing exigent moral dilemmas. You may be fortunate enough never to be amid such stark predicaments, but for millions of others, these are their present moments.

Among other ideas running through this chapter, the two texts introduce the concepts of acts of commission and omission and how they fold into the principle of moral responsibility. We all contend at times with these choices. Acts of commission are those we commit, even enthusiastically, when we actively partake in obeying orders to kill, maim, destroy, or forsake any benevolence or empathy for other human beings, our environment, indeed, the biosphere. Acts of commission occur when we engage with the perpetrators to victimize and dehumanize others.

Acts of omission are primarily committed when we remain silent and passive even when we know that evil and mayhem surround us. Acts of omission occur when we are afflicted by moral blindness and turn away from or even fail to acknowledge the victims, although they are often in plain sight. We, by our inaction, may help to situate them further as victims.

Acts of bravery, empathy, and humanity counterbalance morally destructive acts of commission and omission, such as when we speak out and risk punishment or even death, follow our beliefs, our credos, and defend others. If there is no counterbalance, a vacuum exists that is readily filled by the apathy and moral blindness of people particularly guilty of the acts of omission.

In the last century, among many mass atrocities, the worst in terms of audacious scope, terrifying outcomes, and sheer hubris, was the Nazi attempt in the 1930s and the first half of the 1940s to establish a Thousand Year Reich, to "cleanse" the descendants of the original Aryan people (mainly German) of "impure" blood (primarily the Jews of Europe as well as other minorities) and to expand the territories of the Reich. This is the milieu of Primo Levi's account. Perhaps, to a somewhat lesser degree, that of Schlink's novel, too, set in the aftermath of this monumental tragedy.

Hitler and his henchmen mass murdered millions of innocents in concentration camps by gassing them in huge ovens or through starving and general mistreatment of them in concentration and labor camps. In the Levi memoir, the chapter "The Gray Zone" that we explore, exhibits morally reprehensible acts of commission in the camps. These are firsthand witness bearing accounts, albeit filtered through Levi's mind structure.

Acts of Omission and Commission in *The Drowned and the Saved* by Primo Levi

"Evil is not the absence of the good, as theology and philosophy maintain. It is the invention of the bad." So, wrote James Wood, an essayist for the *New Yorker* magazine in an article "The Art of Witness,"[1] paraphrasing a Primo Levi observation from one of his early books, *If This is a Man,* published in 1947.[2] As we will see, the above paraphrase presents an apt comment on the Nazi mind structure.

Primo Levi (1919-1987), an Italian of Jewish descent, was an industrial chemist who was born and died in the same house in Turin. A simple, humble man, his life was interrupted by the advent to power of Hitler in Germany in the 1930s. In his early twenties, Levi joined the Italian resistance to the government of Nazi collaborator Benito Mussolini. Levi managed to evade capture until 1944. Subsequently, he was sent to Auschwitz, where he survived for eleven months until the camp was liberated in 1945.

His Auschwitz experience was the singular, devastating event in Primo Levi's life. It was the great "Ah-ha" moment for him, an epiphany into the possibilities of evil that he explored in his writings until his death.

In book after book, he bears witness to the still barely imaginable atrocities he experienced and witnessed while in the camp. A scientist by training and profession, he tries to use words to make order out of chaos. Levi possesses a narrative ability to catalyze truth from horror; literary artistry that keeps readers turning the pages even if what they are reading is horrific.

In *The Drowned and the Saved*,[3] Levi's final work, like all his other work, written originally in Italian, returns to his singular obsession, the nature of evil as he experienced its manifestation at Auschwitz. The book was published in 1986, the year before he died, and has the reflective perspective provided by time passed. The book is not autobiographical, as are his previous works, instead he writes a series of essays grouped around themes. The book's power lies in the intellectual analysis and philosophical discernment of his experience of the Holocaust. Levi does not question the absolute reality of the events of the Holocaust; after all, he lived them. He examines the ambiguities of judgment, the will to power, how memory affects memoir, among other considerations.

In the Preface, Levi outlines some aspects of the Nazi mind structure—including the xenophobia against non-Aryans, specifically Jews, and committing dehumanizing acts against these people. Another is the German concept of *Lebensraum* ("living space"), restoring the German people to their ancient lands by using policies and practices of settler colonization. These two priorities of the Nazi German regime—annexing European countries and annihilating Jews and others deemed impure—led directly into the Holocaust of Europe but not the establishment of an Aryan Thousand Year Reich.

The element he describes first is the "Nazi annihilation camps" themselves. In 1942, as they were being built and the first victims arrived in boxcars. All the rumors about their existence, Levi writes,

> ...delineated a massacre of such vast proportions, of such extreme cruelty and such intricate motivation that the public was inclined to reject them because of their very enormity. It is significant that the culprits themselves foresaw this rejection well in advance.[4]

The killing camps were called *Lagers* (German for prisons). Levi records that many survivors had recurring nightmares that their witness bearing testimony would not be believed because it was so horrifying and inhumane. Yet despite the Nazis attempts to destroy all evidence of the Lagers during the last months of the collapse of their Reich—by burning records and blowing up crematoria—the ruins of the gas chambers remain at Auschwitz and other camps, skeletons of hundreds of thousands of bodies exist in mass graves all over Germany, Austria, Poland, and other European countries, and smuggled and buried historical records bear mute witness.

Levi writes,

No one will ever be able to establish with precision how
many, in the Nazi apparatus, could *not know* (Levi's italics)
about the frightful atrocities being committed, how many
knew something but were in a position to pretend that
they did not know, and further, how many had the possibility of knowing everything but chose the more prudent
path of keeping their eyes and ears (and above all their
mouths) well shut. Whatever the case, since one cannot
suppose the majority of Germans lightheartedly accepted
the slaughter, it is certain that the failure to divulge the
truth about the Lagers represents one of the major collective crimes of the German people and the most obvious
demonstration of the cowardice toward which Hitlerian
terror had reduced them…without this cowardice the
greatest excesses would not have been carried out, and
Europe and the world would be different today.[5]

This is a clear indictment of acts of omission. On the other hand,
all those who wore Nazi uniforms and worked in the concentration
camps were guilty of acts of commission.

Levi writes at some length on omission as an aspect of the German
zeitgeist at that time: the population's significant silence and collusion
to hide the truth of the existence of concentration camps. He highlights, for instance, that the general citizenry must have been aware of
the atrocities in these camps, as they supplied the Lagers with everything from materials to build the gas ovens to hydrocyanic acid in such
large amounts more than enough to kill thousands of people,

At the very least those orders could not have gone unnoticed. Their doubts were…stifled by fear, the desire for profit, the blindness, and willed stupidity, and in some cases (probably few) by fanatical Nazi obedience.[6]

Levi introduces yet another aspect of the Nazi mind structure, the willingness to evoke terror—the fact that the prisoners themselves were unable to gain an objective perspective on what was happening around them and to them while they were fixated on trying to ensure their day-by-day survival. He writes,

> At a distance of years, one can today definitely affirm that
> the history of the Lagers has been written almost exclu-
> sively by those who, like myself, never fathomed them
> to the bottom. Those who did so did not return, or their
> capacity for observation was paralyzed by suffering and
> incomprehension.[7]

In the chapter "The Gray Zone," Levi conveys the perplexity and complexity of Jewish prisoners inside the Lagers collaborating with their Nazi guards. Levi begins this chapter with a short treatise, a simplistic statement, of the role of black-and-white thinking in history,

> We also tend to simplify history; but the patterns within
> which events are ordered are not always identifiable in a
> single, unequivocal fashion, and therefore different histori-
> ans may understand and construe history in ways that are
> incompatible with one another. Nevertheless, perhaps for
> reasons that go back to our origins as social animals, the
> need to divide the field in "we" and "they" is so strong that
> this pattern, this bipartition—friend/enemy—prevails over
> all others. Popular history, and also the history, taught in

schools, is influenced by this Manichaean tendency, which shuns half-tints and complexities: it is prone to reduce the river of human occurrences to conflicts, and the conflicts to dual—we and they, Athenians and Spartans, Romans and Carthaginians.[8]

Levi also uses the example of spectator sports as a simplification of this duality: we want victors and vanquished, and we want the saved and the drowned. In the same way, it is easy to assume the human situation inside the Lagers as one of victims and persecutors. However, Levi reveals that the network of human interaction was not a simple or singular mindset. There was no clear-cut good-and-evil paradigm or Judeo-Christian righteousness for the saints and condemnation for the sinners in the Lagers. This deliberately confusing world was what the prisoners experienced, and that granular truth was a shock. They anticipated beatings, but not by fellow prisoners. As Levi writes,

...It is difficult to defend oneself against a blow for which one is not prepared.[9]

Part of the implementation of the grand scheme of extermination of the Jews was to break even the germ of an idea of organized resistance in their belief system. All vestiges of "home" were obliterated. Prisoners received a tattooed number on one of their arms. (Levi's number was #174517). Their spirit was broken, their assumptions and perceptions were upended.

On arrival, prisoners were subjected to blows, insults, simulated rage, stripped of clothes, heads shaven, all actions conducted by seasoned prisoners, staged to intimidate, and destroy any spirit of resistance, any assumption that someone was coming to save them. The purpose of the Nazis administering the camps was the extermination of most of the inmates and salvage the more able-bodied for slave labor.

Who were these Jewish collaborators? Levi identifies a central motivation for these people: the perception that they could gain some vestige of privilege even while counted among the underprivileged. He explains that in the Lagers, the division of masters and servants both diverged and converged. The camp commander and a small coterie of fellow officers held power. As the war effort turned to failure for the Nazis and more men were called to the front, the commander needed auxiliaries to implement his power. So, they made some prisoners into collaborators.

(A similar perception of the pecking order on a larger scale was the collaboration of citizens in abetting the Nazis in rooting out Jews and resisters in occupied countries of Europe such as Poland, France, Norway, Italy, Ukraine, and Balkan states. While these collaborators never served in combat, they abetted the Reich in the most onerous tasks, such as supplying lists of Jews in their territory, finding, and rounding them up, and identifying targets for extermination, digging mass graves and shooting the victims. Most collaborators in occupied countries did not face the same depravation or threat of extermination of prisoner collaborators in the concentration camps. Many were ideologues who supported Nazi aims and ambitions.)

Levi warns us not to cast hasty judgment on the camp collaborators who showed such a lack of empathy for their fellow Jews. He quotes the nineteenth-century Italian novelist and poet Allessandro Manzoni's argument that oppressors are guilty of the evil they commit and the perversion into which they lead the spirit of the oppressed. Only a mind structure of pure evil could construct this psychological twist.

Levi says,

I would lightheartedly absolve all those whose concurrence in the guilt was minimal and for whom coercion was of the highest degree.[10]

He casts prisoners without rank in this category, like those who checked that the covers on all the cots were squarely set every day and became inspectors of lice and other pests and diseases, as well as camp messengers. Their reward—a smidgeon of privilege—however meager, did not remove them from the everyday hardships and suffering of everyone else. Yet they were not regarded as enemies.

As an aside, I wonder if Levi would count himself among this group. He survived Auschwitz mainly because the Nazis used his training and experience as a chemist in their local rubber factories. This role provided Levi with a little more food than he would otherwise have been rationed, but it did not ease any of the other sufferings of his daily camp life. He wrestled with guilt at this slight privilege while he concurrently thought of himself as a victim. But his motivation to survive by any means aided him to accept this situation.

Should Levi have refused to work for the Nazis? There is no easy answer. If he had resisted, he would have been fed to a gas chamber by one of the collaborators. Like many other Lager inmates, Levi's goal in the camp was to survive to bear witness to these monstrous atrocities. The survival motivation is universally regarded as a noble act of resistance, a countervailing aspiration to accept the inevitability of death surrounding you. To survive and bear witness is an act of courage and empathy for oneself and one's fellow victims.

Levi did survive. He did bear witness. Forty years later, in *The Drowned and the Saved*, he reflects on his experience with a sincere attempt at intellectual objectivity.

While he maintains that we should not judge the ordinary camp collaborators, he posits a more stringent standard of judgment for those Jews who ascended to command positions: the chiefs, also known as *kapos*. Levi does not explain why he holds these men to a different standard. What elements of prejudice his mind perceived remains a mystery.

Kapos ran the labor squads, the barracks, the punishment cells, and were clerks who often worked with sensitive political material. Many later wrote about their experiences. These *kapos* became significant witness bearers who shed light on both secrets of the Reich and their experiences as collaborator prisoners. However, Levi does not maintain that witness-bearing later absolved them or lessened the impact of their choice.

Levi tells us that *kapos* were free to commit among the worst atrocities, and they often beat fellow prisoners to death. He continues,

> Thus, the Lager, on a smaller scale but with amplified characteristics, reproduced the hierarchical structure of the totalitarian state, in which all power is invested from above and control from below is almost impossible. ...It is understandable that power of such magnitude overwhelmingly attracted the human type greedy for power...and that the latter became fatally intoxicated by the power at their disposal.[11]

Levi asks the question, who became a Kapo? Some men were common criminals taken from prison; others were political prisoners who had served five to ten years imprisonment and were morally broken, deadened to empathy. Yet others were Jews who saw in their authority role survival from the gas chambers. Still others aspired to power and the ability to wring suffering on others. Levi calls the last group, "gray, ambiguous persons, ready to compromise."[12]

He singles out the collaborators referred to as the SS (Special Squad) for examination. (They are not to be confused with the Schutzstaffel, the Nazi SS, a paramilitary force supporting Hitler—the men, and some women, who also administered the Lagers.) These Jewish men were responsible for running the crematoria. Levi labels their actions as extreme collaboration,

> They maintained order among the new arrivals (often completely unaware of the destiny awaiting them) who were to be sent into the gas chambers. They were sent into the gas ovens to extract corpses from the chambers, to pull gold teeth from jaws. To cut women's hair, to sort and classify clothes, shoes, and the contents of the luggage, to transport the bodies to the crematoria, and oversee the ovens, to extract and eliminate the ashes.[13]

In Auschwitz, the Special Squad (SS) numbered seven hundred to one thousand men. To maintain the secrecy of their mass extermination operation by any of the SS men surviving and later bearing witness, the Nazis had the current SS cadre dragged to the ovens every few months and exterminated, while a new batch was being trained, "As its initiation, the next squad burnt the corpses of its predecessors."[14]

Scarcely any SS men survived, and as of 1986 when Levi wrote this book, none had come forward and told of his moral plight—cremated if you refused to join the Special Squad and cremated if you did. Levi shares that the information about the Special Squad comes from depositions of other camp survivors and hastily written diary pages buried and later uncovered in Auschwitz and other camps near the crematoria. He describes a dilemma we must all grapple with as we read these horrific details,

> All these sources agree, and yet we have found it difficult, almost impossible, to form an image for ourselves of how these men lived day by day, saw themselves, accepted their condition.[15]

Levi himself found it impossible. The judgment he holds in his mind structure in this instance is unforgiving,

> Conceiving and organizing the squads was National
> Socialism's most demonic crime. Behind the pragmatic
> aspect (to economize on able men, to impose on others
> the most atrocious tasks) other more subtle, aspects can
> be perceived. The institution represented an attempt to
> shift onto others—specifically, the victims— the burden of
> guilt, so that they were deprived of even the solace of inno-
> cence. It is neither easy nor agreeable to dredge this abyss
> of viciousness, and yet I think it must be done, because
> what could be perpetrated yesterday could be attempted
> again tomorrow.[16]

Levi examines, in the final pages of this chapter, the allure of power for certain men who will stoop to any action to exercise supremacy over fellow human beings. He shifts his focus away from Auschwitz and the Lagers, using examples from other writers who lived through different periods of atrocities, particularly in the nineteenth century, and he expounds on a fable in *The Brothers Karamazov,* the novel by Fyodor Dostoevsky that touches on questions about God, free will and morality. Akin to these writers, Levi tries to understand the mind structure of those drawn to power over others. But unlike those writers, he writes not of a fictitious character but the real-life, self-proclaimed president (and master collaborator) of the Lodz ghetto in Poland, Chaim Rumkowski.

Nazi authorities established the Lodz Ghetto (also called Litzmannstadt Ghetto) for Polish Jews and Roma following the 1939 invasion of Poland. It was the second-largest ghetto in German-occupied Europe after the Warsaw Ghetto. In all, about 200,000 people were stripped of their homes and belongings and herded into a space covering only several city blocks. Disease and starvation were rife. The Nazis used the Lodz ghetto prisoners as a labor force for the German war machine, mainly to sew uniforms. In the spring of 1944, the Nazis decided to destroy the ghetto and transport what was left of the starving population to Auschwitz and other concentration camps, where they were gassed to death and cremated in the camp ovens.

When the Soviet army liberated the ghetto in January 1945, there were only several hundred survivors. Many people in the ghetto had buried diaries, while others hid photographic evidence of life in the ghetto. Some Jews were able to escape and join the underground Polish resistance army. After the war, they were witness bearers to the truth of the deprivation, mistreatment, and murder of the occupants of the Lodz ghetto.

Chaim Rumkowski, a Nazi collaborator, ran the ghetto and the lives of the one hundred and sixty thousand Jews living there. For Levi, Rumkowski presents a case study of a mind structure corrupted absolutely by the allure of power.

Rumkowski's collaboration with and obeisance to his Nazi overlords, demanded absolute obedience and loyalty from the ghetto residents, even as living conditions grew more and more exacting each day. Yet, in 1944, Rumkowski and his family, like the other Jews from Lodz, were deported in a boxcar to Auschwitz and the gas chamber.

Rumkowski's story serves to epitomize the questions surrounding the very existence of "the gray zone." These questions can be crystallized into a single overarching dilemma: understanding mind structures that embrace humanity's inhumanity to other humans.

Rumkowski, in many ways, typifies a person in the gray zone. As a Jew, he was not allowed to wear a German uniform, yet he aided and abetted the Nazis in implementing their grand scheme of the Thousand

Year Reich. On the other hand, the small number of Jews who escaped the ghetto and worked for the Polish resistance embodied the bravery aspect inherent in the principle of moral responsibility.

Levi ends the chapter with a cautionary note,

Like Rumkowski, we too are so dazzled by power and prestige as to forget our essential fragility. Willingly or not, we come to terms with power, forgetting that we are all in the ghetto, that the ghetto is walled in, that outside the ghetto reign the lords of death, and that close by the train is waiting.[17]

Empathy and Apathy in *The Reader* by Bernhard Schlink

Let's first address the question of whether great art can be fashioned from great horror. Through the ages, artists working in several mediums courageously tackled and continue to grapple with the challenge of how to make art from unspeakable evil taken from life. Faced with portraying horrible events, writers tackle the task of creating artistry with their words to convey that horror.

Unquestioningly, as we see through Primo Levi's mind structure, nonfiction can accomplish this. But what about fiction? German author Bernhard Schlink's best-selling novel *The Reader*,[18] first published in German in 1995, attempts to do so. The novel is set in the early years of post-Nazi Germany (sometime in the early 1950s, we are not given an exact date). The protagonists, Hanna and Michael, fictional creations, struggle with the burden of guilt the Nazi regime engenders on the mind structure of their generation living amid the ruins of their once renowned country. A country that for centuries celebrated and honored leading philosophers, writers, composers, and musicians, among other humanitarian luminaries.

Bernhard Schlink was born to a German father and Swiss mother in 1946. Schlink's father, Edmund, was a world-famous and influential Lutheran theologian and a professor of theology at Heidelberg University. His mother, Irmgard, was one of his father's students when they married. Bernhard Schlink was brought up in Heidelberg and studied law, becoming a judge in the constitutional court of North-Rhine-Westphalia and later a professor of law at Humboldt University in Berlin. His career as a writer began with a series of detective novels with the main character Selb (German for Self.)

The Reader, first published in Switzerland, became a worldwide best seller winning several literary prizes.

The Drowned and the Saved and *The Reader* are grounded in Nazi Germany and deal with issues concerning perpetrators and victims. In the macrocosmic world of Nazi Germany, Levi's chapter "The Gray Zone" makes that distinction clear in his delineation of acts of commission and omission.

In the microcosmic world of *The Reader,* these lines are blurred.

The narrative pivots on a sexual relationship between an adult and a minor. In this novel, the ramifications of moral responsibility, namely, empathy and apathy in these circumstances, are less clear-cut. Another connection between the two books is the presence of Nazi guards and concentration camps, although the contexts are hugely different.

Schlink's novel informs on several conceptual levels. On a literal level, it is the story of mid-thirty-year-old Hanna who seduces a willing fifteen-year-old schoolboy, Michael, and their intensely passionate and short-lived affair. The novel then grapples with the after-effects of the affair from Michael's point of view: his inability to commit or open himself to others, an element of his mind structure that lasts a lifetime.

On a symbolic, historical level, we may read Hanna representing the Third Reich in her over-reaching attempt at a *putsch* of Michael's body and spirit. In this regard, Hanna is portrayed as the symbol of the German *ubermensch*, an iconic figure still powerfully attractive to many Germans of her generation. The idea of the *ubermensch* can also muster grandiose and dangerous allure for the following generation, represented by Michael, who grew up in a bleak post-war and defeated Germany.

A third level allows readers to delve into the many interpretations of the word "reader."

In the opening chapter of the novel, Michael is fifteen and ill with the onset of hepatitis. He vomits in the street. A woman emerges from a bombed-out building and comes to his aid. After ascertaining his address, she carries his school bag in one hand and, supporting him with the other, walks him home. She calls him "kid." And tells him her name is Hanna.

Months later, when he has recovered from his illness, Michael's mother insists he brings the woman a bunch of flowers and thank her for his rescue. Michael is reluctant, embarrassed that he vomited in her arms, but ultimately agrees to the gesture. Accepting the flowers, a surprised Hanna invites Michael into her dingy apartment and continues ironing a huge pile of laundry.

The first intimation we have of the novel's time scheme is that Michael tells us that years later, he can remember every detail of the building on that first visit: Hanna's apartment, the furniture and, Hanna herself, "In later years I dreamed about the building again and again."[19] From that first visit, Hanna is firmly entrenched as an element of Michael's mind structure.

We know then that the novel is essentially the telling of recollected memory that haunts Michael over decades. And, as the narrative unfolds and Michael is positioned as the reliable narrator, we enter the associative memories of his mind structure. Of Hanna, we know little, only discovering tidbits that Michael shares in his narration.

As the story unfolds, Michael slowly becomes entrapped in the web Hanna spins. At least, this is his perception of what is happening. Hanna may simply be apathetically floating on the surface of life, going wherever it carries her, utilizing whatever it brings her. In Michael's belief system, he rationalizes that if feeling desire is the same as satisfying that desire, why not commit the act. He is willingly seduced. After their first sexual encounter, he cannot keep away from Hanna, encouraging his visits.

Society regards a liaison such as this as a predatory criminal act on the adult perpetrated on the underage victim. Yet, the possibility exists that love, as well as lust, can occur between the partners. Perhaps at times, such a relationship can be more complicated than that of predator and prey.

Hanna seduces Michael. Their trysts fulfill most fifteen-year-old schoolboys' dreams. But he does not share stories of their encounters with anyone. Michael has guilty qualms about the affair. He knows something is "off," but he ignores the prompts from his internalized moral code.

After school, Michael visits Hanna every weekday when she returns from her work as a tram conductor. After a steamy encounter, Hanna asks Michael to read to her from one of his textbooks, *Emilia Galotti*. He is taken aback and offers to give her the book to read, but she argues that she loves to hear his voice. He cannot discern with any clarity what is amiss in this scenario and concurs and becomes her reader. As he reads, he is aware of her deep involvement with the characters, as if she were present at an opera. This empathy impresses him but also raises red flags in his psyche: what is her reality? She trudges through such a sedentary routine life of being a tram conductor and managing daily chores that cover the passion and imagination, now so evident to him.

Gradually Michael learns scant details about Hanna's life. She has worked since she was sixteen; she has no parents or siblings. Previously she worked at Siemens, and currently, she has the possibility of promotion to tram driver. She presses him for information on his life, his family, and Michael eagerly divulges many details. Michael's eagerness to speak of these details perhaps expresses a subconscious need to normalize their relationship.

As narcissistic as many other teenagers, Michael accepts their arrangement seemingly contentedly. Hannah is one part of his daily activities. He appears to be comfortable compartmentalizing his life. They never leave the apartment to venture anywhere together, and they spend months meeting in secret. This is strange behavior for them both. Michael does not want to jeopardize their sexual encounters. He knows a hint to anyone that they exist will mean the end of the liaison. He cannot see beyond sexual pleasure into his guilt or the ramifications of both his and Hanna's exploitation of one another. He is exploiting Hanna for what he believes is mutually enjoyable sex. Sexual partner is the compartment she occupies in his mind structure. As for Hanna, we can only guess at her motivation.

Michael also believes that Hanna has the upper hand in the relationship, and she can end it at any time. As Hanna's motivation for continuing the relationship is a blank, we must rely mainly on Michael's perspective. As the novel progresses, our assumptions about Hanna may display more projections from our mind structure onto her than we have any way of learning hers.

There is one exception to this pattern of visits. Michael lies to his parents that after Easter, he plans a cycling tour with a friend. In reality he has persuaded Hanna to take the four-day bike trip with him, posing as his mother and he as her son. Reluctantly she agrees. Their plans run smoothly until one morning when Michael wakes early and hopes to surprise Hanna. He creeps downstairs to arrange their breakfast. He leaves her an innocuous note, "Good morning! Bringing breakfast, be right back."[20]

When he returns, Michael finds a furious Hanna, who asks how he could leave her. She is so overwrought she picks up a belt with a metal buckle and lashes out at Michael, injuring his face and leaving bruises on his body. Michael's perceptions about Hanna are shattered with every blow; her violence far exceeds the parameters of the situation. Although disturbed by Hanna's response, Michael enjoys their relationship too much to delve further and risk more fury from Hanna. When her storm of outrage passes, Hanna clings to Michael and tends to his wounds. These widely disparate responses do not yet, shake Michael's assumptions that Hannah's behavior on the cycling trip is an anomaly, and he is content to return to their previous patterns of behavior.

Hanna's actions may begin to fill in some clues as to her inner world. Abandonment produces deep anxiety in her, so much so that she loses complete self-control. Then, distraught at the possible outcome of her fury (she may have severely hurt Michael, she may have shocked him so that he may leave her.) In the aftermath of her physical violence, Hanna morphs back into her sexual role that is also partially maternal.

Hanna's initial reaction to his absence, Michael feels, tilts the balance of power in their relationship in some mysterious way. There is a shift toward him being in command of the relationship, no longer the willing follower in their sexual lives but the leader. Later, Michael asks Hanna if she read his note, and she denies there was a note. He is puzzled at her cover-up but shows some empathy for her in not pursuing the matter.

Throughout their relationship, he hides any inkling of his liaison from his family (aside from cursory details shared with his sister) or friends. Michael never questions himself if he may be short-changing both himself, Hanna, and his family and friends, by compartmentalizing this part of his life. Hannah shields the facts of her life from him; Michael does the same with those who share his life. Both Michael and Hanna are complicit in hiding their secret love affair; both share guilt for acts of omission.

This secrecy has consequences, for Hanna and Michael's affair ends abruptly in the summer of the year of their meeting. The last time he sees her is when she appears at the public swimming pool where he is with his friends. Michael ignores Hanna.

Perhaps shame is now part of his mind structure or an instinctual avoidance of complications and explanations to his family and friends if he acknowledges her. At that moment, he seems to have no thought or care about how his actions impact Hanna. He feels no empathy for her. The next time he looks her way, she has disappeared.

He chooses the selfish adolescent normalcy of interacting with a pack of friends at that critical moment, over sexual excitement. Whatever that choice manifested in his mind structure will have consequences for the rest of his life. Hanna vanishes from the town that afternoon.

Many years later, Michael learns of the reason why she left abruptly. But that afternoon and in the immediate aftermath, he surmises it was because he did not acknowledge her at the pool. Michael sets himself up for a lifetime of buried feelings of guilt concerning Hanna, buried so deeply he is unaware of them.

Instead, Michael displays all the physical symptoms of profound loss: nausea, tears, sleeplessness, and superficial guilt—berating himself for not rushing to her when he saw her at the pool. That glimpse was his last sight of her—but mostly, his body yearns for their physical contact. Of Hanna, we know nothing.

After his school years end, Michael embarks on legal studies at the university. One semester, as part of a professor's seminar, he attends as an observer, along with other students, a local Holocaust trial of several women, previously concentration camp guards, accused of the murder of hundreds of Jewish women and children.

Michael realizes that the trial is also a symbolic trial of the mass madness and hysteria that gripped an entire generation of millions of Germans to reframe their lives in ideological terms of a belief system that supported Hitler. They served the Reich either on the battlefield or from positions in the judiciary and local government. This generation of guards and enforcers in the camps was the generation who, during the war, took no action to obstruct the Hitlerian horror machine, and after the war had not banished active participants from their midst, as they could have done. Their compliant silence and apathy were their act of omission compounding their acts of commission during the Holocaust.

Michael's parents' generation symbolically were in the dock along with the accused women. Michael represents one of the following or "next" generations who "explored them, subjected them to trial by daylight, and condemned them to shame."[21]

During the Nazi years, Michael's father, a philosophy professor, had lost his position at the university for scheduling a lecture on Spinoza, a 16th-century Jewish philosopher. The family survived the Nazi era, supported by his father, who became an editor for a publisher of hiking books. "We all condemned our parents to shame, even if the only charge we could bring was that after 1945 they had tolerated the perpetrators in their midst."[22]

Varying degrees of guilt and lack of empathy can be laid on those complicit in acts of omission.

In the courtroom for the first time, Michael notes that the defendants and their lawyers sit with their backs to the student observers behind them. Unexpectedly he sees Hanna among the defendants, "I did not recognize her until she was called, and she stood up and stepped forward. … I recognized her, but I felt nothing. Nothing at all."[23]

If Michael truly feels nothing, if he is not deceiving himself, he has incrementally developed into someone without empathy, who struggles within the strictures of moral responsibility.

Eight years have passed since their last encounter. Michael strives to continue to shut down past feelings and memories of Hanna and to play the impartial observer.

But his actions belie this cool indifference, for he becomes obsessed with the trial and returns daily, exceeding the professor's requirements. Not given to introspection, we have little idea of Michael's internal dialog at this moment. We can only muse about his reactions and whether or not he is lying to himself. His interest in the trial representing the Third Reich may be his rationalization for his obsession, or he may sub-consciously still be in Hanna's thrall. His fascination with her, buried for several years, comes to the forefront again.

Hanna is one of five defendants for the murder of hundreds of women and several children during the waning months of WW2. When questioned, the court learns from her that she turned down a promotion to foreman at Siemens and joined the Nazi SS as recruiters were looking for guards. Yes, she had served at Auschwitz until early 1944 and then at a small camp near Cracow until 1945. Yes, when the female prisoners were marched west, she went with them, and, yes, since the end of the war, she had lived at one place or another.

Hanna's lawyer argued that she should be released on her recognizance. Michael allows us a first glimpse into his thinking process when he acknowledges that he wants her safely in a cell so that she cannot contact him. We can make several assumptions, among them that he wants her to remain intact in his memories, as she was years earlier, and not as this accused concentration camp guard. Or that he becomes aware of a thread of thought that can lead to their lives becoming entangled again. He does not want that responsibility, knowing, as he now does, that she was possibly a murderer for the Nazi regime.

To his fellow students' amazement, Michael continues to attend the trial every day. He is aware he is striving to observe the proceeding through a haze of detachment,

> We should not believe we can comprehend the incompre-
> hensible, we may not compare the incomparable... Some
> few at the trial would be convicted and punished while we
> of the second generation were silenced by revulsion, shame,
> and guilt—was that all there was to it now?[24]

In the second week, the indictment is read. The five accused women had been guards in a small camp near Cracow, a satellite camp to Auschwitz. As the Allies approached, the guards marched the women westward to evade capture for themselves and liberation for the prisoners. They were bombed, but the guards and two prisoners (a mother and her daughter) did not die. The most important witness was the daughter who wrote a book about their ordeal and published it in America.

One of the main charges involved the night of the bombing,

> The troops and guards had locked the prisoners, several
> hundred women, in a church.[25]

A bomb landed on the steeple, and the roof collapsed in a blaze. The church caught fire,

The heavy doors were unbudgeable. The defendants could have unlocked them. They did not, and the women locked in the church burned to death.

Except for the mother and daughter who hid in a small space under a staircase.[26]

Hanna is questioned about her earlier role at Auschwitz and her part in the women's selection process leading to their death in gas chambers. After a lengthy back and forth, Hanna asks a question of the judge that silences the court,

"I… I mean…so what would you have done?"

After a long silence, he answers,

"There are matters one simply cannot get drawn into, that one must distance oneself from, if the price is not life and limb."…

But she herself was lost in thought. "So should I have…should I have not…should I not have signed up at Siemens?"[27]

This is an "ah-ha" moment for Hanna. A cipher until now, she is taking her first steps on a journey of self-awareness, a journey into trying to fathom her motivations and decisions,

It was not only a question directed at the judge. She was talking aloud to herself, hesitantly, because she had not yet asked herself that question and did not know whether it was the right one, or what the answer was.[28]

Hanna's self-doubt confounds Michael. He realizes that she is one of life's survivors who drifts on the currents wherever they take her. A decade previously, he washed up with other debris into her life. There was little predatory intent on her part toward him; he was only passing flotsam and jetsam. Whereas, for unclear reasons he cannot distinguish, she remains a central figure in his psyche, solidifying herself as a part of his moral responsibility to another human.

The trial winds on, and the other defendants' lawyers sense that Hanna is the weak link and focus on her as she struggles to find her truth, while the other defendants are willing to lie to avoid conviction. These women, when giving testimony, accuse Hanna of playing favorites among the young concentration camp victims.

The witness daughter confirms their accusation,

"Yes, she had favorites, always one of the young ones who was weak and delicate, and she took them under her wing and made sure that they didn't have to work, got them better barracks space and took care of them and fed them better, and in the evening she had them brought to her. And the girls were never allowed to say what she did with them in the evening, and we assumed she was…also because they all ended up on the transports, as if she had had her fun with them and then got bored. But it wasn't like that at all, and one day one of them finally talked, and we learned that the girls read aloud to her, evening after evening. That was better than if they…and better than working themselves to death on the building site. I must have thought it better, or I couldn't have forgotten it. But was it better?" She sat down.[29]

This revelation sears Michael like a lightning bolt. He knows now that understanding why she had children read to her was a key to unraveling her mysterious behavior. This question nags at him. This is another epiphany that years later, he still probes,

And who had I been for her? The little reader she used, the little bedmate with whom she'd had her fun? Would she have sent me to the gas chamber if she hadn't been able to leave me, but wanted to get rid of me?[30]

These rhetorical questions are significant problems for Michael to resolve concerning Hanna's attitude to him. But he still suppresses any inner questioning as to why he had engaged with her when he was fifteen, covertly disobeying his parents and their mores, using her for sex, and then so casually turning his back on her.

The judge asks each defendant the same question as to why they did not unlock the door to let the women out of the burning church. Each had an excuse—they were hurt in the bombing, they lost the key, there was confusion and chaos, and they didn't hear the women screaming. As evidence, the court presents a report the women filed after the event that completely ignores what had occurred that night. One of the defendants points to Hanna and screams that Hanna wrote the report and dragged them all into the cover-up.

The judge asks Hanna the question about unlocking the doors he had asked the others, and she struggles to answer. She searches for reasons and excuses and ends with a confused statement that if they had let out the women, there would have been chaos and the women would have tried to escape. Those actions were against their orders.

The judge raises the question of the report and asks Hanna for a sample of her hand- writing to compare with the report. Michael is aware that Hanna becomes increasingly agitated and admits she wrote the report.

Michael catches onto the fact that Hanna is illiterate. This epiphany explodes in his mind. Her illiteracy was the reason she wanted children to read to her, the reason she refused the foreman job at Siemens, the reason she did not want to train as a tram driver when the offer came at a point near the end of their affair—the real reason why she left him, without a word, at the swimming pool eight years earlier. The reason she never read his love letters and why she had become so angry when he went to fetch breakfast on their long-ago cycling trip. She must have seen the note and assumed he was leaving her.

But beyond all these instances, he realizes, her shame at her illiteracy drove her to admit falsely that she wrote the report: she could not provide a sample of her handwriting. She preferred a lengthy prison sentence to the shame of being known as an illiterate, a fact of her life from which she had kept running.

These understandings bring other realizations to Michael,

> ...But I had betrayed her. So, I was still guilty. And if I
> was not guilty because one cannot be guilty of betraying a
> criminal, then I was guilty of having loved a criminal.[31]

One moral dilemma resolved—Michael admits the profound sense of guilt secreted in his mind structure—leads to another unresolved. Whether or not to tell the judge about Hanna's illiteracy in the hope of lessening her sentence. That Michael is even contemplating this step delivers some modicum of a sense of empathy, of moral responsibility to the surface of his motivations. But Michael struggles with whether he has a right to interfere in the trajectory of Hanna's case. He still will not acknowledge to himself that even after all the time that has passed, the urge to do so would expose his prior involvement with her.

He asks his father, the philosophy professor, for advice, but his father will not give a forthright answer and poses several alternative moral scenarios. Ultimately, Michael did speak to the judge but balked at mentioning Hanna's secret illiteracy. He understood that the choice was hers, whether to reveal this secret.

Hanna is given a life sentence.

After the trial, Michael has a compulsion to visit a concentration camp, the scene of Hanna's crimes; perhaps then he can better understand Hanna. He would have gone to Auschwitz, but it was too far from the university and his studies, so he hitch-hikes to a small concentration camp near him, Struthof, in Alsace. The camp was used—at least in a tiny house on the property—as a gas chamber and crematorium.

On the road to Struthof, Michael and the stranger who gives him a ride engage in a heated confrontation about the camps and the Holocaust. The driver, an older man, at least as old as his father, asks Michael why he wants to visit Struthof. Michael answers that he was at the trial and wants to see a camp. Then driver says,

> "But people who were murdered in the camps hadn't done
> anything to the individuals who murdered them? Is that
> what you want to say? Do you mean that there was no
> reason for hatred and no war?"[32]

A rhetorical question that Michael treats as such. The man continues answering his own question,

> "You're right, there was no war, and no reason for hatred.
> But executioners don't hate the people they execute, and
> they execute them all the same. Because they're ordered to?
> You think they do it because they're ordered to? And you
> think that I'm talking about orders and obedience that the
> guards in the camps were under orders and had to obey?
> …No I'm not talking about orders and obedience. An
> executioner is not under orders. He's doing his work, he
> doesn't hate the people he executes, he's not taking revenge
> on them, he's not killing them because they're in his way or

threatening him or attacking him. They're a matter of such indifference to him he can kill them as easily as not."[33]

Michael listens but again doesn't respond. The man elaborates,

..."Once, I saw a photograph of Jews being shot in Russia. The Jews were in a long row naked; some were standing at the edge of a pit and behind them were soldiers with guns, shooting them in the neck. It was in a quarry, and above the Jews and the soldiers there was an officer sitting on a ledge of a rock, swinging his legs and smoking a cigarette. He looked a little morose. Maybe things weren't going fast enough for him. But there was also something satisfied, even cheerful about his expression, perhaps because the day's work was getting done and it was almost time to go home. He didn't hate Jews. He wasn't..."[34] (Michael interrupts, "Was it you? Were you sitting on the ledge and..."[35]

The driver stops the car and orders Michael out. Michael walks the remainder of the way to the camp, seething at the driver's mindset. His apathy was so typical of so many Germans during the War. He is aware of his impotence to change the history of what had happened to his country.

"Just doing a day's work." The driver's words haunt him. As Hannah Arendt[36] famously commented later, on more trials of Nazi war criminals, "the terrifying banality of evil". The driver's words are an epiphany for us all. The realization that the collective Hitlerian mind structure was steeped so casually in such work-a-day horror.

After that visit, Michael wants nothing more to do with Germany's recent past. He reads and rereads only classic literature such as *The Odyssey*.

Time passes, years go by, Michael becomes a legal historian, marries Gertrude, and has a daughter named Julia, but he divorces Gertrude when Julia is five. He never remarries, and his encounters with other women inevitably remind him of sex with Hanna. She may have left him physically years earlier, but her presence—as an archetypal female figure—looms large in his mind structure throughout his life.

His avoidance tactics of commitment and his reclusiveness are the obvious psychological scars of Hanna's early seduction that haunt him still. Or they may signal his proclivity not to connect deeply to another, to keep his inner world secret, even, largely from himself.

More years pass, Michael does not visit Hanna in prison,

> I wanted simultaneously to understand Hanna's crime and condemn it. But it was too terrible for that. When I tried to understand it, I had the feeling I was failing to condemn it as it must be condemned. When I condemned it as it must be condemned, there was no room for understanding. But even as I wanted to understand Hanna, failing to understand her meant betraying her all over again. I could not resolve this.[37]

Michael berates himself that he is a selfish, moral coward for not visiting Hanna. Yet, he cannot delve deeper and admit that his lack of understanding of *her* motives stymies any impulse of human empathy he may have towards her.

As a compromise to his inaction but driven by the acknowledgment that he carries some moral responsibility for her, he begins to read to her again by sending tapes of the classics he reads and rereads. As it always was, reading is the bridge between them, spanning the distance of their differences.

Seventeen years later still, Michael receives a letter from the prison director. Hanna will be released in one year, and the director asks if Michael can take care of finding her housing and some form of employment. She also asks that Michael visit Hanna.

Enough time has passed for Michael to come to some détente with the lingering psychological effects of their lengthy past relationship. A week before Hanna's release, he does visit her and sees an old woman. Hanna is in her early sixties and Michael his early forties. On the day of her release, Hanna is found dead in her cell, having hung herself.

In the cell, they find books on the Holocaust and the concentration camps, and classical literature. Hanna taught herself to read by listening to Michael's tapes as she turned the pages of those books. She wrote a will leaving several thousand Deutsche marks to the American mother and daughter who escaped from the concentration camp.

The mother was dead, but Michael traces the daughter to Manhattan. They meet there and agree to transfer the funds in Hanna's name to the Jewish League Against Illiteracy. Michael receives a letter the League sends acknowledging the donation. He places the letter on Hanna's grave, the first and only time he visits the cemetery.

But will he be rid so conveniently of his succubus?

The reader understands the story of Hanna and Michael's relationship, all the way to her death, only from Michael's point of view. We are never made privy to Hanna's inner life. We know only about her apathetic affect. To sketch her image, we glean glimpses from what others say of her, her musings in the courtroom, and her act of naming the escaped mother and daughter as beneficiaries in her will. There is much left unstated.

Undoubtedly, we can see Michael as the victim of an adult sexual predator. But as we learn over the course of the book, that is only a superficial understanding. Michael also bears his share of guilt. Ultimately, he escapes Hanna physically when she is imprisoned, but psychologically she possesses him for the remainder of his life and shapes many of his emotional, interpersonal responses.

Michael had taken care of fitting out a tiny apartment for Hanna and imagining her life once she left prison. But her suicide ends all speculation of what the possibility of a joint future for them might have held.

In a more symbolic level of interpretation, we can find, perhaps, further clues to the relationship. In the novel if Hanna symbolizes the collective mind structure of pre-war and Nazi Germany in the 1930s and early 1940s, she represents (to the following generation of Germans) the last vestiges, the last curling tentacles of the glory promised by the Third Reich. Likewise, Michael's mind structure represents that of the following generation, straddling the interregnum between the end of the War and the birth of modern Germany. In that case, we can see him in his impressionable teenage years being clandestinely attracted into a relationship of sorts with Nazi rites and rituals, the history and glory of the Reich. Like so many young people who became members of the Nazi youth. He is entranced for several months until he grows bored and shrugs off that siren call by slowly returning to his circle of school friends, rooting himself in the present and future. Still, he is symbolic of the generation that needs to come to terms with the horror and shame of the past that the Reich perpetrated.

The symbolic Hanna frees herself by reading the truth. The truth of what was perpetrated in her name is so overwhelming she kills herself—and symbolically, to some small degree, the specter of the Nazi mindset. Michael lives his remaining life reconciling the truth of the past with his state of being in the present.

Nazi Germans (including Hanna) and their collaborators lived among illusions reflected from their belief system that they accepted as reality. They committed monstrous acts of inhumane horror and hubristic attempts at social engineering on a colossal scale to bend reality to fit their make-believe scenarios. But essentially, they were illiterate. They did not read the tea leaves of history. They did not read the countervailing forces of moral responsibility their evil unleashed. They did not read the truth about themselves. They did not read what the future was for generations after them.

Perhaps Hanna sensed this truth, and that is why she made her victims read to her. Some part of her wanted to reach beyond the horror and chaos of what her life wrought to the artistic purity of great literature. Perhaps the saddest impact lies in her inability to read herself, her lack of self-awareness of her inner motives, her ignorance of consequences. Her mind structure was opaque to her, a closed book. But she was a survivor. She floated on the surface of the waves of her life, letting them take her where they would. Once she began to read, aspects of her mind structure opened, and she could not bear what they revealed.

Ultimately, we can ask the question—who is "the reader" of the title? The girls in the concentration camps, Michael, Hanna, or you reading this chapter now?

* * *

The following chapter is set in South Africa after the government's transition from white supremacy (apartheid) to a multi-racial democracy. The South African apartheid government was a brutal, racist regime. We follow the protagonist David Lurie on his journey involving black and white South Africans trying to accommodate their mind structures to living in post-apartheid South Africa.

2

REDEMPTION

The issues discussed in this chapter revolve primarily around the notion of redemption and its implications for mind structures. The idea of redemption is embodied or made manifest when a person demonstrates a mind structure shift—consciousness of changes in attitudes and behavior—that signals one is atoning for a fault or mistake. Then one is in the state of being redeemed. This can happen over time and occurs mostly subconsciously.

As we progress through the text of *Disgrace*, my commentary follows the journey of the protagonist, David Lurie, a professor of literature, as he moves from being a morally blind racist, an exploiter of women, and a remote father figure, to a flawed but humbled and compassionate human being.

Nobel prize winning author, South African, J. M. Coetzee, in this post-apartheid novel creates a fictional witness-bearing account. In this narration he eviscerates the mind structure of the passive, white oppressors of the apartheid regime, as well as that of displaced and disorientated black South Africans trying to cope with the aftershocks of four hundred years of racial oppression.

We explore David Lurie's role as a symbol of apartheid's white citizenry. Coetzee also crafts one man's journey to redemption for the sins of omission he has borne all his life. David was not directly guilty of the sins of commission; he did not wear a police or army uniform, but he was guilty of the sins of omission. By exploiting his privilege, by being blind to the plight of others, by orientating himself to Europe and never Africa, by refusing to apologize and accept the power swing of the country's political pendulum, David cripples himself by clinging to an outdated mind structure.

Disgrace by J.M. Coetzee

After four hundred years of Dutch and British colonial, and finally, tyrannical white rule, in 1994, South Africa held its first fully democratic elections. Nelson Mandela, the anti-apartheid leader who spent twenty-seven years in prison on Robben Island, assumed the presidency of what he called "the rainbow nation."

J.M. Coetzee's Booker Prize-winning novel *Disgrace*[1] is one of his *oeuvre* of literary works for which he was awarded the Nobel Prize in Literature in 2003. Published in 1999, *Disgrace* is placed in the immediate post-apartheid years during a momentous transference of political power. This occurs when the South African government morphs from the predominant mind structure of a privileged, wealthy, Eurocentric, white minority whose repressive supremacy was upheld brutally by a white army and a white lead, mainly black police force, to government by a well-educated black elite. These leaders were either released from prison or returned to South Africa from political exile and who were supported, with a huge majority, by an impoverished, ill-educated, black population. Such a shift was sure to produce seismic socio-political and cultural differences and events.

Much like the work of Fyodor Dostoevsky, the Russian master and one of Coetzee's major literary influences, Coetzee uses historical processes only as a backdrop to individual moral dramas. This microcosmic focus contains many elements of the greater national dynamic. *Disgrace* ranks among the significant novels to exploit this technique.

The fictional scenarios of post-Nazi Germany (*The Reader* in Chapter One) and post-apartheid South Africa explore, at least in part, the mind structure of a sexual predator: a female in *The Reader* and in *Disgrace* a male—and how their victims, in both cases, members of the "following" or next-generation functions in the aftermath of immoral quagmires. In *The Reader,* we grappled with many open-ended moral questions in the relationship of Michael and Hanna. In *Disgrace,* protagonist Professor David Lurie's self-interested exploitation of eighteen-year-old Melanie Isaacs, a so-called "colored young woman" and one of his students, leads us into the unexplored moral territory.

In precise, almost desiccated—yet powerfully evocative prose—Coetzee spotlights the family of fifty-two-year-old, divorced Lurie and his adult daughter Lucy, and on mainly one part of the country, a small town in the rural interior of the Eastern Cape. The narrative of David, Lucy, and the "dog-man" Petrus, a black man who lives on Lucy's farm, will pose several questions of moral choice and responsibility.

Spinning from this microcosm are many strands Coetzee interweaves with masterly skill. Among these are:

- David as a symbol of white patriarchy and racist order;
- David's journey to redemption;
- David's predatory sex drive that reflects many of the misogynistic impulses in the society and culture as a whole—black and white;
- David's assimilated love of western culture and his lack of knowledge of anything African mirrors the general attitude of most apartheid-era whites;

- David's obsession with writing an opera on the Romantic poet Lord Byron, whom he regards as his *doppelganger* (alter ego). His insistence on teaching Byron's work and that of other Romantic Poets to his mainly black students. Most black South Africans have never heard of Lord Byron or Romantic poetry or generally the Western literary tradition.

David begins his fall from grace by sexually abusing one of his students. His colleagues and the media treat David as a pariah; this is his disgrace.

Lucy, his daughter, lives on a smallholding near a rural *dorp* (small town). She is a lesbian (whose partner has left her) and a latter-day hippie. Lucy runs a kennel for guard dogs and grows vegetables and flowers to sell at the town's weekly farmers' market. She barely ekes out a living.

Lucy was the sole owner of the land. Since "the freedom," as Petrus, her main help on the farm, calls it, he has acquired legal rights to portions of the land where his family squatted for generations. Before they were squatters, white settlers with guns appropriated Petrus' ancestral land almost a hundred years earlier. Lucy, Petrus, and questions of land ownership and rights replicate one of the most significant disputes in shifting power from white apartheid overlords to black majority South Africans.

Without Petrus' help, Lucy could not exist on the land. They have established an uneasy partnership to work the kennel and the land—rather than Lucy trying to uphold the status quo of their previous master-servant relationship.

These central themes are stitched with other threads: the mistreatment of animals by the general population—white and black; and a searing rape incident where David is rendered a helpless witness.

Perhaps the most important thread is the arc of David's moral redemption from a selfish, self-satisfied, and morally blind antagonist to a humbled, contrite, and slowly awakening protagonist.

The opening sentence of the book,

> For a man of his age, fifty-two, divorced, he has, to his mind, solved the problem of sex rather well.[2]

The phrase "to his mind" intimates that David lives within a mind structure that declares him a self-serving egoist. From his point of view, this is a construct that has served him well. Once a week, he visits Soraya, a twenty-something prostitute, and finds her olive-skinned allure fascinating. So much so that he begins to stalk her and sees her with two small boys, her sons. David never thinks that maybe Soraya is only prostituting herself to support her family. His deluded and morally blind mind structure leads him to believe that she enjoys their liaisons as much as he does. When she sees him following her, she cuts off their arrangement. David is disconcerted but nothing more. He was often unfaithful to his long-divorced wife, Rosalind; all his life he was never without women. He remembers with pride, many with whom he had sexual encounters. After Soraya, he is once again alive to other possibilities.

Soraya is not the only prostitute. Due to the fall of the apartheid regime, in these uncertain times of transition to a new government, jobs are hard to find for everyone. David, too, feels he is prostituting himself in his current position. A Western-trained, culturally elite intellectual, he rigorously defends the Western literary canon. Formerly he taught literature at Cape Town University College, which is now morphed into Cape Technical University. He was re-allocated to the Technical University. Among the budding plumbers, electricians, hairdressers, and other trades, he, once a professor of Classics and Modern

Languages is now an adjunct professor of communications, allowed to teach one "special-field" course a year. In David's mind structure, this situation is a demotion, and it does not sit well with him.

This year for his unique field course, he chose to teach Romantic poets. A student in his class, Melanie Isaacs, a beautiful young woman, catches his attention. Their paths cross one day on the lawns of the school. Sexual predator David makes his first move; he invites Melanie to his flat for a drink; uncertain but flattered, she accepts. As she leaves, she sees the books in his study and is drawn to his collection on Byron. She asks about Byron, David replies,

> "He died young, thirty-six. Away from his home. They all
> died young. Or dried up. Or went mad and were locked
> away. But Italy wasn't where Byron died. He died in
> Greece. He went to Italy to escape a scandal and settled
> there. Settled down. Had the last big love-affair of his life."[3]

This information presages the same life passage for David, who often imagines he is Byron's alter ego.

On her way out of his flat, David grabs Melanie and kisses her, but she "slips away." A few days later, he invites her to lunch, and reluctantly she agrees. Her reluctance is often a response that arises when an older person of authority enters a younger person's life. Melanie's mind structure is confused between knowing she should refuse David's advances and fear that doing so will jeopardize her future at the university.

They re-enter the flat and have sex. David finds Melanie's young body "perfect." He does not have any sense of Melanie's discomfort; he thinks only of satisfying his desires. Rapaciously he intends to pursue Melanie as Byron might have done. After this encounter, he is aware that she continues to sit in his lecture hall as he teaches the Romantics, moving from Wordsworth to Lord Byron.

He tracks her to her flat. Melanie is too surprised to resist the intruder who thrusts himself upon her. David completes the rape as reluctant Melanie doesn't fight but averts herself and lies passive beneath him,

> Not rape, not quite that, but undesired nevertheless, unde-
> sired to the core. As though she had decided to go slack,
> die within herself for the duration, like a rabbit when the
> jaws of the fox close on its neck. So that everything done to
> her might be done, as it were, far away.[4]

This time David is aware of Melanie's discomfort and momentarily contrite. Surprising him that evening, a distraught Melanie arrives at his door. He makes up a bed for her in his daughter's room. Melanie asks if she can stay with him for a while, and David finds the idea alarming,

> Mistress? Daughter? What, in her heart, is she trying to be?
> What is she offering him?[5]

David has sex with Melanie one more time, on the bed in his daughter's room. David seems blind to Melanie's state of mind, of why she ran to his protection; he only wants to use this unexpected opportunity to satisfy his lust. Indeed, this scene is replete with intimations of incest (copulation on his daughter's bed). Still, the more prominent insinuation is that David has no sense of the power play in the dynamic—he is so used to either paying for sex or using his authority to satisfy his desire. He has no thought for his prey.

The following afternoon he is visited in his office by Melanie's boyfriend, Ryan, who knows about David's sexual encounters with her. He tells David that Melanie fled to David's flat, to his protection, to escape from Ryan's wrath. The boyfriend warns David off Melanie.

She does not return to David's flat, and during the night, David's car is vandalized. David understands the threat of violence. A week later, Melanie reappears in class, but this time with her boyfriend. The class is quiet, and David understands that all the students know about his exploits with Melanie. He feels something, maybe even a slight shame.

Yet, he persists with his lecture and teaches Byron's poem, *Lara*, into silence, receiving no response from the students. David answers his question about the appearance of Lucifer in the poem. He says,

> "Lucifer.[6] The angel hurled out of heaven. Of how angels
> live we know little, but we can assume they do not require
> oxygen. At home, Lucifer, the dark angel, does not need
> to breathe. Suddenly, he finds himself cast out into this
> strange 'breathing world' of ours. 'Erring': a being who
> chooses his path, who lives dangerously, even creating
> danger for himself."[7]

The inference of the nexus of David/Byron/Lucifer is obvious. David may not know it yet, but he is about to be thrust from the ivory tower of academia into the "breathing world."

Melanie withdraws from his class and then from the University. By now, David is aware of universal campus gossip involving him. Unexpectedly, Melanie's father accosts him in his office. He says,

> "We put our children in the hands of you people because
> we think we can trust you. If we cannot trust the univer-
> sity, who can we trust? We never thought we were sending
> our daughter into a nest of vipers. No, Professor Lurie,
> you may be high and mighty and have all kinds of degrees,
> but if I was you, I'd be very ashamed of myself, so help me
> God. If I've got hold of the wrong end of the stick, now is

your chance to say, but I don't think so, I can see it from your face."[8]

The university's sexual harassment committee, a committee whose deliberations echo the Truth and Reconciliation Commission procedures chaired by Bishop Desmond Tutu, requires him to apologize to the victim and her family, show remorse, and commit to hours of community service. David accepts his disgrace but refuses to comply with their demands and to admit any guilt. This stubbornness is symptomatic of his self-absorbed mind structure; he thinks he can bend reality to his will. And like Lucifer, he is hurled out of heaven.

When an older authority figure embroils a much younger victim in his power only for sensual pleasure, once again, we are faced with dilemmas of morality and immorality, moral questions, and questionable choices. If David admitted to his guilt, it would not lessen his disgrace, but it would display a degree of self-awareness he does not yet possess. Melanie's situation is more complex. She was young, impressionable, out of her depth, and—terrified.

After he refuses to admit his guilt, the college asks him to resign. David, his mind structure only slightly mangled by self-doubt, retreats to the country to visit his only child, his almost estranged daughter, Lucy,

> Once he has made up his mind to leave, there is little to
> hold him back. He clears out the refrigerator, locks up
> the house, and at noon is on the freeway. A stopover in
> Oudtshoorn, a crack-of-dawn departure: by morning, he is
> nearing his destination, the town of Salem on the Graham-
> stown-Kenton road in the Eastern Cape.[9]

David's journey to the country's interior may signal a trip into his still dormant inner self, his own heart of darkness. Coetzee, by choosing Salem's settlement (Salem meaning "peace" according to the preacher in the 1830s who founded the territory in the Eastern Cape), foreshadows perhaps some intimation of the underlying mind structure David is not yet aware he is seeking.

Lucy's name may conjure intimations of Lucifer for the reader. For, as Coetzee writes, in David's mind, she has thrown herself out of heaven by choosing to live on the edge of what he regards as civilization; a lesbian, alone, surrounded by black Africans, and a pack of attack dogs.

Lucy, a down-to-earth, unassuming person who by choice quietly treads the moral path she forges, greets David's sudden arrival as if his visit was long planned. He is not sure if she is pleased or not to see him. (Always, his egotistic mind structure places him at the center of any situation.) Matter-of-fact about his disgrace (she is used to his peccadillos) she listens without comment to his version of the episode.

Lucy leads him on a tour of the premises, then shows him the kennels and David notes improvements to the dog pens,

> The dogs are excited to see her: Dobermans, German shepherds, ridgebacks, bull terriers, Rottweilers.[10]
>
> The very breeds used to guard white property during apartheid.
>
> Lucy adds, perhaps redundantly, "…Watchdogs all of them…working dogs on short contracts…[11]

They walk companionably about the farm, and Lucy points out the new dam, the extensive fields of vegetables and flowers. When David questions Lucy about her safety in such an isolated place, she says the dogs will protect her. There will be pandemonium if any stranger approaches the house. Besides, she has a gun, she tells him.

On their return to the house, David meets Petrus, once the hired help now Lucy's partner in running the farm. David assumes Petrus is about forty-five. "I am the gardener and dog-man," says Petrus by way of introduction. David admits to Petrus that he is concerned about Lucy's safety. "' Yes,' says Petrus, 'it is dangerous. Everything is dangerous today. But here it is all right, I think.' And he gives another smile."[12]

One afternoon during that week, Lucy finds David asleep on the concrete slab next to the cage of Katy, an old, listless, mongrel bitch. Lucy is surprised but pleased that David seems to have an affinity to be near Katy. Lucy tells David that Katy is in mourning because no one wants her. David hears it as a referential comment on his situation. Lucy says,

> ... "The irony is, she must have offspring all over the
> district who would be happy to share their homes with
> her. But it's not in their power to invite her. They are part
> of the furniture, part of the alarm system. They do us the
> honor of treating us like gods, and we respond by treating
> them like things."[13]

The parallel to how David regards women is apparent. They discuss whether dogs have souls and whether Lucy ever euthanizes her dogs. "No, I don't. Bev does."[14]

David had briefly met Bev when he and Lucy took produce and flowers to town on market day. Bev, helped by volunteers, runs a minimalist Animal Welfare League clinic behind the main street. Lucy keeps telling David that he underestimates Bev, but he remembers her as "That dumpy little woman with an ugly voice that deserves to be ignored?"[15] During this conversation, he is aware of being momentarily "shadowed" with grief at his judgmental attitudes, at his lack of empathy for Bev. Surprising himself, he offers that he will volunteer to help Bev Shaw. This may be the onset of an incremental epiphany for David.

He begins work at the clinic; he admires Bev's skill and prag-
matism as she deals with animals, and she says he has a "presence"
that animals respond to. David is appalled at the serious injuries and
ailments the animals present. Bev calls it a disgrace the way animals are
mistreated in the country. At day's end, he tells her of his disgrace and
asks if, knowing now of his recent past, she stills wants him around.
Stoically admitting she needs all the help she is offered; she replies in
the affirmative. Non-judgmental Bev works with injured and maimed
animals; perhaps she regards David as such.

Days later, on the farm, Lucy and David take two Dobermans for
a walk. When they return to the house, the other dogs are in a frenzied
uproar in their cages, as three strangers, black males—two men and
an adolescent—wait at the house for Lucy and David. They relate a
story of a pregnant woman, a relative nearby, who needs medical help
urgently, and they have no phone or transport to ferry her to the hospital. Lucy agrees to let them use the phone to call for an ambulance.
David looks around for help from Petrus, but he is not on the farm.
Unlike in years gone by when he was trapped in master-servant bond-
age, he is free now to come and go as he pleases.

Once inside, the men lock David in the toilet,

> His child is in the hands of strangers. In a minute, in an
> hour, it will be too late; whatever is happening to her will
> be set in stone, will belong to the past. But *now* is too late.
> *Now* he must do something.[16]

The men gang-rape Lucy. As hard as he tries to free himself, there
is nothing David can do.

Shortly after that, the toilet door opens, and after some alterca-
tion, David is forced to give over his car keys, as he thinks, "He speaks

Italian, he speaks French, but Italian and French will not save him in darkest Africa. He is helpless."[17]

Locked in once again, he glances out of the window slit. He hears his car engine tick over. One of the men has Lucy's rifle and is walking to the kennels. David witnesses the dogs massacred one-by-one; blood and brains scattered everywhere.

The two men return, together with the adolescent, eating from a tub of ice cream. David is doused in methylated spirits and set alight,

> He and his daughter are not being let off lightly after all!
> He can burn; he can die, and if he can die, then so can
> Lucy, above all Lucy.[18]

David plunges his burning hand into the toilet bowl and uses the water to douse the other flames on his clothes; he smells singed hair. He screams for Lucy. After a while, the key turns, and he stumbles out. Lucy has taken a shower and is covered only in her dressing gown. She rushes to the carnage at the kennels while David tries lamely to stop her.

The damage to both Lucy and David is immense: goods stolen, physical injuries, and psychic trauma. Lucy cannot or won't speak of what happened to her. David intuits her rape, against which act his injuries fade to little consequence. But his eye injury is severe, and they phone Ettinger, a farmer on a neighboring farm, for help. He drives them to the nearest hospital. They spend the night at Bev Shaw and her husband's house.

In David's microsphere of life, the rape signals momentous changes. During the rape, David had no thought for himself but only of Lucy. Slowly his mental pendulum is swinging away from his self-referral self. The massacre of the dogs and the capricious nature of morality are thrust into the forefront of his mind structure.

The following day with Lucy insistent and David reluctant, they return to the farm. Lucy spends most of the day and night in her bedroom, and David realizes she must find her way from her darkness,

> For the first time he has a taste of what it will be like to
> be an old man, tired to the bone, without hopes, without
> desires, indifferent to the future. ...It may take weeks, it
> may take months before he is bled dry, but he is bleeding.[19]

Two young policemen came by. Lucy does not tell them of the rape but lists all the other outcomes of the incident. Lucy's secret reveals that she views her rape as her disgrace. Ettinger comes around to see how they are coping; he tells David that they are lucky the men did not abduct Lucy. Ettinger sends someone to fix Lucy's old kombi. David buries the dogs. We can wonder what else he is burying.

Petrus returns with a load of building material strapped to his old van. David walks to where Petrus is working at the dam. He informs Petrus of the robbery, and Petrus says with equanimity that he has heard,

"It is very bad, a very bad thing. But you are alright now."[20]

They discuss whether Lucy will go to the market the following day. David knows that Lucy,

> ...Would rather hide her face, and he knows why. Because
> of the disgrace. ...That is what their visitors have achieved;
> that is what they have done to the confident, modern
> young woman. ... How they put her in her place, how
> they showed her what a woman is for.[21]

David can understand the layers of Lucy's reactions. But he cannot admit to himself that he shares the rapists' attitude "this is what a woman is for in many ways."

David falls into a routine of helping Petrus keep the farm sustainable. They often talk as they work. David is annoyed at Petrus' phlegmatic acceptance of the incident. He wants everyone to feel as devastated as he does.

But Lucy is not improving. In the face of her non-communication, David's thoughts return to his Byron opera project. Most of his material was in the trunk of his stolen car. The local library has none of the books he needs. Still, in old Ravenna, Byron and his great love, Teresa, haunt him; he longs to bring them to life. Will this be where that happens, he muses, not in Cape Town but old Kaffaria.[22]

For David, Cape Town represents civilization, culture, opera, theater; the city is carried on the coattails of what he views as Western culture. Kaffaria is the colonial name for the eighteenth-century borderlands between the expansion to the northeast of the British Cape Colony from Cape Town into the territory of the indigenous Xhosa people.

In self-exile from Cape Town, David straddles the border between the life he has rejected there and his venture across a psychological frontier into what he considers (and has avoided) "darkest Africa." Can his creativity flourish here; his opera take root in soil other than where a Western mindset exists? As he works on the opera, he may be sloughing off the skin of his former self.

Some weeks later, Petrus invites David and Lucy to a party at his compound. David encounters an unfamiliar mind structure; one he has been living alongside all his life. Petrus has tethered two sheep before their slaughter. With his newfound empathy for suffering animals fomented by his contact with Bev, David cannot bear to hear their bleating and untethers them so they can graze near the dam. But Petrus re-tethers them in the morning.

Lucy guesses that the party is to celebrate the recent land transfer of ownership rights to Petrus. She says they should attend and bring a present. David suspects that Lucy's dark moods and erratic behavior have one cause—pregnancy. At first, she denies his observation and then relents, saying she cannot be sure yet.

On Saturday, they join the party, and David is pleased to see Lucy dancing and enjoying herself. He cannot eat the muttonchops Petrus offers him. Suddenly Lucy is at his side, shaken, exclaiming that the youngest of their assailants is present—at the party.

David confronts the adolescent and threatens to call the police and identify the young man as one of the break-in attackers. Petrus intervenes, trying to protect the young man and dissuade David from involving the police. Back at the house, David is about to act on his threat, but now Lucy stops him. They argue why Lucy is protecting the adolescent, who they agree is obviously inside Petrus' sphere of influence. Lucy responds, "This is my life. I am the one who has to live here."[23]

David appeases Lucy by saying he understands she wants to make up for the wrongs of apartheid's past and accept the new order, but it is wrong not to stand up for herself. After further argument, nothing is resolved about the adolescent. David articulates no awareness that he was a passive recipient of white privilege in apartheid's past and still clings to that mindset. He admits to the only change, his empathy with mute animals; not even Lucy's horror can break his self-centered carapace.

Petrus feels the matter is in abeyance and nonchalantly appears the following day to ask for David's help with pipefitting. While they work together, Petrus tells David that he must not prosecute the boy because Lucy is safe now on the farm; he will protect her. David is puzzled. Her father cannot protect her, but Petrus can? Can he in any way shape a role for himself in this alien territory?

One day at the clinic, he unburdens himself to Bev, emphasizing that while he and Lucy are not communicating, he feels he cannot leave her because she is unsafe. She encourages him to leave, "You have to let go of your children, David. You cannot watch over Lucy forever."[24]

But they disagree on Petrus' role in the situation, with Bev calling him "a good old chap."[25]

As to the attack, Bev's sympathy is all with Lucy. David is outraged,

Do they think he has not suffered with his daughter? What more could he have witnessed than he is capable of imaging? Or do they think where rape is concerned no man can be where the woman is? Whatever the answer, he is outraged at being treated like an outsider.[26]

It is telling that David continues to blind himself to any parallels of his conduct with Melanie or her father's response to his daughter's violation. His outrage is reserved for how *he* is treated.

He continues to try to grapple with his opera project on the farm, but the harder he tries, the more he feels the characters slipping away from him. This seems to reflect his old life slithering into the past, as well as in the present his troubled relationships with Lucy, Bev, Petrus, and the farm.

He is untethered in the interregnum of psychological borderlands.

On Sundays, the clinic's doors are locked, and he helps Bev with euthanizing the "superfluous" animals; Bev treats each with love and care in its last minutes. David is convinced that if Bev cannot charm a dog, it is because of him. He emits the bad smell, the smell of shame. Nonetheless, he holds the dogs in their dying moments,

He had thought he would get used to it, but that is not what happens. The more killings he assists in, the more jittery he gets. Yet, he is the one who drives the loaded kombi to the hospital incinerator and feeds the black plastic bags with the corpses to the flames.

One Sunday evening driving home in Lucy's kombi, he actually has to stop at the roadside to recover himself. Tears flow down his face that he cannot stop; his hands shake. He does not understand what is happening to him.[27]

David may not be aware of what is happening, but he is slowly embarking on his existential journey into himself.

Bev calls and asks to meet him at the clinic at four, but he knows the clinic is not open on Mondays. David surmises why she is calling: like a bitch in heat, she is announcing she is ready for adultery,

The choice is between the operating table and the floor. He spreads out blankets on the floor. …He switches off the light, leaves the room, and checks that the back door is locked, waits. He hears the rustle of clothes as she undresses. Bev. Never did he dream he would sleep with Bev.[28]… Let me not forget this day, he tells himself, lying beside her when they are spent. After the sweet young flesh of Melanie Isaacs, this is what I have come to. This is what I will have to get used to, this and even less than this.[29]

Maybe because Bev was the provocateur in this instance, David has a more realistic view of his changing status.

Petrus borrows a tractor, and to David, seeing him sitting on the machine plowing his land, Petrus becomes an iconic image of the

New South Africa. In a moment of clarity, David senses that Lucy is defeated; if she stays, she will grow old as a thrown-away thing on the entire farm that Petrus will own. White South Africans like himself may have to atone for the sins of apartheid by living as the minority in a country they once ruled with oppressive force.

Once again, David begs Lucy to take a trip out of the country at his expense, to Europe where they have relatives, to replenish her vitality. But Lucy refuses,

> "If I leave now, David, I won't come back. Thank you for
> your offer, but it won't work. There is nothing you can sug-
> gest that I haven't been through a hundred times myself."[30]

The conversation turns to the events of the day of the attack; Lucy continues,

> "I think they have done it before, at least the two older
> ones have. I think they are rapists first and foremost.
> Stealing things is just incidental. A sideline. I think they *do*
> rape. …I think I am in their territory. They have marked
> me. They will come back for me. …What if that is the
> price for staying on? They see me as owing something.
> They see themselves as debt collectors, tax collectors. Why
> should I be allowed to live here without paying? Perhaps
> that is what they tell themselves."[31]

The conversation continues, and David learns that the two older men raped her, and she assumes the younger was there to watch and learn. The discussion, especially by Lucy, chastises David's pointed remarks that he's a man, a father; he must know of these things. He senses an epiphany, a shift in his mind structure. For the first time, he tries to imagine what *she* was experiencing during the rape. (He has never thought of Melanie or any other woman from their perspective.) Shaken again, he asks her to leave the farm, and again she refuses, saying it will be a defeat she'll regret the rest of her life.

He and Lucy have cut too deeply into one another; it is time for him to depart.

David leaves the farm to drive to Cape Town; he needs to revisit his old life. Spontaneously, he detours through George and finds himself outside the family home of Melanie Isaacs. Her younger sister, Desiree, greets him and tells him that her father is at the middle school where he is principal. David feels a flicker of desire for her and hates himself at that moment.

Isaacs is stunned to see David, and tersely, he asks why David is visiting him. David tells Isaacs he wants to speak from his heart and give his side of the story. He explains that what started as an adventure turned into something else because Melanie "struck up a fire in him."[32] He asks after Melanie and learns that she was allowed to re-enroll in the university and is finishing her studies with special dispensation. Then, surprisingly, Isaacs asks David to dine with the family that evening.

At dinner, it is clear the family has discussed him, 'The unwanted visitor, the man whose name is darkness.'[33]

The meal progresses after a long pause when they link hands, and Isaacs leads them in a lengthy, mumbling prayer. David is not surprised to learn the family is Christian, that the father is a deacon or something. He is the recipient of Christian charity, and it makes him uneasy. The meal is filled with stilted conversation, during which David mainly talks about Lucy and Petrus and their activities on the farm.

After dinner, as he makes the gestures of leaving, Isaacs stops him. Facing him, David says to Melanie's father that with Melanie, he failed to provide something lyrical,

"Even when I burn I don't sing, if you understand me. For
which I am sorry. I am sorry for what I put your daughter through. You have a wonderful family. I apologize
for the grief I have caused you and Mrs. Isaacs. I ask for
your pardon."[34]

Isaacs says he has waited for a long time for the apology. "The
question is what does God want from you, besides being very sorry.
Have you any ideas, Mr. Lurie?"[35]

David fumbles through a response that he is not a believer, but if
he were, then perhaps it is enough that he lives in disgrace, a profound
state of punishment from which it seems impossible to lift himself,

"I am living it out from day to day, trying to accept disgrace as my state of being. Is it enough for God, do you
think, that I live in disgrace without term?"[36]

This is a profound statement, not only an admission of David's
developing sense of self-awareness but of his associative connection to
the archangel Lucifer, the light bearer fallen into the darkness of Hell.
His associative response includes Byron, the unsavory sex scoundrel,
his previous alter ego, whom he can no longer make sing, especially in
his opera. His "disgrace" is also associated with the guilty conscience
of white South Africans whom David symbolizes, the upholders of the
disgraceful policies of apartheid.

On his way out of Isaac's house, David blunders past the door of
a room where the mother and daughter sit. He says nothing but kneels
before them and touches his forehead to the floor,

"Good night," he says. "Thank you for your kindness,
thank you for the meal."[37]

David arrives in Cape Town the following day. He is "home again," but it does not feel like home; he must sell the house close to the university and move to a smaller apartment. His life is in shambles; he has not paid bills, the garden is neglected, and he finds the house has been ransacked,

> No ordinary burglary. A raiding party moving in, cleaning
> out the site, retreating laden with bags, boxes, suitcases.
> Booty; war reparation; another incident on the great cam-
> paign of redistribution. …Have Beethoven and Janáček
> found homes for themselves, or have they been tossed out
> on the rubbish heap?[38]

Numbly David goes through the motions of making sense of his life—he deals with the robbery—police and insurance—sees his bank manager, organizes an alarm system, and calls Lucy. He tells her he can come back any time she needs him.

When he has bought the simplest of items to make the house livable again, he turns to work on the opera,

> He had thought of it as a chamber-play about love and
> death, with a passionate young woman and a once pas-
> sionate but now less than a passionate older man. As an
> action with a complex, restless music, behind it, sung in an
> English that tugs continually toward an imagined Italian.[39]

But now, as on Lucy's farm, the project fails to compel him to further composition. He foregoes the image of Teresa as a dashing young woman and re-imagines her as a dumpy widow living with her aging father. He re-imagines Byron as dead, and Teresa treasures his letters and trinkets that she always keeps near her. David hopes his older Teresa will capture his creativity.

The parallels are apparent; Teresa has become Bev. Byron, the exiled David, is now dead to his old self. But there is more. Teresa's heart shatters when she learns that Byron denigrated her to his friends and that once he had ravished her, he grew bored. Teresa is distraught,

> Her years with Byron constitute the apex of her life. Byron's love is all that sets her apart. Without him, she is nothing: a woman past her prime, without prospects, living out her days in a dull, provincial town, exchanging visits with woman-friend sleeping alone.
>
> Can he find it in his heart to love this plain, ordinary woman? Can he love her enough to write music for her? If he cannot, what is left for him?[40]

He finds he can do so; Bev is his unlikely muse. He writes some glorious arias for Teresa/Bev, "That is how it must be from here on: Teresa's giving voice to her lover, and he, the man in the ransacked house, giving voice to Teresa."[41]

For days David follows the distraught Contessa and finds, he is not called by the erotic nor the elegiac, but the comic. "Disconcertingly he hears the plink of the banjo whenever Teresa sings."[42]

As he writes words and music, David finds his work plays out the opera of his current life as a tragi-comedy. He follows Teresa's voice at a gallop interspersed with banjo notes until one day he hears another voice, one he did not know was about to appear: that of Byron's daughter, Allegra.

> Allegra is dying of malaria and sings to Byron, "*Why have you left me?*"… But Byron will not answer; he is too tired of life, "*My poor little baby.*" Sings Byron too softly for her to hear.[43]

Despite his obsession with his opera, David has not forgotten Lucy but suspects she believes her life is easier when he is not around. Finally, his mind structure is changing enough that he thinks about their situation from Lucy's point of view, another incremental step on the journey to redemption.

Aside from composition, David picks up the threads of his life; he lunches with his ex-wife, gossips with some former colleagues, walks on the mountain. And he attends a performance at a local theater where Melanie appears in a play. But Ryan, the boyfriend, recognizes him, and David flees the theater. Ryan waits for him in the parking lot and once again warns him off Melanie.

David stays in terse contact with Lucy, but something in her voice bothers him. He calls Bev to check if Lucy is coping. Bev says she is, but there have been 'developments' that she cannot talk about. He makes up an excuse to visit Lucy and asks if he can stop by for a few days. David returns to the uncomfortable frontier of his new life.

There are changes at the farm; a wire fence marks Lucy and Petrus' property. Petrus has built a scrawny house, as yet unfinished. Lucy wears an old smock. She tells him she is pregnant. Immediately they argue again. David thought she had taken care of any possibility of pregnancy, and Lucy denies she had given him that idea. She tells him that she makes the decisions about her life, and she decided to keep the baby. David does not take kindly to the idea of Lucy carrying the seed of her assailants, a baby of African origin. This is a shock to his rapidly fraying belief system.

But there is more; the young man is back. He lives with Petrus as part of an extended family arrangement because it appears he is Petrus' nephew. And even more, a seismic shock, Petrus has offered to marry Lucy. He tells David that she must be under his protection; it is too dangerous for her to live alone.

David tries in vain to argue with Lucy on this next step, he calls it blackmail to gain her land, and besides, Petrus already had two wives.

Always pragmatic, Lucy shares her point of view,

"I don't believe you get the point, David. Petrus is not offering me a church wedding followed by a honeymoon on the Wild Coast. He is offering an alliance, a deal. I contribute the land, in return for which I am allowed to creep under his wing. Otherwise, he wants to remind me, I am without protection. I am fair game."[44]

David once again tries to dissuade Lucy, but she will not listen. She asks him to tell Petrus that she will marry him but only if he accepts the child as part of his family. She will sign over the land, but the house remains hers,

"I will become a tenant on his land. … No one enters the house without my permission. Including him. And I keep the kennels."

"How humiliating," he says finally. …

"Yes, I agree, it is humiliating. …Perhaps that's what I must learn to accept. To start at ground level. With nothing. No cards, no weapons, no property, no rights, no dignity."

"Like a dog."

"Yes, like a dog."[45]

David feels superfluous; how long can he straddle his two mind structures. Where does he belong? He cannot hold his balance like this for much longer; he must fall back into liberal Cape Town or forward, like Lucy, into African soil. The cultural divide is immense.

The following morning David takes Katy, the mongrel bitch,

for a stroll, and sees the adolescent, Petrus' nephew, spying through a window on Lucy as she dresses. David punches him, and they wrestle on the ground. Lucy is annoyed at what she regards as David's interference, and David realizes that he and Lucy have lost all but the politest connection. Another strand of his old mind structure snaps—his belief that even though he was an absent figure in her life, he, in some way, was entitled to be her protector.

David wants to stay in the area to be near her if there is an emergency and rents a room at a boarding house in town. But he spends almost all his days helping Bev at the clinic. At night he struggles to complete the opera. He and Bev are no longer lovers but warmly affectionate. He decides, "Until the child is born this will be his life."[46]

The unborn baby must already carry the burden of being a pawn in David's decisions. He buys a van mainly to be able to continue to transport dead dogs in their plastic bags to the incinerator. The dead dogs also carry some of the weight of David's re-formatting mind structure. He is literally burning his old mind structure in the incinerator. It would be unthinkable for urbane Professor David Lurie of several months earlier strutting around the university campus to have contemplated, let alone carry to fruition, such a task.

In a small, enclosed yard at the back of the clinic, David spends many hours sitting in the sun, dreaming of Teresa, whose cries to Byron to be rescued from her sad life. David knows he had lied to himself when he told others that the opera was a hobby, now it consumes him night and day. Yet, he also knows how little his effort is and does not have the talent or energy to make it soar. David accepts his limitations,

It would have been nice to be returned triumphant to
society as the author of an eccentric little chamber-opera.
But that will not be... Though it would have been nice for

Lucy to hear proof in her lifetime and think a little better of him.[47]

He is also failing Teresa whom he brought back from the dead. He trusts she will forgive him. For David accepting his limits as a writer of opera is a significant step into his new self. The opera has become a tragi-comedy. He is beginning to view his life that way. This perspective may birth a new, more realistic era for him.

As he works at menial tasks around the clinic or plays his banjo, a young dog with three legs befriends him. The dog is fascinated by the sound of the banjo. David wonders how he can incorporate the dog's howls into the opera. Animals, too, have a role in the new opera of life.

Once a week, he helps Lucy with her stall at the farmers' market. He learns that Petrus has finished his house and that one of his wives is about to have her baby. Petrus has not pushed his marriage proposal any further, and David suggests that once Lucy's child is born, "…after all, a child of this earth…"[48]

Petrus may come around to marrying her. He asks Lucy how she feels about the child—does she love it? She replies, not then, but once it is born, she's sure her love will grow. She adds that she's determined to be a good mother. She suggests that David should try to be a good person. He replies, "I suspect it's too late for me. I'm just an old lag serving out my sentence."[49]

Tacitly, David is signaling he is atoning for his past fault-filled life.

Weeks later, he visits Lucy at the farm. He sees,

> Lucy with her back to him, has not yet noticed him. She is wearing a pale summer dress, boots. And a wide straw hat. As she bends over, clipping or pruning or tying, he can see the milky, blue-veined skin and broad, vulnerable tendons

of the backs of her knees: the least beautiful part of a woman's body, the least expressive, and therefore perhaps the most endearing. Lucy straightens up, stretches, bends down again. Field-labour; peasant tasks, immemorial. His daughter is becoming a peasant.[50]

As Lucy works, David's mind flows forward to the reality of him becoming a grandfather. The wry question arises in his mind,

What pretty girl can he expect to be wooed into bed with a grandfather?[51]

He muses that as he is not much of a father, what can he expect of himself as a grandfather? He recognizes that almost his entire life, his predominant interest has been pretty girls. He wonders if it is too late to learn a broader perspective on life.

Lucy acknowledges him, and his reverie is broken. They have tea. David likes this new way of being together, visiting, a different beginning,

The following Sunday, he and Bev are practicing their ritual euthanasia of the animals that are designated for death: first cats, then dogs. They work silently, attuned now to one another's movements and needs. There is one dog left, the young, three-legged one who would soon be in the theater about to meet his death amid the smell of expiration, the soft, short smell of the released soul.

He could persuade Bev to a week's reprieve for the dog, but death is inevitable. As with all the others, he will wheel the dog in its plastic bag from the van, throw it into the flames, and see that it is burnt to ashes. He is unaware that it is also the smell of his released soul,

He crosses the surgery, "Was that the last?" Asks Bev Shaw.

"One more."

He opens the cage door. "Come," he says, bends, opens his arms. The dog wags its crippled rear, sniffs his face, licks his cheeks, his lips, his ears. He does nothing to stop it. "Come."

Bearing him in his arms like a lamb, he re-enters the surgery. "I thought you would save him for another week," says Bev Shaw. "Are you giving him up?"

"Yes," I am giving him up."[52]

This final scene is filled with pathos and significance. This redemptive—almost Christ-like gesture of Jesus carrying a lamb—signals David's entry to a period of grace. The transference of his self onto the dog, has metamorphosed in his subconscious mind as a way of seeking absolution by burning his past. The dog, a scapegoat that carries David's sins into the wilderness, so he can return from the frontier where his soul has wandered, innocent and untainted.

In his new world order, his mind structure incrementally changed by his atonement, David accepts Lucy as a symbol of the next generation of whites, which adapts more quickly to the new political order that he is slowly embracing. Being the grandfather of a black child may become his anchor in this new world. As for Lucy, she owns African land, works the African soil, and carries an African baby; she is an African.

Petrus, on his tractor, with his two, and possibly soon, three wives, and his land rights, has inherited South Africa's future.

* * *

Across the Indian Ocean from South Africa lies the sub-continent of southeast Asia, including the country of India. In that ancient country, 2500 years ago, a young prince known as the Buddha grew famous with his teachings that soon spread across the entire Asian continent. The mind structure of Buddhism is constructed from different premises than those that underlie our Western precepts. This is our next chapter.

3
EXPLORING ASPECTS OF OUR INNER LIFE

The books in this chapter, *Siddhartha* by Hermann Hesse; *Shambhala: The Sacred Path of the Warrior* by Chögyam Trungpa, focus on East Asian mind structures. They are framed by the philosophy of the Buddha and practices of Buddhism, particularly meditation and meditation practices, and shed light on some essential insights into East Asian mind structures. Buddhism focuses on self-mastery and advocates a path that enhances inner awareness achieved through self-reflection and meditation practices; exploring concepts related to understanding aspects of our inner life.

Meditative consciousness can inculcate wisdom and compassion to help form a cultural mind structure.

Wisdom and compassion practices are based on the Buddha's teachings of the Four Noble Truths and the Eightfold Path. The purpose of this aspirational path is self-reliance through self-reflection and self-control to align and balance many mind states. The Four Noble Truths and the Eightfold Path describe aspirational steps to that end.

As defined in Buddhist terms, wisdom is generally accepted as "insight" or "inner sight," a mind state beyond the dualities and uncertainties inherent in our sensory reality. The word "dualities", as used in this context, involves many of the paradoxes we grapple with throughout our lives, such as birth and death, darkness and light, sadness and joy, good and evil—they are each side of the same coin. For example, we cannot know happiness if we do not know unhappiness, and so on. When you achieve a deep level of meditative concentration, you are open to new realizations that move you beyond dualities to their underlying unity.

People who embody insight can maintain that awareness while functioning simultaneously on their sensory reality. In other words, they are embodied practitioners who operate in the "marketplace" while maintaining consciousness of insight.

Meditators can achieve this metaphysical understanding of "wisdom" through ontological experiences that vary from meditator to meditator. They are individual, personal experiences. Personal experience—garnered through my layperson practice—affirms that humans can achieve embodied insight.

As a meditator since a teenager, I did not immerse myself or become an adherent of any of the great meditation traditions. Instead, I viewed myself as a SAT—a seeker after truth. To become a practicing meditator, one does not have to become an adherent of a particular "-ism."

I studied different meditation traditions in university courses, continuing education classes, and retreat centers in cities and rural settings. I found that the basis of every meditation tradition and many practices center on "quieting the mind" and "following the breath." Reassured by this understanding, I ventured far afield to experience meditation retreats and teachings from different teachers.

One such retreat found me in 2007 at Kopan Monastery in the

Kathmandu Valley, Nepal. This monastery is a replica of the largest monasteries—ancient sites of learning—destroyed by the Red Army when China first invaded Tibet in the 1950s.

Kopan is home to about three hundred and fifty Buddhist monks, lamas, teachers, and workers. The monks come from all areas of Nepal and Tibet and range from seven to over seventy. They devote their lives to the study and practice of the teachings of the Buddha. Also, at the monastery are international retreatants attending courses designed for them.

Several times during the two-week retreat, our learned lama entered the *gompa* (temple) with a beaming smile and a sideways rocking gait. He was an elderly abbot or head lama, a lifelong monk, a revered figure in Tibet, and a Tibetan refugee, settled in Nepal, who helped found Kopan monastery.

This lama led several of our *dharma* (Buddhist teachings) talks aided by a translator. He cycled a *mala* (a string of prayer beads) wrapped around his left hand deliberately and constantly between his thumb and forefingers. Seated cross-legged on a high platform so we could all see him, he ran his gaze over the entire group (about forty people), his eyes lingering on each face. His energetic presence was palpable. There was something different about this man.

Overall, he said little and never stopped smiling, except to utter concise responses to questions. Generally, I'm a skeptic, but I could feel the energy field when he asked us to join him in guided meditation.

"Be happy," the lama repeated into the silence. These were moments of great clarity for me.

Here was a being, a living philosopher who personified experiential inquiry—ontological practice—simply by his presence; and epistemology, by his knowledgeable responses to questions: a man of wisdom in all meanings of the word. Merely being in his embodied presence induced a sense of greater self-awareness in a meditator—but meditating with him—expanded the possibilities of being human. This man belonged to a special order of human beings I had not encountered before. He was a living example of what we can aspire to be.

In their book *The Monk and the Philosopher*,[1] French philosopher, Jean-Francois Revel, and his son, Buddhist monk, Matthieu Ricard discuss similarities and differences in Western and Eastern mindsets. Ricard described how in East Asia (mainly Nepal and India) he found people, living examples of wisdom,

> I had the impression of seeing living beings who were the
> very image of what they taught. They had such a striking and
> remarkable feeling about them. I couldn't quite hit on the
> explicit reasons why, but what struck me most was that they
> matched the ideal of sainthood, the perfect being, the sage—a
> kind of person hardly to be found nowadays in the West.[2]

This is exactly my experience as described above.

On other retreats in the United States and elsewhere, I've had similar responses when sitting with practitioners. Many were awakened to deep levels of meditative consciousness through sustained practice, but never to the extent as when I was in the presence of this lama. Practitioners who are "awakened" simply mean people open to ontological experiences that manifest when they bring such single-pointed, focused attention to the breath that their thoughts, although still present, fade into the background.

Anyone can practice meditation and achieve these states anywhere they live. You don't have to be in a temple, an ashram, monastery, nunnery, meditation hall, ice cave or cave of any description.

Initially, the historic Buddha transmitted spiritual wisdom gained from his own experiences to his, eventually, seven thousand *arhats* (initiated followers). They moved with him around northern India, changing locations with the changing seasons. From the Buddha, they learned that practicing meditative consciousness (wisdom) is one of two arms of his teachings—the other is compassion.

Compassion can be universally understood as kind-heartedness, sympathy, empathy, all emotions related to the wellbeing of others, as well as for ourselves.

For instance, local kings and princes fed and housed the Buddha's nomadic gathering, largely supporting this massive spiritual army, thereby demonstrating one way of embodying the very compassion the Buddha taught.

Supporting the Dharma and Buddhist teachers enables compassion for self and others to grow, for as the Buddha communicated, the dharma demonstrates a way to end our existential, psychological suffering.

One *dharma* tradition is that teachers do not charge for their teachings. Students support the teacher and the teachings. They contribute *dana*, a donation, of whatever they can afford for the value of the teachings they receive.

Many of the Buddha's acolytes embarked on meditation retreats on their own and acquired wisdom through solitary meditation practices in ice caves in the Himalayas and other caves while on solitary retreats on the lower slopes of mountainsides, in temples, monasteries, and nunneries. Eventually, they returned to towns and villages to share their wisdom in the marketplace of human interaction. After the Buddha died, his teachings spread as generations of teachers continued to transmit the teachings. Centuries later, these teaching and practices flourished and grew in Asia, Europe, and the United States.

The Buddha taught in the oral tradition. This tradition of passing stories and societal lore to succeeding generations down the ages is prevalent in societies where literacy is not widely present. Many societies hold storytellers in high esteem. They are the carriers of folklore, customs, and beliefs.

The following well-known story features the Buddha in the form of the Buddha of Compassion. The story of Deer Park is akin to Aesop's fables or biblical parables.

As the story unfolds, once upon a time, two magnificent deer were born in the Kingdom of Benares in north India. One was called King Banyan Deer and the other Branch Deer. Eventually, each led a herd of over five hundred deer.

The King of Benares and his followers hunted deer for the table. The daily beating of drums and general harassment drove the herds into panic, and many deer were injured and died. The kingdom's people were also upset; they had to interrupt their tasks when the King hunted nearby, as they were pressed into serving as his bearers and beaters. To stop this routine, they built him a deer park and herded the deer into the park. The king was pleased with the vast herds and his park.

He saw two perfect, golden deer there, and he granted them immunity from the daily killing forays. But the herds' panic returned whenever they sensed the royal hunters in the park with their bows and arrows. Eventually, the two golden deer gathered their herds, and all agreed that each day one deer would volunteer for death and place their head on the killing stone so that the other deer would be spared disastrous panic.

One day a pregnant doe approached Branch Deer and asked for immunity from volunteering to protect her unborn fawn. But he refused, saying he could not change the rules that were for everyone. He chose logic over compassion. She went to King Banyan Deer, who responded to her supplication by saying he would put another deer in her place.

In an act of genuine compassion, King Banyan Deer then went to the executioner's block, where he laid his head. But the royal cook would not slaughter him because of the immunity the King had granted this deer. When the king learned of the event, he was surprised and went to the park to meet with King Banyan Deer.

The two conversed, and the deer told the King of Benares about the pregnant doe. Banyan addressed him as king of men and said he wept as he thought of the fawn never being born and never experiencing the natural wonders of the park. He also described how he felt the doe's maternal sorrow and suffering and offered himself in her place. He added that he was in a quandary because of the king's immunity order not to be killed. Yet he could not force another deer to take her place, knowing that all deer felt safe for another day. He assured the king that he offered his life for the sake of the doe and unborn fawn and not for any other reason.

The King of Benares was overcome. Tears rolled down his cheeks. Then he replied, addressing the deer as a great lord, the golden king of deer, and added that even among men, he had not seen such a being as this deer, capable of great compassion, generosity, and kindness to give his life for another. He decreed that the doe would never be killed. The king told Banyan to rise.

Without hesitation and with his head still on the block, the golden deer responded by asking questions as to the fate of other deer in the park and if they too, could be saved. Addressing Banyan again as "My lord", the king said that he could not refuse the request and granted safety and freedom to all the deer in the park. When pushed by Banyan to save all the deer not only those in the park, the king replied that all the deer in his kingdom would be spared.

Still, the golden deer did not rise. He pleaded for the safety of all four-footed animals and the birds and fish. The king responded that they would be safe, and he granted immunity from hunting and killing all the animals in his kingdom.

Having successfully pleaded for the lives of all creatures, the great being arose.

Through the example of this tale (and many others), we learn of compassion in the Buddha's teachings.

Siddhartha by Herman Hesse

Siddhartha,[3] first published in an English translation in 1951 (originally published in German in 1922), is a fictional account of a man's spiritual journey as he seeks inner peace. The author, Hermann Hesse (1877-1962), was a Nobel Prize winner in literature. *Siddhartha* wielded significant influence on young people worldwide in the tumultuous late1950s-1960s, an era of profound social changes in Western countries. These shifts particularly impacted American mind structures. Notably, it was an era of progressive steps in civil rights aspirations in the United States. A truism exists that young people of that era carried in the back pockets of their blue jeans, a copy of Jack Kerouac's 1957 best-seller, *On the Road,* and Herman Hesse's *Siddhartha.*

For millions of Western seekers searching for another way to perceive the world and escape their egotistical and consumer-driven mind structure and culture, reading *Siddhartha* is often the Open Sesame experience to their inner worlds.

The work is carefully crafted to read as if one hears Hesse's words spoken in the oral tradition. His story unfolds almost like a replica of the life journey of the historical Buddha. The living Buddha appears as a historical figure in the book, so we can assume the novel was set in northern India two and a half thousand years ago. The Buddha's birth name was also Siddhartha.

The novella opens with a young man of a high caste Brahmin family speaking to his friend, Govinda, as they attend morning meditation in Siddhartha's family's home on the banks of a river.

The narrator tells us that Siddhartha was an advanced meditator,

> Already he knew how to pronounce Om silently—this word of words, to say it inwardly with the intake of breath, when breathing out with all his soul, his brow radiating the glow of pure spirit. ...[4]

("Om" can be translated as Perfection.)

His father took pride in his intelligent son...thirsty for knowledge and he saw him growing up to be a great, learned man, a priest, a prince among Brahmins. [5]

Yet Siddhartha was not content,

> He had begun to feel the seeds of discontent within him...He had begun to suspect that his worthy father and his other teachers had already passed onto him their wisdom, they had poured the bulk and best of their wisdom and the sum total of their knowledge into his waiting vessel...but his soul was not at peace, his heart was not still.[6]

Siddhartha concluded that what he sought couldn't be found in his current milieu,

> "One must find the source within one's own Self, one must possess it. Everything else was seeking—a detour, error."[7]

Siddhartha knew that to fulfill this realization, he must leave his father and the familiarity of his household and seek further wisdom elsewhere. Eventually, his father gave his blessing, and Siddhartha, accompanied by Govinda, began their search for the wise men that live in the forests—the Samanas.

They lived with the Samanas, practitioners of an ascetic form of Hinduism, for several years: walking barefoot, wearing only a loincloth, living outdoors in all weather, fasting many days, and barely eating on others, never cutting their hair or beards or nails. Every moment they were awake, they moved slowly, usually in meditative silence.

Siddhartha and Govinda grew to be skeletal and unkempt. The goal of their practice was to move beyond all pain in the physical body,

> Silently Siddhartha stood in the fierce sun's rays, filled with pain and thirst. Silently he stood in the rain, water dripping from his hair onto the freezing hips and legs. And the ascetic stood until his shoulders and legs no longer froze, till they were silent, till they were still. Silently he crouched among thorns, blood dripped from his smarting skin, ulcers formed, and Siddhartha remained stiff and motionless, till no more blood flowed, till here was no more pricking, no more smarting.
>
> ...He waited with new thirst, like a hunter at a chasm where the life cycle ends, where there is an end to causes, where painless eternity begins. He killed his senses, he killed his memory, he slipped out of his self, in a thousand different forms.[8]

Siddhartha learned much from the Samanas but he did not feel fundamental consciousness changes in his mind structure. After all these years of practicing self-denial as a path to release the soul, Siddhartha asked Govinda if he thought they were any further on their quest. Govinda shared with Siddhartha that he saw his friend as an exemplary ascetic who exhibited that he had learned much and was still learning. Govinda predicted that one day Siddhartha would be a holy man. Siddhartha disagreed and replied that he did not feel as though he had learned anything more than if he had been living among thieves and gamblers. He questioned self-denial's rationale, saying that thieves and gamblers achieved the same sense of escape from their bodies when they fell asleep in the tavern over their wine vessels.

With their begging bowls for food, the pair moved among the villagers, Siddhartha continuing constantly to question Govinda whether they were on the right path and to warn him that he, Siddhartha, would soon leave the Samanas.

They heard a rumor that a holy man had appeared called Gotama, the Illustrious, the Buddha. In Sanskrit, the word "Buddha" translates as "awakened teacher within." The rumor proclaimed,

> He had conquered in himself the sorrows of the world
> and had brought to a standstill the cycle of rebirth. He
> wandered through the country preaching, surrounded by
> disciples, having no possessions, homeless, without a wife,
> wearing the yellow cloak of an ascetic, but with a lofty
> brow, a holy man, and Brahmins and princes bowed before
> him and became his pupils."[9]

Siddhartha and Govinda found the rumors compelling, and when they learned the Buddha was to teach near the forest where they lived with the Samanas, they told the group they wanted to hear him. The Samanas scolded them but eventually gave their blessings.

The Buddha and his vast array of followers were in Savathi (Savasti) in northern India, in Jetavna grove—land and garden that a wealthy merchant, a devotee of the Buddha, gave him. During many days in Jetavna grove, they often saw the Buddha in the distance surrounded by monks, all with their begging bowls. Finally, they heard the Buddha teach,

> They heard his voice, and this was also perfect, quiet and
> full of peace. Gotama talked about suffering. Life was pain,
> the world was full of suffering, but the path to the release
> from suffering had been found.[10]

Many pilgrims came forward and asked to be accepted into the community. Among them was Govinda, fully expecting Siddhartha to follow. But Siddhartha declined. He told Govinda that he had often wondered whether Govinda, driven by his conviction, would ever separate from him. Siddhartha said,

> "Now, you are a man and have chosen your own path.
> May you go along it to the end, my friend. May you
> find salvation!"[11]

Their parting was sad, and Govinda wept, but Siddhartha was resolute. Wandering through the grove, unexpectedly he met the Buddha and asked respectfully if he could address the Illustrious One. He tried to explain why, unlike his friend, he was not joining the Buddha. Siddhartha asked if he could speak freely, and the Buddha agreed to listen. Among much else, he articulated his questions and concerns about following yet another teacher. He used epistemology, logic, and reason to reveal what he thought was a flaw in the Buddha's teaching. In his ontological teachings, something new could not be proven, only experienced: a path to end mental suffering and perceptions of duality.

The Buddha listened patiently for a long time and answered that Siddhartha should think hard about the perceived flaw. He told Siddhartha to be wary of "only a thirst for knowledge, and to be wary of opinions and the conflicts of words. Opinions mean nothing."[12] He defended his teaching, saying it was not "...my goal was not to explain the world to those who are thirsty for knowledge. Its goal is quite different; its goal is salvation from suffering."[13]

In other words, what the Buddha taught was experiential. How Siddhartha argued was based on knowledge and reason. To step from one mind structure and open himself to another would be a giant leap for Siddhartha.

They argued politely back and forth, and the Buddha ended their interaction,

> "You are clever, O Samana, you know how to speak cleverly, my friend. Be on guard against too much cleverness."[14]

Among the Samanas, Siddhartha had followed a path to more knowledge. The Buddha's teachings were anathema to him. As the Buddha walked away, Siddhartha thought,

> I have seen one man, one man only, before whom I must lower my eyes. I will never lower my eyes before any other man. No other teachings will attract me, since this man's teachings have not done so.[15]

For many weeks, Siddhartha wandered without a destination, without Govinda, and without a teacher. After years of suppressing his sensory reactivity, he delighted in the cornucopia of sensory delights that nature offered, arousing all his senses. He sustained himself with his begging bowl and the generosity of villagers as he passed through their hamlets. He had but one aim,

> What he had said to the Buddha—that the Buddha's wisdom and secret was not teachable, that it was inexpressible and incommunicable—and which the Buddha had

once experienced in his hour of enlightenment, was just want he had now set off to experience… He must gain experience himself.[16]

One afternoon, Siddhartha came to a river and asked an aging ferryman to take him across. The ferryman agreed and did not charge Siddhartha whom he knew from his tattered clothes and begging bowl was a Samana. He assured Siddhartha that they would meet again. When Siddhartha asked him how he could be so confident of that meeting, the ferryman said,

> "I have learned from the river that everything comes back. You, too, Samana, will come back."[17]

Skeptical, Siddhartha did not want to be impolite and did not question the ferryman how he could learn from a river.

Eventually, in one of the larger villages, Siddhartha encountered a lovely courtesan, Kamala. He fell instantly in love forgetting his previous life and his vows to experience what the Buddha had experienced. Under Kamala's influence, Siddhartha became the assistant to a wealthy merchant and then a wealthy merchant himself. For months, Kamala instructed him in the art of lovemaking.

During the next several years, Siddhartha indulged in the sensory delights of this world. He gambled, had many women (although he always returned to Kamala), became a wealthier and wealthier man, gained weight, and sated every physical desire he imagined. Yet,

> …At times he heard within him a soft, gentle voice, which reminded him quietly, complained quietly, so that he could hardly hear it. Then he suddenly saw clearly that he was leading a strange life, that he was doing many things that were only a game, that he was quite cheerful

and sometimes experienced pleasure, but that real life was flowing past him and did not touch him. … His real-self wandered elsewhere, far away, wandered on and on invisibly and had nothing to do with his life."[18]

Siddhartha's discontent and impatience with his luxurious lifestyle presaged significant changes. His disgruntlement forced him to speak harshly to Kamala. Kamala said that she understood his feelings. Siddhartha praised her for her inner stillness and shared some of his deepest thoughts,

> "Most people, Kamala, are like a falling leaf that drifts and turns in the air, flutters and falls to the ground. But a few others are like stars which travel one defined path: no wind reaches them, they are within themselves their guide and path."[19]

Kamala responded that once again he was talking like a Samana. She said,

> "You do not really love me—you love nobody. Is not that true?"[20]

Siddhartha spoke enigmatically,

> "I am like you. You cannot love either, otherwise how could you practice love as an art? Perhaps people like us cannot love. Ordinary people can—that is their secret." A shudder passed through his body; he felt like something had died.[21]

His life in the town and his relationship with Kamala continued until he knew, "That the game was finished, that he could no longer play."[22]

Although he was not consciously aware of deep changes in his psyche, his mind structure had shifted. That same night Siddhartha left his house, his garden, all his belongings, and Kamala, never to return,

> He was full of ennui, full of misery, full of death; there was nothing left in the world that could attract him, that could give him pleasure and solace. He wished passionately for oblivion, to be at rest, to be dead.[23]

In our lifetimes, we may experience many deaths to our inner selves, through hardships and joys, and the different roles we play at various stages in our lives. Siddhartha had fully experienced both the asceticism of the mystical Samanas and the indulgent and sensuous lifestyle of a wealthy merchant and found both unsatisfactory. Now, he sought oblivion by heedlessly rushing through forests and fields until exhausted; he passed out on a riverbank. But, unknown to him, he was ultimately seeking a middle way between these extremes.

As he regained consciousness, Siddhartha heard the word Om resonant in his ears. He became aware of his querulous wish for oblivion,

> ...all the despair, had not affected him so much as it did the moment the Om reached his consciousness, and he recognized his wretchedness and his crime.[24]

Metaphorically, in his life till this moment he had fallen into a deep sleep and now awakened, he felt renewed. He reflected on the change he felt within, a gentle yet seismic, mind structure change,

> Now, when I am no longer young, when my hair is fast growing grey, when strength begins to diminish, now I am beginning again like a child. ...He was going backwards, and now again he stood empty and naked and ignorant in the world. ... He did not grieve about it, no, he even felt

a great desire to laugh, to laugh at himself, to laugh at this strange foolish world![25]

Siddhartha realized that his struggles as a Hindu Brahmin, then an ascetic, and most recently a voluptuary, were illusionary. Long ago, his inner voice had been correct when it told him that no teacher could bring him deliverance. He had died and a new Siddhartha awakened from his sleep. He had experienced the mind shift the Buddha taught. He saw through new eyes.

Siddhartha was transitory, all forms were transitory, but today he was young, he was a child—the new Siddhartha—and he was very happy.

Happily, he studied the flowing river,

Never had he found the voice and appearance of flowing
water so beautiful. It seemed as if the river had something
special to tell him, something which he did not know,
something which still awaited him. The new Siddhartha
felt a deep love for this flowing water and decided that he
would not leave it again so quickly.[26]

In time, he thought, he would come to know what the river would teach him. At that moment, he realized that the water flowed continuously from where he sat on the riverbank, but it was new at every moment. He asked himself who could understand this phenomenon. He did not, yet, but he was aware of a slight recognition of the truth the concept contained.

A ferryman appeared from across the river and seemed surprised to see Siddhartha, and then he recognized him as the young ascetic he ferried across this same river years before. After conversing on pleasantries, Siddhartha apprised the elderly ferryman, Vasudeva, that he would like to live there at the river with him and learn how to be a ferryman and read the river's currents, as well as to listen to the voices in the water. The old man agreed that Siddhartha could stay.

If we think metaphorically, the river becomes life flowing from individual creeks, to streams, to ever wider rivers that all flow into the ocean and all oceans are inter-connected. A ferryman learns to become one with the currents and tides, the wind and rain as he rides the river. He can chart a steady course over the river; he has found the middle way.

Siddhartha began his life as a ferryman. Vasudeva, his steadfast companion, occasionally offered enlightening commentary on Siddhartha's musings. On one occasion, Siddhartha asked Vasudeva if he had learned from the river that there is no such thing as time. In general, Vasudeva spoke sparingly,

> "Yes, Siddhartha, is this what you mean? That the river
> is everywhere at the same time, at the source and at the
> mouth, at the waterfall, at the ferry, at the current, in the
> ocean and in the mountains, everywhere and that the pres-
> ent only exists for it, not the shadow of the past, not the
> shadow of the future."[27]

And Siddhartha understood then what Vasudeva had taught him; the same river flowed by, but the water was always different.

Siddhartha spent many years with the ferryman. Dressed in a loin cloth and turban, he became one with the river learning its moods and voices and understanding the ecology of all life that dwells there or close to it. He found the rhythmic poling action of the ferry meditative. Siddhartha had dreams in which he conversed with Govinda, Kamala, and his father.

On one occasion, the Buddha was teaching near the river

crossing, and Siddhartha and Vasudeva were ferrying many people back and forth. One such pilgrim was Kamala and with her a ten-year-old child. When she overcame her shock at seeing Siddhartha, she introduced him to the child, telling Siddhartha the boy was his son. Siddhartha was instantly smitten with love for his son. But the boy shunned Siddhartha.

A few days later, Kamala died from a snakebite. Siddhartha tried to comfort the boy and offered him a home in his hut. The boy stayed for a while but eventually ran away to the nearest village. Siddhartha was overwhelmed with the loss of both Kamala and his son. Then he understood the pain his father must have felt when he, Siddhartha, left his ancestral home. As the ferryman had said many years before, "All things return."

Vasudeva counseled him,

"Forgive me, I am speaking to you as my friend. I can see you are worried and unhappy. Your, son, my dear friend, is troubling you and also me. The young bird is accustomed to a different life, to a different nest. He did not run away from riches and the town with a feeling of nausea and disgust as you did; he has had to leave all these things against his will. I have asked the river, my friend, I have asked it many times, and the river laughed, it laughed at me and it laughed at you; it shook itself with laughter at our folly. Water will go to water, youth to youth. Your son will not be happy in this place. You ask the river and listen to what it says."[28]

Siddhartha listened to the river and the river laughed and told him,

"Everything not suffered to the end and finally concluded, recurred, and the same sorrows were undergone."[29]

Mind structure changes that are fully embraced, in many ways, mean relinquishing old egotistical scaffolding and revealing the self, encased behind the frame.

Many years passed before Siddhartha became accustomed to living with the inner void that the loss of his son opened in his life. He had loved the boy blindly and then lost him. Nothing before had caused this much pain. Finally, Siddhartha realized that all the interlocking lives in his life, all the pain, joy, sadness, love, ill fortune, fortune, and happiness were all together in this Life,

> All of them together within the stream of events, the music
> of life…When he did not bind his soul to any one partic-
> ular voice and absorb it in his Self, but heard them all, the
> whole, the unity; then the great song of a thousand voices
> consisted of one word: Om—perfection.[30]

He understood what Vasudeva said about the river being everywhere and simultaneously beneath his ferry,

> From that hour Siddhartha ceased to fight against his
> destiny. There shone in his face the serenity of knowl-
> edge, of one who is no longer confronted with conflict of
> desires, who has found salvation, who is in harmony with
> the stream of events, with the stream of life, full of sympa-
> thy and compassion. Surrendering himself to the stream,
> belonging to the unity of all things.[31]

Shortly thereafter, Vasudeva knowing that his death was near, left their abode, as he wanted to die in the woods. He told Siddhartha, "Yes, I'm going into the woods; I am going into the unity of all things."[32]

Years passed. Govinda, living miles away from the river, eventually heard of an old ferryman several day's journey away, who lived by the river and was a sage. Govinda, now a revered senior monk himself was still restless to gain more knowledge. He wanted to meet the sage. The old ferryman-sage ferried Govinda across the river, and he asked the ferryman to share some of his wisdom. They conversed about spiritual seeking and how sometimes the most challenging part of the path is acknowledging what is staring directly at you.

Siddhartha revealed himself to Govinda, who was overjoyed to find his friend. The next day before he departed, Govinda asked Siddhartha where he found his happiness, his serenity. Siddhartha said,

> "Knowledge can be communicated, but not wisdom. One
> can find it, live it, be fortified by it, do wonders through it,
> but one cannot communicate and teach it."[33]

As he spoke, Siddhartha realized that even the Buddha's words returned, as Vasudeva had told him, "Everything returns." In his own words to Govinda, he heard the Buddha's voice in his head telling him to be wary of seeking knowledge or cleverness for its own sake.

By way of illustrating his point on wisdom, Siddhartha bent and lifted a stone,

> "This is a stone, and within a certain length of time it will
> perhaps be soil and from soil it will become plant, animal
> or man. Previously I should have said: This stone is just
> a stone; it has no value, it belongs to the world of Maya,
> but perhaps because within the cycle of change it can also
> become man and spirit; it is also of importance. That is
> what I should have thought. But now I think: This stone
> is stone, it is also animal, God and Buddha. I do not love
> and respect it because it was one thing and will become
> something else, but because it has already been everything

and always is everything. I love it just because it is a stone, because today and now it appears to me a stone."[34]

Govinda nodded, understanding evident in his shining eyes. Still holding the stone, Siddhartha continued,

> "I see value and meaning in each one of its fine markings and cavities, in the yellow, in the gray, in the hardness and the sound of it when I knock it, in the dryness or dampness of its surface. There are stones that feel like oil or soap, that look like leaves or sand, and each one is different and worships Om in its own way; each one is Brahman. At the same time it is very much stone, oily or soapy, and that is just what pleases me and seems wonderful and worthy of worship."

He paused, clearly pleased that Govinda was receptive to his words. He said,

> "But I will say no more about it. Words do not express thoughts very well. They always become a little different immediately they are expressed, a little distorted, a little foolish. And yet it also pleases me and seems right that what is of value and wisdom to one man seems nonsense to another."[35]

The two old men conversed further, and as Govinda took his leave, he had a vision of a thousand faces and unity in the interconnectedness of all that is. Siddhartha watched his friend's face as he came to this realization and smiled. The realization is profound,

> …Unity overflowing forms, this smile of simultaneousness over the thousands of births and deaths—this smile of

Siddhartha—was exactly the same as the calm, delicate, impenetrable, perhaps gracious, perhaps mocking, wise, thousand-fold smile of Gotama, the Buddha as he perceived it with awe a thousand times.[36]

The novella ends with Govinda bowed low to the ground in front of his friend,

> ...Whose smile reminded him of everything that he had ever loved in his life, of everything that had ever been of value and holy in his life.[37]

Siddhartha, the novella, carries universal resonance for any seeker open to uncovering through their ontological realizations, their inner teacher, inner peace, wisdom, and unity that comes from understanding the interconnectedness of all that is.

Another fundamental teaching of Buddhism—the Middle Way—can become a mind structure reinforcing a way to live your life. If you live your life "the middle way," you are not strung too tight as to be overly intense or strung too loose as to be lackadaisical. You find equilibrium between these extremes. This teaching can be found in the following oral tradition story.

A Samana sat on a riverbank dressed in a tattered loincloth, unkempt, skeletal, his only possession a begging bowl. He meditated on the flow of the river. The river carried many small vessels with passengers, as the river was the only way for people to pass through the dense tropical forests.

The Samana noticed a boat drifting on the current near the shore with a standing ferryman and two seated occupants—one a man, and the other a boy holding a stringed instrument and bow. As they floated by the Samana snatched a moment of their conversation. The man said, "If you string the instrument too tight the strings cannot move enough to make music. If you string the instrument too loose the strings cannot make music because there is no tension. You must find the middle way between too tight and too loose and then the instrument will make wonderful music."

This was the moment of enlightenment for the Samana. He had lived a life of luxury and worldly pleasure and found it too loose. He had lived a life of physical deprivation and abuse and found it too tight. Henceforth he would strive to live in the middle way.

At that moment, a girl passed by on the bank, herding goats. She filled his begging bowl with rice. The man ate every grain, and for the first time in years, he felt satisfied and felt free.

Thus, the Buddhist path is often referred to as the Middle Way.

As mentioned earlier in the chapter, foundational Buddhist principles that become the dharma path are present in the Four Noble Truths, and the Eightfold Path. These precepts build the Buddhist mind structure.

The Four Noble Truths are known as doctrine and the Eightfold Path as practice. They interlock and are not an intellectual exercise but practical, incremental steps on a spiritual path.

The First Noble Truth is that we all suffer. All humans experience psychological suffering because all conditional (cause and effect) phenomena are not substantial or fulfilling. Actions have consequences. Decisions have consequences. Desires have consequences.

The Second Noble Truth identifies the cause of suffering. Craving and clinging to what is pleasurable and avoiding that what is not cause psychological suffering. Craving and clinging generate hindrances to meditative consciousness: ill will or aversion; sensory desire or greed; sloth or torpor and restlessness; worry or lack of confidence; and doubt or confusion. Inevitably, we accept physical decrepitude, aging, and death. But we struggle to accept as the causes of our suffering, the psychological afflictions of craving for what we do not have, clinging to what we do have, and their emotional offshoots, such as anger, greed, and fear.

The Third Noble Truth is that we can end this suffering. The cessation of psychological suffering ends this craving and clinging.

The Fourth Noble Truth shows the way. Simply follow the Eightfold Path.

Arising from an understanding of the Four Noble Truths, these following eight steps are logically structured so that the previous one folds neatly into the one that follows:

Right View

Understand the Four Noble truths in order to practice
Right Intention.

Right Intention

Dedicate yourself to becoming a just, kind, courageous
and wise person with the aim of achieving liberation from
suffering. Be aware of the impact of your words in order to
practice Right speech.

Right Speech

Think before you speak. For example, do not lie, slander,
insult or mislead others. This will lead to Right Action.

Right Action

Channel your speech in positive ways. This inevitably leads
to Right Action in your communication and interactions
with others, including generating your livelihood.

Right Livelihood

Earn your living, honestly. Quash any self-serving motivations, such as cheating or not paying your taxes. This is achieved through Right Effort.

Right Effort

Strive to achieve a level of balance and fairness in your mind and hence in your interactions with others. Right Effort is the step that requires placing your attention, psychological energy, and other inner resources into training your mind.

Right Mindfulness

Meditate daily with Right Mindfulness. Concentrate on your breath, try to cease clinging to your thoughts, swinging wildly through your mind. Begin to see and name thoughts as thoughts, feelings as feelings, sensations as sensations; and so on. In other words, you become aware of your mind as it slips into habitual thinking.

Right Concentration

Meditation practice now brings insight, inner stillness and unbreakable concentration. This infuses your daily life as you carry a sense of equanimity, mindfulness, and objectivity. As described previously. there are other more developed stages of meditation where all sense of duality fades. Master meditators can achieve these awareness states at will and often their minds are in Right Concentration even as they go about their daily tasks.

Shambhala: The Sacred Path of the Warrior
by Chögyam Trungpa

As the Buddha teaches and Siddhartha and Govinda show us, wisdom and compassion may be attained through meditation practice and accompanying mind training. Chögyam Trungpa's book *Shambhala*[38] is a handy, introductory guide to these practices.

Shambhala describes a utopian vision. Two significant ideas permeate *Shambhala: The Sacred Path of the Warrior. Shambhala* describes the terrain of our consciousness of an Eastern Buddhist utopia present in everyone. The other describes step-by-step Trungpa's training program for the spiritual warrior. As we will see in Chapter Seven of this book, Plato's *The Republic* follows in many ways, although for divergent ends, both these precepts.

The significant difference between the works is that Plato aimed to develop a society based on individuals educated to uphold The Good. In contrast, Trungpa builds a "how-to" model for everyone to find Shambhala within us, no matter where or when we live and who we are. He shares methodology to conquer mind states that negatively impact our inward journey. The battles spiritual warrior wages are not external and physical but psychological and spiritual.

Unlike in Plato's hierarchical schema, no one in the Buddhist tradition, must be of "select" or elite caliber. The Buddhist mind structure includes all humans under the rubric—spiritual warrior.

Author Trungpa, (1940-1987), a Tibetan high lama, a refugee after the Communist Chinese invasion of Tibet in the early 1950s, eventually made his way to the United States via India (living in a refugee camp) and Scotland (a teaching stint for several years). He arrived in the United States in 1970. In 1974 he established a Tibetan Buddhist center in Boulder, Colorado, called the Naropa Institute. Decades later, the institute founded Naropa University, a fully accredited higher education school since the mid-1980s that, among many other disciplines, maintains a core curriculum with an emphasis on East Asian Buddhist culture, history, philosophy, and teachings. The institute also established a publication arm, Shambhala Press. The Press has published thousands of books on Eastern philosophy, literature, history, and culture, and publishes several quarterly journals. These activities are ongoing.

The following quote is by Carolyn Rose Gimian in her Editor's preface to *Shambhala,*

> Trungpa's interest in the kingdom of Shambhala dates back to his years in Tibet, where he was the supreme abbot of the Surmang monasteries. As a young man he studied some of the tantric texts that discuss the legendary kingdom of Shambhala, the path to it and its inner significance. As he was fleeing from the Communist Chinese over the Himalayas in 1959, Chögyam Trungpa wrote a spiritual account of the history of Shambhala, which was unfortunately lost on the journey.
>
> Although Trungpa uses the legend and imagery of the Shambhala kingdom as the basis for this book, he states that the teachings draw on ancient, perhaps even primordial, cultural and spiritual wisdom and principles of human conduct. Whatever its sources, the vision that is presented in his book has not been articulated anywhere else. It is a unique statement on the human condition and potential.[39]

I love teaching people to meditate and have done so in many settings with adults, as well as adolescents. Teaching gifted high school seniors, a literature and philosophy elective provided me with a perfect opportunity to help them embark on a meditation journey.

As we begin our meditation practice, I ask my students to take a deep breath, place their fingers over their larynxes, and say the word "Om" until all their breath is expelled. We do this breathing exercise several times. Once their self-consciousness dissipates, we can feel and hear the vibrations in our larynx and ears. In the Eastern mindset, the Sanskrit word "Om," meaning perfection, is one of three seed syllables of universal energy thought to be present at the birth of our universe.

By repeating these words, you align yourself with those elemental energies. Then, I play recordings of Buddhists monks chanting "Om" and the two other seed syllables, "Ah" and "Hung." Together the vibrational energy is palpable.

During these weeks of meditation practice, we read and discuss Trungpa's book as a way in which to anchor our practice. We discuss his detailed explanations of the various steps towards self-mastery and self-awareness. After each meditation session, students noted their experience, journaling what was the same and/or different for them during that session. They wrote 3,000-word papers on their experiential learning encounter. Below are short paragraphs from two papers.

From an essay by Evan Garnick: *Reflections on Meditation*[40]

For me, our introductory study of meditation proved to be an exercise of tremendous value. Unlike most experiences I have encountered before, meditation enabled me to truly understand –that is, to comprehend ontologically – the extraordinary ability of the human brain to transform its perception of reality. Consciousness, it seems, is neither rigid nor unalterable; rather, it is strikingly flexible, able to morph from one state of being to another. The means by which these metamorphoses occur can vary between different traditions and individuals, but it seems almost axiomatic that transcendental, spiritual undertakings – whether accomplished through the consumption of mind-altering drugs, the participation in religious worship, or the practice of meditation – hold a central position in the human experience.

From an essay by Addie Oursler: *Eastern Philosophy: A Response*[41]

The diamond mind of sharp, concentrated focus and the profound physical state of relaxation create a terrifyingly brilliant experience. Meditation, deeply and intricately connected to Eastern philosophical cultures, allows an individual to follow their own breath to find an inner state of harmony and to develop an awareness of one's basic goodness. Compassion for one's self and for others is crucial in a harmonious society.

Through meditation, one can leave the chaos and distractions of the external world for inner tranquility, guided away by the breath. Few things are universal. However, the gentle inhale and exhale of breath, bringing oxygen to the bloodstream and thus enabling life, is a common, shared experience throughout the human species. In accordance with Eastern teachings, inner goodness—or the innate and natural tendency toward good—also exists within every person, just like the breath. With attention to the breath, one can journey to find his or her inner goodness and gain the experiential knowledge that comes from meditating.

Meditation gave me refuge as I have seen a glimpse of the universe within myself.

Meditation allows me to be aware of my ego and the

societal cultivation of empty materialism to align myself
with the metaphysical or the universal spirit of goodness.
Through meditation, I see myself and those around me in
relation to the earth and the sky.

Questions may arise after reading this chapter. The most common
encompasses the thought: Why don't we in the West pay more attention to imparting ontological experiences in our daily lives?

To track an answer, we must return to the days of the ancient
philosophers in Athens.

In the age of classical Greece there was no fundamental difference
between Western and East Asian philosophy. The schism arose after
Plato and Aristotle died and philosophy slowly drifted in the west to
a neo-scientific methodology that relies almost entirely on establishing
scientific explanations using models and tested theories of how natural
laws work. Ontology, metaphysics, and cosmology essentially became
the purview of Eastern philosophy.

After around a thousand-year hiatus, in the 12th and 13th centuries, a golden age of philosophy arose in Spain in Andalusia, where
Christian, Jewish, and Islamic scholars lived, worked, and philoso-
phized together. This was a period of significant renewal and flowering
for Christian and Jewish philosophy as well as Islamic philosophy and
literature. In Andalusia, we see this symbiosis manifested, although
with a twist of Christian, Jewish and Islamic interpretation.

Then and for several hundred years after that, as many intellec-
tuals and thinkers studied Plato's work for the first time in a millen-
nium, schools of Neo-Platonism arose at many of the great European
universities.

In the late 19th century, philosophers, literary luminaries, and now
cultural icons, American Transcendentalists—Ralph Waldo Emerson,
Henry David Thoreau, and Herman Melville—discovered East Asian

philosophy and incorporated many concepts into their work. In the early 20th century, philosopher and psychologist Carl Jung, a disciple of psychologist Sigmund Freud, explored East Asian philosophy and included these ideas. The ontological nature of and possibilities for philosophy began to recapture the mind structure of Western thinkers.

* * *

Let us turn now to Chapter Four, the play *Hamlet*.

Siddhartha and *Hamlet* in tandem present a fascinating investigation into contrasting mind structures. If Hamlet is the prototypical Western man beset by questions and doubts, the eponymous Siddhartha in Herman Hesse's novella embodies an Eastern mind structure. Both protagonists are of princely birth and exemplars of the mind structures of his time and place. Both have companions on their journeys, Hamlet and Horatio, Siddhartha and Govinda.

Siddhartha, a seeker after truth, receives his father's permission to leave his luxurious life in the palace, and embark on a life-changing journey to find inner peace. He succeeds.

Siddhartha comes to understand that Nirvana (awakening from illusion through listening to your inner teacher) and Samsara (mental phenomena we wrestle with every day) are of the same nature.

Initially, Hamlet fights his fate to revenge his father's death,

O cursed spite that ever I was born to set it right.[42] (Act 1, scene 5, lines 210-211).

By the end of the play, Hamlet arrives at acceptance that his fate is pre-ordained,

There's a divinity that shapes our ends,
Rough-hew them how we will —
(Act 5, scene 2, lines 11-12)[43]

Hamlet's philosophizing,

There is nothing good or bad, but thinking makes it so.[44] (Act 2, scene 2, lines 68-70) echoes Siddhartha's awakening but in a Western framework of understanding.

4

EXPLORING ASPECTS OF WESTERN MIND STRUCTURES

The literature we explore in this chapter is the play *Hamlet* by William Shakespeare. Shakespeare lived from 1564 to 1616, mainly in Stratford-on-Avon, his birthplace, and in the City of London, one of England's walled cities. London was the Western world's theatrical epicenter during the Golden Age of English literature.

Drama is not primarily about actors on the stage or characters whose lines we read. Drama is about each of us—our emotions, thoughts, and interactions with those around us, and with the circumstances of our lives. Human drama exists in plays. And there is no more universal character in drama, especially Western drama, than William Shakespeare's character, Prince Hamlet.

I learned firsthand the power of drama. In South Africa, in the aftermath of the black student "uprising" against the apartheid regime in June 1976 and the subsequent government's shutdown of all schools in the so-called "black areas," I volunteered to teach at a makeshift study center at the YMCA hall in Dube, Soweto. Soweto, a vast, sprawling "black township," abuts Johannesburg. We read aloud and acted out the play *Murder in the Cathedral* by T.S. Eliot.

The play centers on Archbishop Thomas Becket residing at Canterbury Cathedral, England in 1170. As well as the chorus and Becket, the other character roles are four knights or tempters. Each represents a facet of authoritarianism and the autocratic power of the King (to whom they have pledged loyalty) in his struggle for dominance over the power of the Church. Becket is murdered in the Cathedral (historical fact), and the people rise against royal authority. The play was first produced in 1935 in Canterbury Cathedral amidst the realization in Britain of the real threat presented by fascism and authoritarianism in Europe. Eliot connected the dots.

I chose this play because it offered many students a part in the chorus. Eliot structured the play in the format of Greek drama, so simultaneously, I taught the origins of drama in the Western tradition.

Additionally, I chose the play because of the students' recent experience of uprising against the authoritarianism of apartheid as enacted by the government's police-state policies and activities. The army and police had reacted to the student uprising, shooting, killing, and maiming many young students, children, and adolescents, mainly as they ran away from police bullets. *Murder in the Cathedral* would be a suitable catalyst, I thought, for students to release some of their anger and psychic pain.

Of course, the students readily made the connection I hoped they would. The play reading progressed rapidly, and we agreed to hold a reading performance in a large hall in Soweto. One afternoon during rehearsals, the Chorus, about twenty strong, drew out real knives and other homemade weapons to attack the Four Knights when they made their appearance. The Chorus's demeanor, intense and purposeful, sent shivers of alarm through me. For them, the Knights embodied the police coming to kill one of their well-respected leaders. The drama's universal significance became life-threatening.

Amid the turmoil, somehow, I managed to stop the rehearsal and avert a crisis. I remember standing in front of the young men playing the Knights, throwing open my arms and shouting at the menacing Chorus, "Stop! Stop!" I don't remember much else aside from many other students rushing to protect me.

We no longer rehearsed the play. Drama has universal significance.

Hamlet by William Shakespeare

Hamlet[1], the dramatic, emotional, and tragic tale of the eponymous Prince of Denmark, first published in 1603, remains William Shakespeare's most famous play. Translated into hundreds of languages, re-issued in numerous editions, produced on stage somewhere almost continuously around the globe, and captured in several movie versions.

If only one of Shakespeare's works is taught in schools everywhere on the planet, that one is *Hamlet*. There are troves of books and theses on Shakespeare and *Hamlet,* found in world libraries and databases. An edition of Shakespeare's First Folio that includes *Hamlet* sold in New York in 2001 for $6.16 million, making it the book with the highest monetary value in the world.

This play carries magnetic appeal. The mores of Hamlet's time and place have resonated across the world for over four hundred years. Precepts of Western mind structures such as individualism and unwavering acceptance of Life's changing circumstances, frame the play. Individualism is a significant aspect of the Western mind structure. The play evokes ideas on existence, being and becoming, death, reality and illusion, and the ceaseless activity of our minds.

The Italian Renaissance birthed Shakespeare's embryonic individualistic man. He molds the character of Hamlet into a proto-typical

Western figure. In *Hamlet*, Shakespeare's anthropocentric vision mirrors the innovative ideal behind the bravura sculptures of the Italian Renaissance created centuries earlier. Shakespeare wields Hamlet's thoughts and words to describe an idealized depiction of the individual human. In other words, sculptors and artists, such as Michelangelo and Leonardo Da Vinci would acclaim the man Hamlet as he ponders aloud on the dual nature of our lives that develop perfected human minds and bodies, only for them to face aging imperfection and the dusty decay of death. Hamlet says,

> What a piece of work is a man, how noble in reason, how
> infinite in faculties, in form and moving how express and
> admirable; in action how like an angel, in apprehension
> how like a god: the beauty of the world, the paragon of all
> animals—and yet, to me, what is this quintessence of dust?
> (Act 2, scene 2, lines 327-332)[2]

Hamlet probes more deeply into the mystery of life and death than the artists of the Italian Renaissance ever did. He asks, "What is this quintessence of dust?"

We ponder this rhetorical question to this day.

Another significant aspect of the Western mind structure is both a blessing and curse, the ceaseless activity of our minds, generating endless thoughts. Hamlet says,

> ...Oh, God, I could be bounded in a nutshell and count
> myself a king of infinite space, were it not that I have bad
> dreams.
> (Act 2, scene 2, lines 273-275)[3]

Through the first three acts of the play, Hamlet cannot shake his "bad dreams," his ceaseless thoughts, as they thrust him into tempestuous arguments with fate, into philosophizing, procrastinating, and then procrastinating again. Simultaneously, he struggles to find validity in not exacting revenge for his father's death.

Hamlet acknowledges that these thoughts currently form his mind state, and he can find no relief from their almost manic charge. Trying to cling to his usual rationality, although having admitted to his "bad dreams", Hamlet does not timidly accept this mental state. He has a profound response to his own rhetoric. His depression, procrastination, doubts and fears, and realization of Man's decay into "the quintessence of dust," result from his following assertion that explains the realistic, fundamental origin of what he calls his "bad dreams,"

> … There is nothing good or bad but thinking makes it so.
> (Act 2, scene 2, lines 268-270)[4]

These lines are among the most important philosophical statements in the play. They explain the formation of mind structures. Our constant flow of thoughts is the cornerstone of all our mind structures, governing how we react to outer circumstances, our inner responses to those stimuli, and directing who we are and who we become.

Hamlet presages the existence of the thinker, the existentialist, an individual responsible for his actions even as he tussles with nihilistic angst, anxiety, and, less often, neurosis and mad obsession. Hamlet grapples bravely with these states that fold into his mind structure.

He struggles to be psychologically free.

The notion of psychological dilemmas is all too familiar to modern readers; we accept the apparent reality that existence encompasses the contradictory struggle between good and evil, life and afterlife, sadness and joy, and so on. We are free to choose between their binary components and/or free to perceive them holistically as two sides of the same coin.

Freedom of choice may be our greatest shackle. As French

existentialist philosopher Jean-Jacques Sartre wrote in 1943, "Man is condemned to be free." The full quote reads, "Man is condemned to be free; because once thrown into the world, he is responsible for everything he does."[5]

A more positive viewpoint frames existentialism as a belief that we are all free to choose, exercise free will, remake ourselves, cast off experience, speak our truth and be sure of it—even as we grow and change again. We can change our mind structure, adapt to individualism, to resolute acceptance of Life's changing circumstances. We can reveal our newly discovered ideas on existence: being and becoming; death; reality and illusion.

Essentially what I am tracing in this chapter is Shakespeare's detailed portrayal of such reactions and responses as he comprehensively constructs Hamlet's mind structure or way of being. From Hamlet's psychological struggles emerge a burgeoning awareness of proto-modernism. The English poet, John Milton, writing his epic *Paradise Lost* about sixty-five years after Shakespeare wrote *Hamlet,* paid homage to the master and this seminal thought with this similar idea,

The Mind is its own place, and in itself
Can make a heav'n of hell, a hell of heav'n.
(Book 1, Lines 254-255)[6]

As for Hamlet, so for us; associative thought processes—for good or ill—that each of us brings to our individual life experience shape our mind structure, and hence our existence.

Modern psychoanalysts cannot express this fundamental tenet of their field in clearer terms. Hamlet knows what hinders his inaction, knows his thinking replaces action, and knows the cause that underlies his ceaseless, stormy thoughts, "Thinking makes it so." Yet he is unable to pivot his mind in another direction.

He struggles with questions relating to regicide and his desperate unhappiness with the changes to his life circumstances. Somehow, he maintains the clarity of mind to declare a universal truth, "There is nothing good or bad but thinking makes it so."

For any bridge figure with one foot planted in the past and one foot in the future, the present feels untenable.

Hamlet, along with the character Hamlet, broke the traditional stranglehold of conventional Elizabethan drama with its heroes and heroics dubbed "the theater of revenge." As the play is carefully scrutinized, we become mindful of the layered depths of meaning in the text.

The character, Hamlet, describes a complete case study of this mentally tortured, young protagonist.

While Hamlet oscillates like a pendulum between expectation and actualization of revenge, Laertes, another young man of rank in the court, epitomizes the hero according to the prevailing revenge code of Shakespeare's day. Deeply embedded in the mind structure of that cycle, Laertes leaps headlong into action, intent on honoring his family by killing the person who inadvertently killed his father, Polonius, and sister, Ophelia. And that person is Hamlet.

As the play opens, Hamlet's way of being in the world is that of a fortunate young man in his early twenties. A famous prince loved and beloved of his parents, King Hamlet and Queen Gertrude, adored by his girlfriend Ophelia, who reveres him but with a futile love, as she accepts he is above her station and cannot contemplate a taboo marriage. He is esteemed and loved by his closest and truest friend, his confidante, Horatio. Together they attend the same university in Wittenberg. Additionally, Hamlet has the love of the people of Denmark who expect him to succeed to the throne when, in time, his father dies.

Then, circumstances shift.

Suddenly, summoned back to court for his father's funeral, and aware of rumors and intrigue about his father's demise, Hamlet plunges ever more deeply into depression over his father's mysterious death and mother's hasty marriage.

Towards the middle of Act 1, one-night, past midnight, Hamlet encounters what is ostensibly his father's ghost, but also plausibly may be a horrific vision erupting from his disturbed state of mind. He acknowledges that he must avenge his father's murder after the Ghost imparts to his ears a grizzly tale of how his father, King Hamlet, was murdered by Hamlet's uncle, Claudius. These words confirm Hamlet's suspicions about his uncle, and he vows to the Ghost that he will avenge his father's death, a customary action for a son.

After the Ghost disappears into the oncoming dawn, Hamlet's devoted friend, Horatio (the audience's reliable witness), accompanied by two castle guards loyal to old King Hamlet and this young prince, reaches Hamlet and forms a protective shield.

Unexpectedly and to their dismay, Hamlet displays deep anxiety tinged with paranoia. None of the three have had any conversation with the Ghost, yet Hamlet forces them to swear not to divulge his furtive meeting, doubling down to ensure that his clandestine *tête-à-tête* will remain only with them.

This is a significant event.

The primary factor that paralyzes Hamlet in his inability to fulfill the task he has sworn to fulfill, rests on his lack of proof for the Ghost's story. As a proto-modern thinker, Hamlet cannot kill wantonly. He needs solid evidence that revenge is justified.

After this dramatic and emotion-fueled encounter, Hamlet, shaken and obsessed with the Ghost's words and with his vow ever-present in his mind, moves warily around the castle. He struggles to hold onto physical reality, terrified that he is becoming insane.

He knows that latterly his manic actions have not gone unnoticed. King Claudius and Queen Gertrude try to convince him that his grief over his father's death has rendered him mad. But, intriguer as he is, Hamlet seizes on this perception and pretends to be madder than he has become, a guise to trap Gertrude or Claudius into indiscreet comments relating to guilt for their possible roles in a murder plot against King Hamlet.

Edgy and primed to catch any hint of deception around him, Hamlet knows that anyone in the castle may have abetted the plot to kill his father; anyone may provide clues as to Claudius' guilt. To create space in which to explore his suspicions further, Hamlet hides behind a metaphorical papier-mâché mask. This he constructs from hyper-activity, semi-crazed speech patterns, and appearances in weirdly odd outfits, camouflage for his mind states that swing from depression to mania.

At the end of Act 1, Hamlet describes how confined he feels—in his very being. After he has wrapped himself in the mantle of presumptive avenger for his father's death, he wrestles with his conscience to accept this new responsibility. Hamlet speaks,

> The time is out of joint. O cursed spite
> That ever I was born to set it right?
> (Act 1, scene 5, line 210-211)[7]

His obsession is further complicated by not knowing when he encountered the Ghost if he was experiencing a lucid dream, a vision, or the work of the devil. Indeed, rhetorically he poses the question of whether the Ghost may be a figment of his own whirling brain,

> The spirit that I have seen
> May be a (devil), and the (devil) hath power
> T' assume a pleasing shape; yea, and perhaps,

> Out of my weakness and my melancholy
>
> As he is very potent with such spirits*,
>
> Abuses me to damn me.
>
> *spirits = emotionally induced psychological states
>
> (Act 2, scene 2, lines 627-632)[8]

The consequences of these events manifest in their tragic conclusion.

I am not delving much further into the intricacies of the plot (intriguing as they are) with devices such as parallel structures, spying, gamesmanship, ambiguities, profiles of various characters—all created with unparalleled use of the English language. I am eager to discuss perceptions of the nature of mind structures as they inform Hamlet's existence.

Fortunately for us, Shakespeare wrote several soliloquies that Hamlet delivers, and these set pieces, akin to intimate journal entries, reveal Hamlet's mind structure. In the soliloquies, many of the sources of the "bad dreams" arise from within Hamlet's consciousness and unite to form the essential "outsider" fabric.

The soliloquies highlight the structure of the Shakespearean dramatic arc. Soliloquies in Acts 1 and 2 introduce the ideas, conflicts, and characters in the play. In Act 3, at the apex of the arc, climatic events occur. And Acts 4 and 5 reveal conclusions to the thematic threads.

As we follow the soliloquies, we trace how Hamlet shifts from an optimistic young man to become a nihilistic schemer who achieves a persistent, even fatalistic peace of mind. Before he reaches this mind state of equilibrium and acceptance, Hamlet morphs into a master manipulator and laces the play with mirrors, masks, feints, and damaging verbal thrusts. We never know if he speaks his truth at any one time or if he sets a trap for someone in any speech he utters.

Shakespeare masterfully spins Hamlet's web of dastardly deeds and duplicity. At times we are justified asking if Hamlet is a hero or a villain; yet, through the soliloquies, Shakespeare skillfully sways the audience into believing that basic goodness underlies Hamlet's perturbation.

Hamlet leaves us puzzled but never loses all our empathy.

Hamlet heroically tries to overcome inner quandaries of suicide and depression and struggles to maintain a grip on sanity in his stressed and disintegrating mind. As chronologically we explore the soliloquies, we see the turmoil bubbling constantly in Hamlet's mind and how he restrains himself from madness even though at times he veers close to mania, maybe even slips into the abyss. Our changing mind structures become our way of being at every stage of our lives. The soliloquies aptly exemplify this progression, and they anchor the developmental arc of Hamlet's tragic struggle.

In the first soliloquy Hamlet's mind state is depressed, suicidal, nihilistic, filled with passive aggressive anger and obsessed by his mother, Gertrude, her sex life, and her perceived infidelity.

Grieving for his father's death, Hamlet dresses in mourning black to attend his mother's wedding to Claudius. Hamlet watches, along with the crowded court as immediately following the splendid celebration, the wedding pair exit to their wedding bed. When the courtiers have all left, Hamlet alone on stage speaks these words, opening an intimate glimpse into his state of mind,

> O, that this too, too sullied flesh would melt,
> Thaw, and resolve itself into a dew,
> Or that the Everlasting had not fixed
> His canon 'gainst (self-slaughter!) O God, God...
> (Act 1, scene 2, line 133-136)[9]

Deeply depressed by the change in his familial circumstances, Hamlet envisions his body under his mourning clothes and wishes it could simply melt away. But his Christian belief system forbids suicide. His suicidal thoughts show us the depths of his dismay and how it has become the seething, distraught focus of his attention. Outwardly he behaves in a princely manner and obeys his mother; inwardly, his depressed thoughts pivot on suicide,

> How (weary) stale, flat, and unprofitable seem to me all the
> uses of this world!
>
> Fie on 't, ah fie!*...
> *fie = expression of disgust
> (Ibid, line 137-138)[10]

Previously of a cheerful disposition with a quicksilver wit and basking in the love of his parents, Ophelia, and the Danish population, Hamlet now faces a changed reality. He exclaims in despair at what these circumstances have wrought as he contemplates with disgust the world (his life) where he now finds himself, compared to the world he engaged with previously.

Later in this soliloquy, Hamlet transfers his disturbed state of mind into a diatribe against his mother and what he labels her "defilement" as he imagines her—at this very moment as he speaks to us—having sex with his uncle,

> Within a month,
> Ere yet the salt of most unrighteous tears
> Had left the flushing of her galled eyes,
> She married. O, most wicked speed, to post
> With such dexterity to incestuous sheets!
> It is not, nor it cannot come to good.
> (Act 1, scene 2, lines 158-163)[11]

In the second soliloquy, Hamlet's mind state is self-denigration, self-hatred, admittance of cowardice, and feverish scheming as he welcomes a troupe of wandering players to Elsinore. He asks the lead actor to recite lines from a famous play, Virgil's *The Aeneid*. The player recites lines that tell the tale of the slaughter of King Priam of Troy at the hand of Pyrrhus, himself seeking revenge[12] for his father Achilles' death. He references Hecuba, King Priam's wife. During his monologue, the actor loses his composure and delivers his lines emotionally through tears.

When the players leave, Hamlet expresses how deeply the player's show of emotion at Hecuba's plight affected him. He berates himself for his perceived lack of feeling,

> Now I am alone.
> O, what a rogue and peasant slave am I!
> Is it not monstrous that this player here,
> But in a fiction, in a dream of passion,
> Could force his soul so to his own conceit
> That from her working all (his) visage waned
> Tears in his eyes, distraction in his aspect
> A broken voice, and his whole function suiting
> With forms to his conceit—and all for nothing!
> For Hecuba!
> (Act 2, scene 2, lines 577-585)[13]

Hamlet expresses his amazed admiration that an actor can be so transported by his emotions that they take the form of physical tears. The actor's outward responses seem to match his inner thoughts: a feat Hamlet yet cannot accomplish. He marvels at this display of emotion for Hecuba, King Priam's widow, with whom the actor only has an artistic, intellectual connection through the ancient Roman poet, Virgil. Whereas he, Hamlet, son of a beloved father, murdered, restrains his emotions and only allows his desperate sorrow to surface when he is alone. Hamlet prosecutes the case for why he should act in likewise a manner as the actor,

> What's Hecuba to him, or he to (Hecuba,)
> That he should weep for her? What would he do
> Had he the motive and (the cue) for passion
> That I have? He would drown the stage with tears
> And cleave the general ear with horrid speech,
> Make mad the guilty and appall the free,
> Confound the ignorant and amaze indeed
> The very faculties of eyes and ears. Yet I
> A dull and muddy-mettled rascal, peak
> Like John-a-dreams, unpregnant of my cause,
> And can say nothing—no, not for a king
> Upon whose property and most dear life
> A damned defeat was made. Am I a coward?
> (Act 2, scene 2, lines 586-598)[14]

Hamlet reaches this damning rhetorical question on the nature of *his* cowardice as the cause that may be hindering his actualization of revenge. He asks how the actor would behave if he had a similar reason, as evident in Hamlet's circumstances. He chastises himself for existing at all—he can find no excuses for himself—while he remains aware of the significant burden he carries; the revenge dynamic he abhors but must obey. Hence, he concludes that he is a coward because he does not act,

> Who calls me (villain)? Breaks my pate across?
> Plucks off my beard and blows it in my face?
> Tweaks me by the nose? Gives me the lie i' th' throat
> As deep as to the lungs? Who does me this?

Ha! "Swounds, I should take it! For it cannot be
But I am pigeon-livered * and lack gall
To make oppression bitter, or ere this
I should have fatted all the regions kites
With this slave's offal.
(Act 2, scene 2, lines 599-607)[15]

* In the Elizabethan worldview the liver was regarded as the seat of bravery. Hamlet compares his liver to that of the tiny organ found in a pigeon.

Hamlet reacts vehemently against the idea that he is a coward. He argues that if someone challenges him to a duel or calls him a villain or a coward then he could act. Instead, he constantly searches for verifiable evidence to harden his resolve to act in his father's unproven cause, must verify he is a coward. He excoriates himself that he is "pigeon-livered"* or else he would long since have killed Claudius and fed all the kites (raptors) with his uncle's intestines.

Then his self-anger is displaced onto his uncle,
Bloody, bawdy villain!
Remorseless, treacherous, lecherous, kindless
Villain!
Ibid (Act 2, scene 2, lines 607-609)[16]

Suddenly, Hamlet's mood swings again and he desists from demeaning his uncle and turns his anger inward recognizing his almost manic behavior. He protests that he is like a "drab" (a prostitute) who speaks words to her customers but feels no emotion as they have sex. He expresses disgust towards himself,

Why, what an ass am I!
This is most brave,

That I, the son of a dear (father) murdered,

Prompted to my revenge by heaven and hell,

Must, like a whore, unpack my heart with words

And fall a-cursing like a very drab,

A (scullion). Fie upon 't. Foh!

About, my brains!...

(Act 2, scene 2, line 611-617)[17]

After he welcomes the Players to Elsinore, his mood shifts yet again, as unexpectedly, he intuits a ploy to trap Claudius. He latches onto the idea. Now he can move into action, use his mind to strategize a plan, and cease questioning himself about cowardice,

The play's the thing

Wherein I'll catch the conscience of the King.

(Act 2, scene 2, lines 633-634)[18]

He will use the Players as unwitting instruments by writing a short scene for them to perform before their main performance for the court. The scene will unfold with action akin to what the Ghost related to Hamlet in Act 1. After a tender interchange between an older King and his wife, the King enters a private garden for an afternoon nap as a stealthy man tip-toes toward him. He pours lethal liquid into the King's ears. As the poison moves through his body, the King writhes in pain and dies in agony. Hamlet hopes Claudius will prove his guilt by recognizing in the theatrical murder a mirror of his regicide and being scared into self-damning reactivity.

Hamlet intends to share his scheme with Horatio. He and Horatio will watch Claudius' reaction to the playlet.

The third soliloquy includes arguably the most famous lines in *Hamlet,* "To be or not to be" (Act 3, scene 1, line 64).[19] The soliloquy portrays Hamlet philosophizing on the nature of existence, on questions of an afterlife, and fear of what lies—if anything—on the other side of death.

Hamlet touches on the magnitude of the possibilities of an afterlife, but as no one returns to tell us what is beyond this life, we are afraid of stepping into the unknown. Perhaps there is no information. Like Hamlet, all we can do is probe more deeply with questions as our understanding of the nature of existence expands. We can feel compassion for Hamlet as he attempts to—but cannot find a way forward.

(A reminder that in his first soliloquy in Act 1, Hamlet contemplated suicide. There are echoes of that mind state in this soliloquy.)

Hamlet must have perceived that Claudius is disturbed by how the negative impact of his stepson's current mind state affects Gertrude. Hamlet believes her sympathy—as it always has—lies with him, despite her actions to the contrary. Is Hamlet blinded to Gertrude's true nature as an adulterer? Does he suspect Gertrude's relationship with Claudius to be long-standing? Does he ever question if she may be culpable in abetting Claudius in her first husband's murder? We have no evidence in the text to answer these questions. We know that Hamlet's moral blind spot relating to Gertrude's motives and actions, hamstring him.

Let me set the stage. To ascertain if Hamlet is truly mad, Claudius, Polonius and Gertrude concoct a scheme. They use Ophelia as bait to trap Hamlet into acting out, or not, his supposed madness. Ophelia, reluctantly accepting her filial duty, obeys her father's request and curtails contact with Hamlet. Hamlet asks her for one last meeting, and Ophelia, with her father's blessing, agrees to an assignation where she intends to return all Hamlet's letters and gifts.

On the stage while waiting for her, Hamlet believes he is alone. Unbeknownst to him, Polonius and Claudius, are now hidden to spy on Hamlet and Ophelia and judge if Hamlet's behavior is truly manic. This is a disquieting moment for the audience to witness as those hidden voyeurs (like a mirror for the audience) become privy to Hamlet's innermost musings,

Hamlet poses the question,

To be or not to be—that is the question:
(Act 3, scene 1, line 64)[20]

Six small words that encompass so much—and leave so much unstated yet strike at the very essence of who and what we are: "to be," to exist, to have a "be-ing" that is constantly "be-coming" itself. Yet in the nanosecond between be-ing and non-be-ing "not-to-be", the nanosecond of death, of ceasing to be—what, if anything, happens,

Whether 'tis nobler in the mind to suffer
The slings and arrows of outrageous fortune,
Or to take arms against a sea of troubles
And, by opposing, end them.
(Act 3, scene 1, lines 65-68)[21]
Hamlet still entertains suicidal thoughts,
To die, to sleep—
No more—and by a sleep to say we end
The heartache and the thousand natural shocks
That flesh is heir to—'tis a consummation
Devoutly to be wished. To die, to sleep—
To sleep, perchance to dream. Ay, there's the rub,
For in that sleep of death what dreams may come,
When we have shuffled off this mortal coil,
Must give us pause.
(Act 3, scene 1, lines 67-76)[22]

Hamlet is tired; his warp speed mind exhausts him. His doubts and fears burden him, he longs for peaceful sleep, but as we know, he is troubled by bad dreams. This, as he says, "is the rub." If living dreams are distressing, who can risk "in the sleep of death what dreams may come"? Hamlet concludes that fear of the unknown after death forms a bulwark against suicide. Otherwise, why do we carry so stoically the burdensome trials of this life? Hamlet itemizes some of these burdens, such as the ravages of time and the injustices we suffer,

> There's the respect
> That makes calamity of so long life.
> For who would bear the whips and scorns of time,
> Th' oppressor's wrong, the proud man's contumely,
> The pangs of despised love, the law's delay,
> The insolence of office, and the spurns
> That patient merit of th' unworthy takes,
> When he himself might his quietus make
> With a bare bodkin?* Who would fardels* bear,
> To grunt and sweat under a weary life,
> But that the dread of something after death,
> The undiscovered country from whose bourn
> No traveler returns, puzzles the will
> And makes us rather bear those ills we have
> Than fly to others that we know not of?"
> (Act 3, scene 1, lines 76-90)[23]
> *bare bodkin = unsheathed dagger;
> *fardels = burdens

The words "But that the dread of something after death/ The undiscovered country from whose bourn/ No traveler returns. ..." are a concise and impactful, practical summation of the significant yet abstract discussion on existence in this soliloquy. As Hamlet says no one has ever returned after death to tell us "what we know not of."

Even the ghost would not speak of what he knows of purgatory and the afterlife.

> Hamlet continues,
> Thus conscience does make'-cowards (of us all,)
> And thus, the native hue of resolution
> Is (sicklied) o'er with the pale cast of thought,
> And enterprises of great pitch and moment
> With this regard their currents turn awry
> And lose the name of action. –Soft you now,
> The fair Ophelia. —…
> (Act 3, scene 1, lines 91-98)[24]

He questions whether the "unknown afterlife" makes cowards of us all, and that is why we bear the injustices and burdens of this life.

Hamlet feels no inclination to commit regicide without proof. His conscience will not let him. In this soliloquy he coaxes out and articulates the reasons for his reluctance to act vengefully, the result of a compulsive conscience over-thinking his dilemma, "the pale cast of thought."

In the fourth soliloquy, Hamlet further philosophizes on the nature of cowardice, his inability to act, and the dawning awareness that action may be the path back to sanity. He reaches a calm resolution to finally commit regicide by killing Claudius. (He had an opportunity in Act 3.)

Prior to this moment, Claudius and Hamlet have been playing deadly mind games. Claudius devises an outlandish scheme to banish Hamlet—to send him on a royal mission to England. Clandestinely, he asks the King of England to execute Hamlet.

On his way to the coast to board the ship bound for England, Hamlet calls a halt for his entourage when they encounter hundreds of Norwegian soldiers and mercenaries marching (with permission from

Claudius) across Denmark to wrest a small parcel of land from Denmark's Polish neighbors. The soldiers leave a somber impression on him. In this soliloquy delivered in a quieter, more measured tone than those before, we sense a tinge of resignation under his self-condemnation; perhaps Hamlet anticipates that in contrast to the mercenaries, he may remain a "coward",

> How all occasions do inform against me
> And spur my dull revenge. What is a man
> If his chief good and market of his time
> Be but to sleep and feed? A beast, no more.
> Surely, He that made us with such large discourse,
> Looking before and after, gave us not
> That capability and godlike reason
> To fust* in us unused.
> *fust = to become moldy
> (Act 4, scene 4, lines 34-41)[25]

Hamlet indulges in philosophical musing in this first part of the soliloquy, as he tries to identify the difference between a man and a beast. Is man content only to eat and sleep. Rhetorically he tries to reassure himself that humankind has been endowed with "godlike reason," an echo of his thought earlier when he references man "in apprehension how like a god." Surely, this godlike acuity is meant to be exercised. Hamlet continues the thought,

> Now whether it be
> Bestial oblivion or some craven scruple
> Of thinking too precisely on th' event
> (A thought which, quartered, hath but one part
> wisdom
> And ever three parts coward), I do not know

Why yet I live to say "This thing's to do,"
Sith I have cause, and will, and strength, and means
To do't.
(Act 4, scene 4, lines 41-49)[26]

Hamlet muses that there is a limit to the utility of "godlike reason." He suggests that thinking consists of one-part reason ("wisdom") and three parts cowardice. He speculates on why he lives after murdering Polonius, yet allows himself to be pursued by his revenge neurosis when he has the psychological and physical means to rid himself of this scourge,

Examples gross as earth exhort me,
Witness this army of such mass and charge...
(Act 4, scene 4, lines 49-50)[27]

As the soliloquy continues, Hamlet broadens his thinking to encompass the external evidence of resolute courage he sees in the passing army. The soliloquy expands on the idea that men are prepared to fight and die over a piece of land and for a meager wage, while he twists and turns handicapped by incessant thinking as he grapples with questions of dying, death, afterlife, bad dreams—and a lack of will to kill his uncle. Yet, an alternative perspective emerges the more Hamlet focuses on his "cowardice." Ultimately, he displays nobility of thought and bravery in accepting that he will proceed carefully and thoughtfully until certain his actions are taken for inviolable motives. Then, he can kill Claudius,

O, from this time forth
My thoughts be bloody or be nothing worth!
(Act 4, scene 4, lines 68-69)[28]

This is the final soliloquy in the play.

We find several instances with echoes of the mind structures we have been following; essentially on the nature of death, revenge, being and becoming; of existence, and resolute courage. These echoes are contained in familiar reprises of earlier speeches.

In Act 5, Hamlet, with his friend Horatio, returns to Elsinore. Hamlet foiled Claudius' plot to have him killed by extricating himself from the ship where Claudius placed him. Yet in a callous maneuver, he altered Claudius' letter to the English king, and in so doing, while saving himself, he sends his two "guards" to their deaths in England. Hamlet can abet murder as long as he does not have to face his victims while doing so.

Nearing the castle, Hamlet and Horatio encounter a gravedigger, and Hamlet diverts himself by gossiping with the man. Surrounded by graves and skulls that have emerged from the soil, Hamlet reflects once again, albeit this time somberly, on the nature of death. He references dust and earth that recall his earlier question, "What is this quintessence of dust?" In the graveyard, surrounded by moldering corpses in various stages of decay, and bleached skulls and bones, Hamlet speaks,

> …Alexander dies, Alexander was buried, Alexander
> Returneth to dust; the dust is earth; of earth
> We make loam; and why of that loam whereto
> He was converted might they not stop a beer barrel? Impe-
> rious Caesar died,
> dead and turned to clay,
> might stop a hole to keep the wind away.
> O, that the earth which kept the world in awe
> Should patch a wall t' expel the (winter's) flaw!
> (Act 5 scene 1, lines 216-223)[29]

Hamlet returns to Elsinore amid enthusiastic welcome and acclaim from the public. Their support thwarts Claudius, who knows that if Hamlet dies, he will be blamed for Hamlet's death. Ever since the Players' visit to the castle, rumors have circulated that Claudius committed regicide in killing his brother, King Hamlet.

Ensconced in his rooms in the castle, Hamlet relates to Horatio how he managed to escape from the ship to England and rid himself of his "guards." Hamlet prefaces his remarks to Horatio with an abstraction: despite the plotting and conniving humanity indulges in, we are only "rough-hewing" the circumstances of our lives. Despite the actions we undertake, our lives are shaped by "a divinity."

This sentiment is a significant shift philosophically for Hamlet, who has strived so mightily to shape his own life with other choices despite cursing that he was "born to set right" the injustice against his father. Hamlet states,

> There is a divinity that shapes our ends,
> Rough-hew them how we will—
> (Act 5, scene 2, lines 11-12)[30]

Claudius devises one more ploy; he persuades the vengeful Laertes to challenge Hamlet to a friendly but competitive duel; both are well-reputed fencers. With Claudius' agreement, Laertes consents to further the certainty of killing Hamlet by rubbing lethal poison on the tip of his rapier.

Horatio begs Hamlet not to accept the challenge. But Hamlet, perhaps weary of the grievous burden imposed on him by his father's murder and murderer, and now with four more deaths on his conscience, fatalistically agrees to the duel. He accepts that his death may be near; he is prepared ("the readiness is all") for whatever Fate has in store for him,

...If it be

(now,) tis not to come; if it be not to come, it will be

now; if it be not now, yet it (will) come. The

readiness is all. Since no man of aught he leaves

knows, what is 't to leave betimes? Let be.

(Act 5, scene 2, lines 234-239)[31]

Of particular note in this passage are the many uses of the word "be." These hearken back to the famous opening line of soliloquy #3— "To be or not to be…" Hamlet parsed that phrase within the parameters of a discussion on suicide. Now he accepts his fate, "Let be."

The phrase "The readiness is all" carries a certain dignity, a high-minded claim from a calm and reflective mind. Has Hamlet's mind returned to a more balanced sense of inner peace?

In the physical, sensory reality we live, two certainties exist: constant change and the inevitability of death. The readiness to accept both may become our mantra.

But there is another significant factor to consider. Shakespeare may be postulating a bold precept that shatters the mutual exclusivity of the freewill vs. determinism enigma. Do these words "the readiness is all" offer one plausible approach that encompasses both? Until the moment of death is upon us, we can practice our free will *as long as* we accept death as part of our lives and are prepared for that inevitable (possibly pre-determined) reality.

Hamlet's mood and thoughts have undergone a significant transformation over the length of the play, from the implausibility of suicide to a discussion on the inevitability of death and the cessation of change. His realization that the time and circumstances of his death are beyond his control frees him *to be,* to exist in the present moment, and to act.

In his final moments, while still standing, even though poisoned by Laertes' sword and armed with his newfound freedom to act, Hamlet finally kills Claudius with the poisoned rapier. He forces Claudius to drink the dregs in a goblet—a lethal potion Claudius had concocted to kill Hamlet—but accidentally killed Gertrude. Claudius dies. Gertrude dies. Hamlet dies. Laertes dies. This revenge cycle ends. As he dies, Hamlet charges his faithful friend, Horatio, with the task of speaking the truth of events that have led to all these deaths. Among the last lines in the play are Horatio's words,

> And let me speak to (th') yet unknowing world
> How these things came about. So shall you hear
> Of carnal, bloody, and unnatural acts,
> Of accidental judgments, casual slaughters,
> Of deaths put on by cunning and (forced) cause,
> And in this upshot, purposes mistook
> Fall on th' inventors' heads. All this can I
> Truly deliver.
> (Act 5, scene 2, lines 421-428)[32]

The Danish court and all of Denmark now know that the chicanery involved in King Hamlet's death, Gertrude's death, and Hamlet's inevitable demise, settle on Claudius.

Now we shift to a discussion of physical and metaphysical reality in *Hamlet*, where starkly drawn distinctions are expressed between physical reality (perceptions of the senses) and illusion (metaphysical reality), those beyond the physical. Illusionary states are usually accessible only to the person experiencing the delusion. Shakespeare tackles this phenomenon without compromise or hesitation.

In the Elizabethan worldview—that of the mind structure of

Shakespeare's day and therefore of his audience—ghosts existed. Many people today believe they do, but no one has yet produced physical evidence of ghostly existence. Yet, a pervasive belief in a spiritual or metaphysical realm beyond our sensory perception steadfastly exists down the centuries.

Literary scholars have no suggestion about what Shakespeare's personal belief in ghosts (and much else) entailed. We know that in the character of the Ghost in Hamlet, he created one of the most dynamic and enigmatic presences to grace any stage.

Early in Act 1, after his first soliloquy is unwittingly intruded on by Horatio and two guards, Hamlet says,

My father—methinks I see my father.

Horatio: Where, my lord?
Hamlet: In my mind's eye, Horatio.
(Act 1, scene 2, lines 191-193)[33]

Horatio and the others earlier, hesitantly, had come to inform him that they thought they saw the ghost of Hamlet's dead father the previous night. Before they can do so, Hamlet unexpectedly states that he sees his father "in my mind's eye." What does Hamlet's intuit?

Does this statement portend that we are entering metaphysical territory? Indeed, in one layer of interpretation, we can clearly understand that the Ghost of Hamlet's father is a plot device to provide the "back" story to King Hamlet's death. A Shakespearean ploy to devise a dramatic *deus ex machina*[34] whereby Hamlet (and the audience) can learn the Ghost's account of his regicide of Claudius. However, simultaneously, the Ghost's visitation sucks Hamlet into a vortex of anguish that generates the revenge cycle for him.

This encounter suggests Shakespeare's preternatural understanding of mind structures. Three hundred years before pioneering psychologists Sigmund Freud and Carl Jung began to crack the code of our miraculous evolution of consciousness; essentially, Shakespeare introduced the phenomenon of an altered mind structure (illusion, delusion, ghost, call it what you will) into what is now known as a disassociated state.[35]

During the episode under discussion—Hamlet's first interaction with the Ghost—he does not experience a sense of loss of reality but rather one with heightened senses beyond reality. His episode with the Ghost is perhaps part of Hamlet's subconscious mind desperate to receive a supportive rationale from an outside source to execute the act of revenge he must perform. Eager for that accommodating message, he may visualize and actualize the Ghost's speeches.

In some instances, disassociation can be regarded as a coping or defense mechanism to master or minimize stress—including conflict. Inarguably in Act 1, Hamlet is under duress. The Ghost episode may stem from the unfortunate realities of Hamlet's changed life circumstances that cause him such mental and emotional distress. However, the highly charged interaction with a ghost intruding his mind further roils Hamlet.

Skeptically, Hamlet agrees to meet with Horatio and the two loyal guards on the castle ramparts that night. They do see a shadowy form that could be clouds or mist or water vapor or a ghost. What are they seeing? The three caution Hamlet not to follow the form.

Nonetheless, Hamlet charges after the shape that seems to beckon for him to follow, even though he is aware of the risk,

> Why, what should be the fear?
> I do not set my life at a pin's fee.
> And for my soul, what can it do to that
> Being a thing immortal as itself?
> (Act 1, scene 4, lines 72-75)[36]

Hamlet runs into the darkness of the night and disappears from the view of Horatio and the two guards. Horatio exclaims that perhaps Hamlet sees something they cannot see,

> He waxes desperate with imagination.
> (Act 1, scene 4, line 97)[37]
> Marcellus, one of the guards, exclaims,
> Something is rotten in the state of Denmark.
> (Act 1, scene 4, line 100)[38]

When Hamlet and the Ghost are far removed from Horatio and the others, the Ghost speaks to Hamlet and spins a tale,

> Sleeping within my orchard,
> My custom always in the afternoon,
> Upon my secure hour thy uncle stole,
> With juice of cursèd hebona* in a vial
> And in the porches of my ears did pour
> The leprous distilment...
> (Act I, scene 5, 67-71)[39]
> Thus was I, sleeping by a brother's hand
> Of life, of crown, of queen at once dispatched,
> Cut off...
> *hebona = lethal plant poison
> (Ibid, lines 81-83)[40]

Hamlet's mind races as his assumptive suspicions about his reviled uncle are "confirmed." He desperately wants to accept as truth (evidence) that his father was poisoned with hebona that his uncle poured into the King's ear. Hamlet's horrifying encounter with the Ghost and hearing or imagining its tale sears into his subconscious mind a plausible scenario explaining his father's murder, one that later he will use to plot Claudius' tacit admission of guilt.

The Ghost continues speaking with these terrifying words,

> O horrible, O Horrible, most horrible!
> If thou hast nature in thee, bear it not.
> (Act 1, scene 5, lines 87-88)[41]

Hamlet's mind heaves with turbulent responses now that he has acknowledged that he is responsible for avenging his father's death; if indeed, he can be resolute enough.

The Ghost then utters the most troubling words of all. He confirms Hamlet's despair, anguish, maybe even voyeuristic jealousy at the sexual pleasure his mother and uncle enjoy. The Ghost warns,

> Let not the royal bed of Denmark be
> A couch for luxury and dammèd incest.
> (Act 1, scene 5, lines 88-89)[42]

Hamlet must be pleased to hear the Ghost's next words because they allow him to separate his uncle's murderous act from confrontations he must eventually have with his mother,

> But, howsomever thou pursues this act,
> Taint not thy mind
> Against thy mother aught...
> (Act 1, scene 5, lines 91-93)[43]

For deeper understanding and verification that this scene portrays a rudimentary and muddled description of a disassociation episode,[44] once more, we turn to the text.

The Ghost speaks almost the exact words as Hamlet did earlier in this Act and thus supports the idea that the Ghost's speech springs from Hamlet's mind. In Hamlet's first soliloquy (in addition to what we parsed earlier), Hamlet describes how he now sees the world,

> ...Tis an unweeded garden
> That grows to seed. Things rank and gross in nature
> Possess it merely. That it should come (to this:)
> But two months dead—nay, not so much, not two.
> So excellent a king, that to this
> Hyperion[45] to a satyr; so loving to my mother
> That he might not beteem* the winds of heaven
> Visit her face too roughly. Heaven and earth,
> Must I remember? Why, she would hang on him
> As if increase of appetite had grown
> By what it fed on. And yet, within a month
> (Let me not think on 't; frailty they name is woman!)
> A little month, or ere those shoes were old
> With which she followed my poor father's body
> Like Niobe[46], all tears—why she (even she)
> (0 God, a beast that wants discourse of reason
> Would have mourned longer!), married with my uncle,
> My father's brother, but no more like my father
> Than I to Hercules.[47]
> *beteem = allow
> (Act 1, scene 2, lines 139-158)[48]

Hamlet compares his father to his uncle and calls his father Hyperion and his uncle a satyr. He compares his father to himself and calls his father Hercules,

> Within a month,
> Ere yet the salt of most unrighteous tears
> Had left the flushing in her galled eyes,

She married. 0, most wicked speed, to post
With such dexterity to incestuous sheets!
It is not, nor it cannot come to good.
But break, my heart, for I must hold my tongue...
(Act 1, scene 2, lines 158-164)[49]

Hamlet cannot come to terms with his mother's betrayal of his father in the unseemly haste of her marriage to his uncle. He obsesses on the sexual nature of their union calling it "incestuous". The Ghost confirms what he suspected; his uncle is involved deeply in King Hamlet's death; his marriage to Gertrude, incestuous,

O, my prophetic soul! My uncle!
Ghost: Ay, that incestuous, that adulterous beast...
(Act 1, scene 5, 48-49)[50]

The Ghost continues with embellishments of the above statement on incest, adultery, shameful lust, and Gertrude's infidelity, the very thoughts whirling in Hamlet's mind for days,

With witchcraft of his (wit,) with traitorous gifts—
O wicked wit and gifts, that have the power
So to seduce! – won to his shameful lust
The will of my most seeming-virtuous queen.
O Hamlet what a falling off was there!
From me, whose love was of that dignity
That it went hand in hand even with the vow
I made to her in marriage, and to decline
Upon a wretch whose natural gifts were poor
To those of mine.
But virtue, as it never will be moved,
Though lewdness court in a shape of heaven,
So, (lust,) though to a radiant angel linked,

Will (sate) itself in a celestial bed

And prey on garbage.

(Act 1, scene 5, lines 50-64)[51]

...O all you host of heaven! O earth! What else!

And shall I couple hell? O fie! Hold, hold my heart...

(Act 1, scene 5, lines 99-100)[52]

Hamlet questions himself if he is forming an alliance with Hell. After the Ghost concludes his story, the visitation exacts a vow of revenge from Hamlet,

Now to my word.

It is "adieu, adieu, remember me."

I have sworn 't.

(Act 1, scene 5, lines 118-119)[53]

This vow, even more than the Ghost itself, haunts Hamlet through the play.

The only other occasion when the Ghost appears in the play occurs during the "bedroom" scene in Act 3.

Hamlet's playlet appears to trap Claudius into acting guiltily. Along with the court, he watches the scene unfold on stage, and then Claudius abruptly rushes out of the hall. He enters a small chapel and attempts to pray to atone for his regicide and fratricide. Simultaneously, Hamlet rushes to confront his mother with what he believes is inalienable evidence of his father's murder. On his way, he passes the chapel and catches a glimpse of Claudius kneeling in prayer. Hamlet has an opportunity to kill Claudius. But he desists, as he does not want to send Claudius to death while he prays when his father died without confession and absolution. Perhaps that is a desperate excuse because, for all his braggadocio in the fourth soliloquy, Hamlet is still not ready to commit murder.

Meanwhile, at Claudius and Gertrude's request, Polonius hides behind an arras in her bed-chamber to further spy on Hamlet. They await Hamlet's imminent arrival.

Hamlet loves his mother, and he hates his mother. He barges into Gertrude's rooms, finally challenging her with all his pent-up anguish, sense of betrayal, and bewilderment. This is the first moment he anticipates being alone with her since his return from Wittenberg.

Irrationally, Hamlet mistakes the slight movement Polonius makes as an erroneous indication of Claudius' presence. He runs a sword through the arras, killing Polonius. If Hamlet were thinking rationally, he would know that Claudius at prayer could not have arrived before him at Gertrude's rooms and hidden behind the arras. But Hamlet—in this scene—is not rational.

Even the death by his own hand of the older man (and his lover's father) will not deny him his opportunity to browbeat Gertrude—who in his previous carefree life enabled his every word and action—into uniting with him against Claudius.

Momentarily unhinged, unable to restrain himself from venting his anger, disappointment, and shock at his mother, he furiously accosts her.

Terrified of her highly charged son, his mother leaves Polonius' dead body unattended on the floor while Hamlet berates her. He harangues and even threatens her physically as his pent-up rage spews verbal lava around her. He forces her to form a comparison between his father and Claudius. Perhaps her looks of fear, amazement, and horror trigger a mini-disassociated state because Hamlet is suddenly reminded that the Ghost commanded him to render his mother blameless. He has failed to obey the Ghost. Whatever the reason, the Ghost appears to him—only—and articulates what Hamlet's conscience already dictates. He speaks while staring into space,

> Save me and hover o'er me with your wings,
> You heavenly guards! —What would your gracious
> figure?
> (Act 3, scene 4, line 118-120)[54]

Alarmed, Gertrude, exclaims while staring at her son, "Alas, he's mad." Hamlet responds (to the Ghost),

> Do you not come your tardy son to chide,
> That, lapsed in time and passion, lets go by
> Th' important acting of your dread command?
> O, say![55]
> The Ghosts speaks words only Hamlet can hear,
> Do not forget. This visitation
> Is but to whet thy almost blunted purpose.
> But look, amazement on thy mother sits.
> O, step between her and her fighting soul.
> Conceit in weakest bodies strongest works.
> Speak to her, Hamlet.[56]

The Ghost departs; Hamlet exerts control over his rage and only takes his leave of Gertrude after he gains her promise not to tell Claudius details of their encounter. Inevitably, almost immediately, she breaks her word and divulges all to Claudius.

In this chapter, we have come somewhat further to an understanding of the nature of mind structures. In Hamlet's situation, we see how he created his reality composed of choices (to kill Claudius or not), circumstances (his father's death, his mother adultery, his lover's betrayal), associative thoughts (encounters with a vision of his father, pretense at being mad, acknowledgment he may be a coward), and acceptance (facing the possibility of his death.)

There is Hamlet's truth and the Ghost's truth, but no universal truth. If universal reality exists, we have two proofs: death and dying; everyone succeeds at dying. The other universal truth, everything else changes. The readiness is all.

* * *

One writer who pondered these matters was Henri-Louis Bergson, a French Nobel Prize winner for Literature at the turn of the 20th century. In several famous books, he explored the nature of ontology (metaphysical reality) and firmly established this branch of philosophy within the purview of Western thought again. His books expounded on the nature of moment-by-moment experience and intuition. He found these processes more significant than rationalism and scientific proof for understanding what we consider reality.[57]

Among his most significant contributions to the intellectual ferment during the period he lived suggested alternative ways for thinkers and writers to express their inner consciousness and tackle perplexing issues such as those around the concept of Time and the passing of Time.

In the next two chapters we will discuss ideas on time that reflect Bergson's influence. These chapters highlight concepts posited by physicist Alan Lightman and those found in masterworks of poet T. S. Eliot; and in Chapter Six, the novelist Virginia Woolf.

5

INTERPRETATIONS OF TIME FILTERED THROUGH CONCEPTUAL POSSIBILITIES

In this chapter, we shift from the world of revenge at odds with reason, the world of ambition, power, ego, and occasionally responsible self-lessness. We swing into the world of time, trying to understand different ideas on what time may hold for our collective mind structure. Here we encounter many challenging enigmas.

What role does time play in our cultures and mind structures? Questions abound, such as, what is time? What is our place in time? Is timelessness a feasible concept? Do memory and history help us understand time? What is the relationship between human existence and time? Does spirituality add to an understanding of time? Among many others who have written on time, we explore how two well-known authors grapple with these questions in their works: *Einstein's Dreams* by Alan Lightman and *The Four Quartets* by T.S. Eliot.

We share this blue and white planet on the outer reaches of our galaxy with over seven billion humans and an infinitely diverse biosphere.

How can you reconcile that universal perspective—time on a vast scale—with the experience of your individual self as a unique universe of consciousness, a universe of your being and becoming—within the scale of a human lifetime?

Almost four hundred years ago, John Milton, one of the most famous English poets in the mid-17th century, penned *the* classic epic poem in the English language, *Paradise Lost*. Among so much else in *Paradise Lost*, Milton tries to envisage the eternal moment before time began. In this pre-lapsarian world, the world of Eden before the Fall, all is perfect and therefore without change. In Milton's Edenic paradise, life remains static—climate, temperature, one season, and no aging. If to be without change means a world without time, Milton envisages a world existing in an eternal moment of timelessness.

Additionally, Milton's reliance on the literary device of the extended metaphor to describe his vision juggles two-time scales. Satan and his followers' fall from Heaven to "Stygian" Book 1, (line 239) darkness, but the darkness of that Greek underworld, Hades, did not exist at the time of the biblical first fall.

In another metaphor (among many others) that describes Satan's immense height, Milton compares Satan's spear to a giant Norwegian fir cut to become the mast of a large ship. In Satan's hand, the spear appears as a wand. Norway did not exist in Satan's purview of Hell.

To describe his vision, Milton relies on metaphorical frames of reference to which his audience can easily relate but which are anachronistic to the era and events he is describing.

So, too, in his way, does physicist and author Alan Lightman.

Einstein's Dreams by Alan Lightman

In *Einstein's Dreams*[1], Massachusetts Institute of Technology physicist, Alan Lightman, imagines the days preceding one of Albert Einstein's gigantic intuitive leaps into luminous fame,

In his hand he holds twenty crumpled pages, his new
theory of time, which he will mail today to the German
journal of physics.[2]

Or were they such intuitive leaps?

Stephen Kern[3], reknown cultural historian, does not think so. In
his book *The Culture of Time and Space*, 1880-1918, he examines this
period in Europe, demonstrating how certain ideas percolated through
the European zeitgeist. He argues that Einstein's theory was not an
isolated event in the field of math and physics but rather a product
of a particular cultural moment. Changes and advances in technology, industry, and travel (railways, motor cars, early flying machines),
as well as in the fields of psychology (Carl Jung, Sigmund Freud, the
arts (Cubism), and many scientific theories, encouraged rethinking
hypotheses on how to conceptualize time.

Alan Lightman indeed considered the theory of relativity as reve-
latory, a breakthrough in its time, to an enlightening societal mind
structure. Decades later, this theory inspired physicist Lightman to
imagine what dreams Einstein may have had around the time he developed his groundbreaking postulations.

Einstein's Dreams is Lightman's first work of fiction and was published in 1993. This highly acclaimed work remains a classic in imaginative explorations on concepts of time. *Einstein's Dreams* attempts to
decouple time from our objective, mechanical understanding conveyed
by watches and clocks. In so doing, Lightman challenges our perceived
concepts of time, much as Einstein did in 1905.

The plot of *Einstein's Dreams* is simple. In 1905, in Berne, Switzerland, a young patent clerk, Albert Einstein, dreams marvelous dreams
about notions of time. What are his dreams in those months? Author
Lightman sets his imagination to work to manifest these allegorical
dreams.

While each dream may seem far-fetched when read literally, they all speak to some aspect of time. We enter each dream as if the described parameters of time genuinely exist. We imagine they are part of a mind structure in which we may live. Lightman's speculations help us frame previously unacknowledged parameters of what time is and what time is not.

The dreams are interspersed with brief scenes that highlight details of Einstein's life in Berne at the time he worked on his theory of relativity. These are fictional interactions with Einstein's real-life friend and fellow patent office worker, an engineer, Michele Besso.

In the Prologue of *Einstein's Dreams,* the intent of Lightman's vocabulary, as evinced in this first paragraph, thrusts us into Einstein's world of time,

> In some <u>distant</u> arcade, a <u>clock</u> tower, calls <u>out</u> <u>six</u> times and <u>then</u> <u>stops</u>. The <u>young</u> man <u>slumps</u> <u>at</u> his desk. He <u>has come</u> to his office <u>at dawn</u>, <u>after</u> another <u>upheaval</u>. His hair <u>is</u> uncombed, and his trousers <u>are too big</u>. <u>In</u> his hand he <u>holds</u> <u>twenty</u> <u>crumpled</u> pages, his <u>new</u> theory of <u>time</u>, which he <u>will mail</u> <u>today</u> to the German journal of physics.[4]

The underlined words imply time (actions and movement) and occur throughout the Prologue on every line. Lightman's purpose is clear. Every verb—in past, present or future tense—implies time but if we examine our own speech and writing closely, we will find it impossible not to share the implication that time is not only in all our verbs, adverbs, adjectives and sometimes nouns.

Time lives in perceptions which language *expresses*.

In *Einstein's Dreams* each dream, and there are thirty in this small book, begins with Lightman stating his thesis for that dream. The first dream,

14 April 1905

Suppose time is a circle, bending back on itself. The world repeats itself, precisely, endlessly.[5]

In the abstract, thesis concepts such as this are not implausible, but Lightman suggests we imagine how that abstraction may play out in our lives,

For the most part, people do not know they will live their lives over.[6]

The phrase "for the most part, people ..." is arresting as it implies there are other possibilities,

How would they know that each secret glimpse, each
touch, will be repeated again and again and again, exactly
as before?[7]

As soon as Lightman cements the abstract into concrete terms of human lives, we almost involuntarily try to compare those lives to the one we know—our own. The lives of these dream people are somewhat akin to that of the protagonist in the movie *Groundhog Day*. Phil (Bill Murray), the weatherman, who, over a period of weeks, has to relive each day until he learns to ameliorate his crass behavior and show warmth and bonhomie to the people he meets that day. However, in this first dream in Lightman's book, no such redemptive acts exist; there is no way to break the cycle, "The world repeats itself precisely, endlessly."[8]
Lightman makes his metaphor even more singular by narrowing his focus to one person,

... How could she know that time will begin again, that

she will be born again, will study at the gymnasium again, will show her paintings at the gallery in Zürich, will again meet her husband in the small library in Fribourg, will again go sailing with him in Thun Lake on a warm day in July, will give birth again, that her husband will work for eight years at the pharmaceutical and come home one evening with a lump in his throat, will again throw up and get weak and end up in this hospital, this room, this bed this moment? How could she know?[9]

Lightman uses the technique akin to that which John Milton employs in *Paradise Lost* by humanizing the dreams. Milton used the dual notion of time for his metaphorical effect, describing, for instance, the size of Satan's spear in anachronistic terms. Lightman uses what I'll call the dual conceptual metaphor. Each dream is a metaphor with the thesis applied to human examples.

In the dreams, he moves from the abstract concept to the concrete using the touchstone of what it is to be human to engage the imaginative capabilities of our mind structures,

(Concept-Thesis): In a world in which time is a circle, every handshake, every kiss, every birth, every word, will be repeated precisely. ...[10]

(Concrete-Human):... And just as all things will be regretted in the future, all things now happening happened a million times before. Some few people in every town, in their dreams, are vaguely aware that all has occurred in the past. They are people with unhappy lives, and they sense that their misjudgments and wrong deeds and bad luck have all taken place in a previous loop of time.[11]

These "some few people" referred to in the phrase above "for the most part" have a sense of regret; a déja vu feeling about their mistakes, but there is no exit for them, no breaking the circular form of time. This possibility belies the idea of free will, the essence of existentialism. This universal form of time, this indestructible circle, represents as deterministic a mind structure as we can have. It questions the very idea of what it is to be human with no ability to make choices. In Lightman's book, only a few people have knowledge of the significance of living in such a predetermined circle, and they are "cursed" and fill the streets with "moans."

> In the dead of night these cursed citizens wrestle with their
> bedsheets, unable to rest, stricken with the knowledge
> that they cannot change a single action, a single gesture.
> Their mistakes will be repeated precisely in this life as in
> the life before. And it is these double unfortunates who
> give the only sign that time is a circle. For in each town,
> late at night, the vacant streets and balconies fill up with
> their moans.[12]

As with this dream, all the others convey multi-layered meaning and understanding of the human condition. All the dreams posit intriguing ideas and are written in charming, light-hearted yet profound prose. They each describe lives within these concepts on a human scale to make the ideas more accessible. I describe a handful below,

16 April

(Concept-Thesis): In this world, time is like a flow of
water, occasionally displaced by a bit of debris, a passing
breeze. Now and then, some cosmic disturbance will cause
a rivulet of time to turn away from the mainstream, to

make connection backstream. When this happens, birds, soil, people caught in the branching tributary find themselves suddenly carried to the past.[13]

Lightman surprises us with the phrase, "Some cosmic disturbance" dropped into this bucolic setting, a disturbance so powerful that it can disrupt the flow of time and the lives of people by transporting them back in time. Those who are transported provide the human element to this dream. They live uncomfortably in the knowledge of having been transported to the past and in great fear that they can alter the future,

> (Concrete-Human): Persons who have been transported back in time are easy to identify. They wear dark indistinct clothing and walk on their toes, trying not to make a single sound, trying not to bend a single blade of grass. For they fear that any change they make in the past could have drastic consequences for the future. ...[14]

When a traveler from the future must talk, he does not talk but whimpers. He whispers tortured sounds. He is agonized. For if he makes the slightest alteration in anything, he may destroy the future. At the same time, he is forced to witness events without being part of them, without changing them. He envies the people who live in their own time, who can act at will, oblivious of the future, ignorant of the effects of their actions. But he cannot act. He is an inert gas, a ghost, a sheet without a soul. He has lost his personhood. He is an exile of time.[15]

"An exile of time" is a compelling image. As is the idea that one's actions in the past carry consequences for everyone in the future,

28 April 1905

(Concept-Thesis): Time is visible in all places. ...[16]

This dream opens with a description of how "clock towers, wrist-watches, church bells" divide mechanical time into years, months, days, hours, seconds, each working in perfect synchronization with each other as the inner workings of mechanized flywheels and gears turn the time of our lives,

> Time paces forward with exquisite regularity, at pre-
> cisely the same velocity in every corner of space. Time is
> an absolute.[17]

Lightman takes this proposition—time is an absolute—further,

> (Concrete-Human): Those of religious faith see time as the
> evidence for God. For surely nothing could be created per-
> fect without a Creator. Nothing could be universal and not
> be divine. All absolutes are part of the One Absolute. And
> wherever absolutes, so too time. Thus, the philosophers of
> ethics have placed time at the center of their belief. Time is
> the reference against which all actions are judged. Time is
> the clarity for seeing right and wrong.[18]

The above paragraph is among the most philosophical to be found in *Einstein's Dreams*. Perhaps Lightman is parodying the inclination of many people and, indeed, cultures, to believe in and concretize systemic ethical belief in absolutes of their own, and societal mind structures. In other words, heterogeneity or homogeneity, democratic mores or dictatorial edict, critical thinking or blind obeisance, and so on. For many, there is "consolation" in safety and certainty,

A world in which time is an absolute is a world of consolation. For while the movements of people are unpredictable, the movement of time is predictable. While people can be doubted, time cannot be doubted. While people brood, time skips ahead without looking back. In the coffee-houses, in the government buildings, in boats on Lake Geneva, people look at their watches and take refuge in time. Each person knows that somewhere is recorded the moment she was born, the moment she took her first step, the moment she said goodbye to her parents.[19]

If we see ourselves in this mirror, we can perhaps refer to the discussion on reality and illusion in the previous chapter. As Hamlet learned, there are no absolutes in life except dying and death.

11 May 1905

(Concept-Thesis) In this world, the passage of time brings increasing order. Order is the law of nature, the universal trend, the cosmic direction. If time is an arrow, that arrow points towards order. The future is pattern, organization, union, intensification; the past, randomness, confusion, disintegration, dissipation.[20]

Lightman seems to propound a theme in many of his dreams that if we try to systemize aspects of time into concepts such as "order" we avoid the chaos of "randomness, confusion, disintegration, dissipation". He never places a value judgement on either end of this cultural spectrum, of these mind structures. He makes the point that even the imaginary world of time contained in dreams exists as a dual metaphor of time tied to human aspirations.

(Concrete-Human): Philosophers have argued that without time a trend towards order, time would lack meaning. The future would be indistinguishable from the past. Sequences of events would be just so many random scenes from a thousand novels. History would be indistinct, like the mist slowly gathered by treetops in evening.[21]

Essentially, this is Lightman's understanding of "the eternal moment", the idea of timelessness,

In such a world, people with untidy houses lie in their beds and wait for the forces of nature o jostle the dust from their windowsills and straighten the shoes in their closets. People with untidy affairs may picnic while their calendars become organized, their appointments arranged, their accounts balanced...If one visits a city in the spring one sees another wonderous sight. For in springtime the populace becomes sick of order in their lives...people meet at unarranged times, burn their appointment books, throw away their watches, drink through the night. This hysterical abandon continues until summer, when people regain their sense and return to order.

To quote poet T.S. Eliot, "Humankind cannot bear too much reality" (from *Burnt Norton, The Four Quartets*). Hence the cyclical nature of political movements, good governance collapses into revolt and revolt leads to good government. Cultural mind structures move from "order "to "randomness" as time does in this dream.

11 June 1905

(Concept-Thesis): This is a world without future. In this world, time is a line that terminates at the present, both in reality and in the mind.[22]

This thesis echoes the famous tenant of Buddhism that all we have is the present moment. The past dissipates, the future is unknown, we exist in the present. But Lightman adds a twist, "time is a line" that *ends* at the present. No concept of a future. The ramifications of that concept are disturbing, unfamiliar, and almost unimaginable,

> (Concrete-Human): In this world, no person can imagine the future. Imagining the future is no more possible than seeing colors beyond violet; the senses cannot conceive what may lie past the visible end of the spectrum. In a world without future, each parting of friends is a death. In a world without future each loneliness is final. In a world without future, beyond the present lies nothingness, and people cling to the present as if hanging from a cliff.
>
> A person who cannot imagine the future is a person who cannot contemplate the results of his actions. Some are thus paralyzed into inaction. They lie in their beds through the day, wide awake but afraid to put on their clothes. They drink coffee and look at photographs. Others leap out of bed in the morning, unconcerned that each action leads into nothingness, unconcerned that they cannot plan out their lives. They live moment to moment and each moment is full. Still others substitute the past for the future. They recount each memory, each action taken, each cause and effect, and are fascinated by how events have delivered them to this moment, the last moment of the world, the termination of the line that is time. ...[23]

The Buddhist construct that all we have is the present moment is fascinating in that it posits that each moment is complete unto itself, past, present, and future. Lightman's postulation is equally fascinating but hugely different. Time is a line with a past, and each passing moment for each person, adds to the line. There is no present, no future, moment-by-moment we dangle at the end of the line of time.

> *Epilogue*: At four minutes past eight the typist walks in. Einstein gives her his manuscript, his theory of time. It is six minutes past eight. He walks to his desk, glances at the stack of files, goes over to a bookshelf, and starts to remove one of the notebooks. He turns and walks back to the window. The air is unusually clear for late June. Above an apartment building, he can see the tips of the Alps, which are blue with white tops. Higher up, the tiny black speck of a bird makes slow loops in the sky.
>
> Einstein walks back to his desk, sits down for a moment, and then returns to the window. He feels empty. He has no interest in reviewing patents or talking to Besso or thinking of physics. He feels empty, and he stares without interest at the tiny black speck and the Alps.[24]

Four Quartets by T. S. Eliot

Thomas Stearns Eliot (1888-1965) was an American-British poet, essayist, playwright, literary critic, and editor. Born in St. Louis, Missouri, he moved to England in 1914 and settled, married, and worked there. He became a British citizen in 1927, and in 1937 renounced his American citizenship. Eliot is one of the 20th century's major poets. His earlier poems are recognized as hallmarks of the Modernist movement. In 1948 he was awarded the Nobel Prize for Literature for his "outstanding, pioneering contribution to present-day poetry."

The *Four Quartets* first published in 1941-1942[25] was written over eight years, with the first quartet originally a stand-alone poem. In this section, I have cherry-picked several extracts from the *Quartets* that contain Eliot's predominant themes on concepts of time. These are by no means the only content in The *Four Quartets* that does so. While we consider his ideas on time, we will also examine some of the symbolism for which Eliot's poetry is famous.

In the *Four Quartets,* Eliot scrutinizes ideas on a universal scale. Eliot studied Eastern spirituality as an undergraduate at Harvard University and later Oxford University and had in-depth knowledge of the teachings of the Buddha. After his time at Oxford, he later became a disciplined Anglican, deeply steeped in Christian dogma, mysticism, and symbolism. Both Eastern spiritual and Anglican Christian influences are evident in the *Four Quartets*: Buddhist teachings in the first quartet, and Christian influence more pervasive in the latter three.

Eliot structures the *Four Quartets* much like a musical composition such as some of Beethoven's quartets. There are motifs, refrains, themes, points, and counterpoints: Beethoven in musical notes and Eliot in words. Eliot's quartets are divided into five movements. Each starts with a series of thematic statements that become counterstatements as the theme develops, often in descriptions of a place or a scene. The fourth movement is usually a short lyric and the fifth a restatement of earlier themes.

Each quartet is named after a locale known to Eliot. The first, *Burnt Norton*, is the name of a manor house in Gloucestershire. Eliot lived in proximity to this house for many years. This quartet contains a major theme—ideas on the nature of the present moment. *East Coker* was the home of his English ancestors in the 17th century and include a significant theme—cycles and centuries. *Dry Salvages* is the name of a group of rocks off the New England coast near Cape Ann, Massachusetts, that Eliot visited as a boy and young man and contains a major theme—time the destroyer is also the preserver. *Little Gidding*, the final quartet, was the eponymous name of a 17th century religious community and an ideal setting for the central theme—spiritual-mystical experiences.

In general, Eliot's poetry relies on readers' understanding of the ideas he works towards without being distracted by the artifice of the poetry. Essentially, his work is stripped down to muscular, unadorned composition, so the poetry does not supersede the sense of the combinations of words. This does not mean Eliot eschews symbolism in his work; on the contrary, broad swathes of symbols are present. As our minds seek to grasp the ideas he communicates through a response in our associative thought processes, the symbols rouse emotion. We respond to his poetry on a visceral, as well as an intellectual, level.

One of Eliot's earlier poems *The Wasteland* (1922), written after the devastation of World War One, offers readers a way to alleviate their suffering present in the wasteland of the collective European post-war psyche. He believed that the after-effects of that apocalypse could be ameliorated through a spiritual revival and mystical experience. These ontological manifestations are contrary to the beliefs of many of his contemporary thinkers, such as Jean-Paul Sartre, an early 20th-century French philosopher, and his followers, including Albert Camus, the Algerian-born writer and philosopher and Simone de Beauvoir, a French philosopher, writer, and pioneering feminist. Sartre focused on the phenomenology of the nature of human existence.

Sartre, in his work, espouses a perspective on human experience that captures the post-World War Two apocalyptic zeitgeist in a philosophical movement called existentialism.[26] This contrasts with Eliot, who in *The Wasteland* expressed comfort for the post-World War One masses through faith in spiritual-mystical experience.

Sartre, de Beauvoir, Camus, and other existentialists perceived humanity as a species spinning on a tiny planet, alone in a cold and dark universe, and, therefore, to survive, self-reliant. According to Sartre, we are the focal point and entirety of our existence.

Four Quartets

Burnt Norton—In this quartet, Eliot expresses concepts of time, time-lessness and the nature of the present moment, and his perceptions of our place in time. Following on from Lightman's theses, you may ask, is living in the present moment even possible? This is an issue T. S. Eliot tussles with in *Burnt Norton*. For a promising line of inquiry, we turn to Eliot's background that encompasses one of the Buddha's seminal teachings on time, as a continuous succession of transient nanoseconds through which our lives pass. We need to be aware of each moment, as our ephemeral future so rapidly becomes our fleeting past.

In *Burnt Norton*, in the lines with which Eliot opens the folio, he positions under his poetic microscope the concept of the present moment,

From: *Burnt Norton 1*
Time present and time past
Are both perhaps present in time future,
And time future contained in time past.
If all time is eternally present
All time is unredeemable.[27]

"All time is unredeemable"—for something to be redeemable you can turn it into something else through trade-ins, buy backs, transfers or the like. Eliot states boldly that all time is "unredeemable", as if it is "eternally present", and therefore an entity unto itself, immutable.

This is a startling proposition. If all time is eternal, then, for instance, the years 1710 and 1910 and 2110 are all in the present. As is all the past and all the future. Present. Now. At this moment.

Eliot is not discussing time in this quartet but timelessness. Time has limits. In *Burnt Norton*, there is only timelessness.

This idea has three obvious implications. Each life of every person that ever was or will be is always present on an infinite scale. But we *know* that our lives *now,* as we live them, are lived in time. We cannot access the eternality of timelessness while we are in time.

The following lines from *Burnt Norton I* further explicate this concept,

> What might have been is an abstraction
> Remaining a perpetual possibility
> Only in a world of speculation.
> What might have been and what has been
> Point to one end, which is always present.[28]

In the second section of *Burnt Norton*, Eliot returns to the "present moment" (focused attention is called "a moment" but may last for varying periods if not measured by mechanical time). He further elaborates on his expression of time being "unredeemable" with a new idea, "the still point",

> From: *Burnt Norton 11*
> At the still point of the turning world. Neither flesh
> nor fleshless;
> Neither from nor towards; at the still point, there the
> dance is,
> But neither arrest nor movement. And do not call it fixity,
> Where past and future are gathered.[29]

These lines somewhat muddy the meaning of being in the *present* moment by introducing this new aspect to the present moment concept ("the still point"), merging past and future. He notes that in each moment as the past meets the future there is no such thing as the present, no "fixity", simply because "fixity" always has a past and future. He is now shifting to the understanding that "the still point" touches eternity, a moment *out* of time. He elaborates on this idea in the lines below,

> Neither movement from nor towards,
> Neither ascent nor decline. Except for the point, the
> still point,
> There would be no dance, and there is only the dance.
> I can only say, *there* we have been: but I cannot say where.
> And I cannot say, how long, for that is to place it in time.[30]

(A word on Eliot's symbology; Eliot uses the symbol of "the dance" throughout the *Quartets.*)

How to explain "the still point." We turn to Plato's famous Cave Allegory in *The Republic* (Chapter Seven in this book). The allegory reveals that insight and full conceptual cognition are achieved only when a light is seen as the source of the shadows, exposing them for what they are. A timeless state is beyond our experience until we realize where the source lies—in Eliot's proposition at "the still point"—for when past and future fade, in that instant, "there is only the dance." The dancer becomes the dance. At that moment we observe the dancer and the dance. What of the dancer? Is s/he able to transcend the moment to know s/he is dancing? At that moment does the dancer cease to exist?

Eliot's "still point" unveils time as a possible dimension of timelessness that arises when we lose all consciousness of whatever we are doing but exist in a moment of focused attention on, for instance, the breath, a tree, a cloud, a bird circling above us. Everything else drops away; only the focus is present.

Can we transcend timelessness by living in time? This is a

conundrum that others have pondered. As with philosophers, literary figures, whether consciously or subconsciously, build on the ideas of other thinkers and writers. Here, poetry can pinpoint this conjunction. Perhaps Eliot was aware of these last four lines of a poem[31] by W.B. Yeats first published in 1928,

> O chestnut tree, great rooted blossomer,
> Are you the leaf, the blossom or the bole?
> O body swayed to music, O brightening glance,
> How can we know the dancer from the dance?

Maybe Eliot was thinking of William Shakespeare who in one of his later plays also expressed this idea of our lives being lived amid timelessness, in a speech by Prospero from *The Tempest*,

> Now our revels are ended
> And like the baseless fabric of this vision,
> The cloud-capped towers, the gorgeous palaces,
> The solemn temples, the great globe itself—
> Yea, all which it inherit—shall dissolve,
> And like this insubstantial pageant faded,
> Leave not a rack behind. We are such stuff
> As dreams are made on, and our little life
> Is rounded with a sleep.
> (*The Tempest*, Act 4, scene 1, lines 140-148)[32]

Eliot also poses other dilemmas "here at the still point" that invite us to see the unity beyond this seemingly inscrutable enigma.

Each of us lives in time; in our existence, we are never outside of time. (Like Plato's allegorical people living their "reality" in the world of shadows.) We live our life span at the interstice of our lifetime and infinity, death and eternity—a timeless space.

Eliot hones the essence of this idea to its conclusion— the almost unimaginable speculation that we live in time but are enmeshed in timelessness. Only if we can forgo the past and the future can we create an eternal moment for our lives. There can be no memory or plans, and as he states, but "little consciousness" of time.

Perhaps we can imagine this concept, but we cannot access its significance as yet in our evolutionary progress. We are calibrated to mark the passage of time. Eliot concludes this section of the quartet echoing the opening of *Burnt Norton 1*,

> Time past and time future
> Allow but a little consciousness.[33]

Only with light are shadows revealed. Only through time is timelessness redeemable by our memory of the lives of those who have died. And redeemable through reflection on past events of our lives.

East Coker—In the first quartet, *Burnt Norton*, Eliot, works his ideas on an almost wholly abstract level. In the second, *East Coker*, he writes of cycles and centuries. He switches gears somewhat as he tries to concretize his conceptual principles by describing life on earth.

East Coker
From: *East Coker 1,*
In my beginning is my end. In succession
Houses rise and fall, crumble, are extended,
Are removed, destroyed, restored, or in their place
Is an open field, or a factory, or a by-pass.
Old stone to new building, old timber to new fires,
Old fires to ashes, and ashes to the earth
Which is already flesh, fur and faeces,
Bone of man and beast, cornstalk and leaf.
Houses live and die.[34]

"In my beginning is my end", encapsulates a stark understanding of the concept that from the moment of our birth we are dying, so too with houses and all the biota around us. For each of us, time moves inevitably forward to an endpoint. But if we view this movement from the perspective of cycles—cycles and not a linear progression—each generation is the iteration of the birth to death process in a seemingly unending cycle.

East Coker 1 continues,

> In my beginning is my end. Now the light falls
> Across the open field, leaving the deep lane
> Shuttered with branches, dark in the afternoon,
> Where you lean against a bank while a van passes,
> And the deep lane insists on the direction
> Into the village, in the electric heat.
> Hypnotised. In a warm haze the sultry light
> Is absorbed, not refracted, by grey stone.
> The dahlias sleep in the empty silence. Wait for the
> early owl.[35]

In these lines Eliot uses the symbolism of fire imagery, yet even fire dies in the embers of its own ashes. In Christian symbology fire purifies as it purges.

The speaker in the above extract envisages that while walking in the early evening in the countryside passed an open field, maybe our minds turn to what occurred there on similar evenings centuries previously. We are all capable of this sort of time travel. These lines underscore the idea of time cycling and recycling over centuries.

To make his point even clearer, in the following lines, Eliot inserts some Middle English spelling of familiar words to place us in a medieval scene. Fire then and fire now are a constant reference point, as is the human activity of dancing, the cycle of the seasons, and birth and death,

> In that open field
> If you do not come too close, if you do not come too close,
> On a summer midnight, you can hear the music
> Of the weak pipe and the little drum
> And see them dancing around the bonfire
> The association of man and woman
> In daunsinge, signifying matrimonie-
> A dignified and commodious sacrament. Two and two,
> necessarye coniunction,
> Holding eche other by the hand or the arm
> Whiche betokeneth concorde. ...
> Keeping time
> Keeping the rhythm of their dancing
> As in their living of the living seasons
> The time of the seasons and the constellations
> The time of milking and the time of harvest
> The time of the coupling of man and woman
> And that of beasts. Feet rising and falling.
> Eating and drinking. Dung and death.[36]
> The daily cycle of dawn appears each new day,
> Dawn points, and another day
> Prepares for heat and silence. Out at sea the dawn wind
> Wrinkles and slides. I am here
> Or there, or elsewhere. In my beginning.[37]

Perhaps the most significant and powerful of these lines "I am here/Or there, or elsewhere" is the declarative statement "I am here". Wherever we find ourselves *we* are the "still point." We are the axis of the temporal and the infinite. *With our allotted few moments of consciousness,* we are the crux of all that has been and all that is still to come.

These continuous, almost unchanging cycles of life on this planet—generation-by-generation—give comfort or can seem deadeningly dull. The enigmatic lines "I am here/ Or there, or elsewhere. In my beginning" encourages us to think not in the broad brushstrokes of annual, centennial, and millennial cycles but in continuous moments. In every moment of our lives, as we reach an end, in the next moment, a new one begins. Are we like snakes sloughing off old skins and emerging anew, only millions of times in our lifetime as the seconds begin and end?

Dry Salvages—In this quartet, Eliot introduces ideas on the formation and destruction of memory and history and couples time as both the destroyer and the preserver. The first difference between this, the third quartet, and the other two already discussed is the difference in tone. Here Eliot conversationally writes in prose poetry.

> *Dry Salvages, 11*
> The moments of happiness—not the sense of well-being,
> Fruition, fulfillment, security or affection,
> Or even a very good dinner, but the sudden illumination—
> We had the experience but missed the meaning,
> And approach to the meaning restores the experience
> In a different form, beyond any meaning
> We can assign to happiness.[38]

In the above two lines, Eliot strives to explain what he means by "happiness." He defines the emotion by what it is not and adds value to what is already experienced by stating that if one searches for the meaning in the experiences that lead to "happiness," we "restore the experience in a different form." In this example, enhanced memory renders more meaning than "happiness" alone. He continues to explicate this understanding,

> I have said before
> That the past experience revived in the meaning
> Is not the experience of one life only
> But of many generations—not forgetting
> Something that is probably quite ineffable:
> The backward look behind the assurance
> Of recorded history, the backward half-look
> Over the shoulder, towards the primitive terror.[39]

This idea echoes concepts in *East Coker* of layers of history resting on one another. For instance, the "open field" contains below the surface geological layers of the remnants of people using the field for centuries to make fires and dance, and to build homes in the summer evenings. The land you live on now, most likely a century or two ago, was forest, savannah, or lake. We live on the detritus of millennia of layers of natural and then human existence.

This knowledge of history stretching behind us may be what Eliot means by us looking back at "primitive terror." Recorded history by witness bearers become our saviors from the terror of the unknown, as well as (in their testimony) reinforcers of that "terror." And the future stretching ahead will become other people's history as well as the history of our descendants.

Philosopher Friedrich Nietzsche addressed this very dilemma in his essay *On the Advantage and Disadvantage of History for Us*[40]. He writes, "History belongs to the living man in three respects: it belongs to him so far as he is active and striving, so far as he preserves and admires and so far as he suffers in and is in need of liberation."

The third respect is particularly apt in *Dry Salvages*. Nietzsche writes further that a critical approach to history serves life itself. We must bring critical judgment to history and understand,

> "Since we happen to be the results of earlier generations, we are also the results of their aberrations, passions, and errors, even crimes; it is not possible to free oneself from this chain. ...At best we may bring about a conflict between our inherited, innate nature and our knowledge, as well as a battle between a strict new discipline and ancient education and breeding; we implant a new habit, a new instinct, a second nature so that the first nature withers away. It is an attempt, as it were, *a posteriori* to give oneself a past from which one would like to be descended in opposition to the past from which one is descended."[41]

Each generation creates a new societal context, a new cultural mind structure from that which is past.

These ideas are also present in the lines below,

Dry Salvages 11
Now, we come to discover that the moments of agony
(Whether, or not, due to misunderstanding
Having hoped for the wrong things or dreaded the wrong
things,
Is not in question) are likewise permanent
With such permanence as time has. We appreciate
this better
In the agony of others, nearly experienced,
Involving ourselves, than in our own.
For our past is covered by the currents of action,

But the torment of others remains an experience
Unqualified, unworn by subsequent attrition.[42]

We know that people lived before us for millennia and experienced the human condition as we do, but we do not understand what contextual meaning they gave their experiences. History can help fill that gap if we rely on sources (witness bearers) and not only commentators who are invariably biased.

French philosopher Jean-Paul Sartre believed that only our experiential past becomes the history of our past, the present is our reality, and the future anticipates further life experiences. However, our existence ends with death. For Sartre, after death we do not have a past, as we cannot experience the present and thus create a past. After death we become our past in the memory of others. Indeed "time the destroyer is time the preserver."

People change and smile: but the agony abides.
Time the destroyer is time the preserver[43]

Time destroys each life but through recorded history—individual and collective—it also preserves previous lives and eras.

Little Gidding

The fourth quartet, *Little Gidding*, introduces ideas on time through spiritual-mystical experiences. This quartet is generally considered the masterpiece of the folio and certain lines herein are the most often quoted. Below are two famous passages,

From *Little Gidding 1*:
If you came this way,
Taking any route, starting from anywhere,
At any time or at any season,
It would always be the same; you would have to put off
Sense and notion.[44]

When you enter the sanctuary of a religious or spiritual space, in order to fully experience the power present to believers there, you must divorce your mind from your reliance on your physical senses and ideas of non-belief. For,

> You are not here to verify,
> Instruct yourself, or inform curiosity
> Or carry report. You are here to kneel
> Where prayer has been valid.[45]

You are in a transcendent space. Your one purpose is to open yourself to the unknown possibilities of spiritual experience. Your first step is to humble yourself by kneeling[46] and praying (whatever that means to you),

> And prayer is more
> Than an order of words, the conscious occupation
> Of the praying mind, or the sound of the voice praying.
> And what the dead had no speech for, when living,
> They can tell you, being dead: the communication
> Of the dead is tongued with fire beyond the language of
> the living.[47]

In prayer, the exact words are repeated over centuries every year at the same time of year. The prayers "tongued with fire" both purge and purify. Every time you utter the words, often unchanged for thousands of years, they reverberate with the voices of hordes of supplicants before you. Still, those are not the voices and sounds easily understood, for they are "beyond the language of the living."

> Here, the intersection of the timeless moment
> Is England and nowhere. Never and always.[48]

Eliot states here, as he does elsewhere, that we find that "timeless" moment at the intersection of the eternal and the temporal. When we lose ourselves in ontological or spiritual experiences, we do so for an eternal moment.

From *Little Gidding* V:
What we call the beginning is often the end
And to make an end is to make a beginning.[49]

This final section of *Little Gidding* opens with these lines. As with the repetition of other lines throughout the folio these lines intertwine themes and render the entire folio unified. Life begins anew every time we die to our old selves. (You no longer have the mind structures of the child you were at five or the adolescent at fifteen or the adult at twenty-five, you've sloughed off those skins.) Perhaps when you encounter a spiritual experience, you are changed (made new) even if you return to old patterns of habitual thinking. We can constantly re-emerge from the chrysalis of old thought patterns. Much like the people in the cave allegory, looking back, we see the previously imperceptible reality that we could not see before. Aided by our new perspective, we create alternative mind structures for ourselves,

The end is where we start from. And every phrase
And sentence that is right (where every word is at home,
Taking its place to support the others,
The word neither diffident nor ostentatious,
An easy commerce of the old and the new,
The common word exact without vulgarity,
The formal word precise but not pedantic,
The complete consort dancing together)
Every phrase and every sentence is an end and a beginning,
Every poem an epitaph.[50]

Words have individual meaning and together they make a sentence. A sentence becomes a paragraph and several paragraphs, a document. Words can make an absolute statement such as an epitaph. Writing, such as you see on a tombstone or monument commemorates the dead. If a poem comprises the right words it can ensure that the essence of the deceased is perpetuated,

We die with the dying:
See, they depart, and we go with them. We are born with
the dead:
See, they return, and bring us with them.[51]

This idea, "we die with the dying" is accessible. We carry the DNA and the genes of our parents and their parents through millennia and pass them on to our children and future generations. In this way we are born with the dead and "they return, and bring us with them."

Eliot continues with this theme of unification, completion, and wholeness,

The moment of the rose and the moment of the yew-tree
Are of equal duration.[52]

In mechanical time a rose blooms for several weeks, a yew tree for many years, yet Eliot states they are of "equal duration." If we perceive this equation out of time, they are both living "moments" in their own natural life cycle.

The "rose" and the "yew-tree" are two powerful symbols in Eliot's overall lexicon. In this folio, the "rose"[53] is one of several recurring symbols. The "rose" can be blood red and connote madness, passion, and death—also love.

In the above extract from *Little Gidding* the rose symbolizes Christian love, Christ's love for humanity in his life and at his death, at the intersection of the temporal and eternal. The two arms of the crucifix are generally thought to symbolize the intersection of the temporal (Christ's life on earth—horizontal) and the eternal (vertical with the base embedded in the earth and stretching to the heavens.) Christ's love for Christians encompasses the possibility of rebirth and resurrection.

The "yew-tree" is a complex symbol found in many of Eliot's works. Here it represents paganism or death. The two used together signify the repeating cycles of birth and death—beginnings and endings—found in many forms that we see throughout the folio.

Later in this section Eliot returns once more to his emphasis on the importance of history,

> A people without history
> Is not redeemed from time, for history is a pattern
> Of timeless moments. So, while the light fails
> On a winter's afternoon, in a secluded chapel
> History is now and England.[54]

Understanding and paying attention to our history helps us "redeem" "time" from "timelessness". History is present in each of us. Despite all our history and all we know,

> We shall not cease from exploration
> And the end of all our exploring
> Will be to arrive where we started
> And know the place for the first time.[55]

The above lines carry this theme forward; humans have an imperative urge to push the boundaries of our understanding. Yet we always return to ourselves—our egos and personalities—but with a different perspective and greater comprehension, as if we regard who and what we are "for the first time."

We can reread the same passage in the prayer book every year, but as we grow older, we read "through the unknown, remembered gate" with a new understanding. This interpretation is underscored in the final lines,

Through the unknown, remembered gate
When the last of earth left to discover
Is that which was the beginning;
At the source of the longest river
The voice of the hidden waterfall
And the children in the apple-tree
Not known, because not looked for
But heard, half-heard, in the stillness
Between two waves of the sea.
Quick now, here, now, always
A condition of complete simplicity
(Costing not less than everything)
And all shall be well and
All manner of thing shall be well
When the tongues of flame are in-folded
Into the crowned knot of fire
And the fire and the rose are one.[56]

In the final four lines of the above quote, Eliot looks to the future when the purging fire and the rose of Christian love unify. Only with light are shadows revealed. Only through time is timelessness redeemable by our memory and reflection.

* * *

Lightman and Eliot express their ideas on concepts of time filtered through various schemas. So too does Virginia Woolf in many of her novels. In the next chapter, we follow Woolf in *To The Lighthouse* as she teases from time passing, the function of memory and time, and how memory retrieves irretrievable loss. She sees time in plastic, not mechanical form. One that can be lengthened, shortened, rolled up, squashed, and stretched thin.

6

TIME PASSES BUT MOMENTS LIVE IN MEMORY

Famed British author Virginia Woolf (1882-1941), a contemporary of T. S. Eliot, is an influential, Modernist writer. In addition to her fiction and non-fiction works, she was an accomplished essayist and literary critic. She is best known for her fiction. Her later novels experiment with the narrative form in non-sequential structures. Her "middle period" novels such as *Mrs. Dalloway* and *To The Lighthouse* are perennially popular. Both Woolf and her writing remain iconic pillars of the literary landscape and the global feminist movement. Many critics and readers believe *To The Lighthouse* to be her masterwork.

In feminist circles, for decades now, her voice has been honored among those at the forefront of the feminist movement, particularly for her extended essay, *A Room of Her Own*. In this famous work, Woolf discusses the standing and status of women artists in the literary or fine arts. She declares that a woman must be financially independent and have her own room to fulfill her creativity. The essay was published in 1929.

In *To The Lighthouse*, protagonist Lily Briscoe emerges as a proto-feminist role model; she eschews marriage and strives to build her life—both artistically and financially—without a husband; as Lily Briscoe is to art, so Virginia Woolf is to fiction. Woolf is a Modernist who finds ways to directly connect with readers, giving them paths to follow as they form, change and develop their mind structures in response to her characters' mind structures that she explores in her semi-autobiographical novel.

Woolf writes in diamond-hard, shatter-proof prose and forges an original voice that (as yet) has not been emulated.

In *Little Gidding*, T.S. Eliot rescues time by placing it in grand historical contexts and cycles. In, *To The Lighthouse*, Woolf uses personal history and memory as a hologram of the entirety of human experience. Love, loss, family connections, human aspirations—dashed and achieved—form the material of the novel, all set against the countervailing force of change that time passing carries. Memory may cast an idealizing patina over loss, which can distort or enhance the mind structures retrieved from time.

To The Lighthouse[1] was published in 1927 on an anniversary of Woolf's mother's death. The novel is an elegy to Woolf's childhood summers with her family in Cornwell at Talland House—although the novel is set on the Isle of Skye in the Hebrides—and to her mother, Julia Stephen. An elegy because she mourns the loss of her mother, who died when Woolf was thirteen, and the innocence and family warmth of Woolf's childhood that died with her. In the novel, Woolf models one of two protagonists, Mrs. Ramsay, on her mother.

A Woolf-ian technique used in the novel is to constantly shift the narrative point of view among the main characters, glimpses of mind structures that build and build. In the first section, 'The Window' (the most extended section; yet set over one day), Mrs. Ramsay plays a prominent role and is portrayed as the rock in the ocean around which, in emotional currents, the other characters swim. Woolf is never out of any of their heads. The authorial voice is never heard; we are in the mind structure of each character. Through this shifting point of view, Woolf achieves immediacy in describing human consciousness, a breakthrough in fiction she shares with Irish novelist, James Joyce, her contemporary.

Despite the central role Mrs. Ramsay plays at the summer home, she remains an enigma to her family and the eclectic group of summer house guests. From where do her magnetism and charisma arise? Woolf digs into Mrs. Ramsay's mind structure,

> But was it nothing but looks, people said? What was there behind it—her beauty and splendor? Had he blown his brains out before they were married—some other, earlier love, of whom rumours reached one? Or was there nothing? Nothing but an incomparable beauty which she lived behind, and could do nothing to disturb. For easily though she might have said at some moment of intimacy when stories of great passion, of love foiled, of ambition thwarted came her way, she too had known or felt or been through it herself, she never spoke. She was silent always. She knew then—she knew without having learnt. Her simplicity fathomed what clever people falsified. Her singleness of mind made her drop plumb like a stone, alight as exact as a bird, gave her naturally, this swoop and fall of the spirit upon truth which delighted, eased, sustained—falsely perhaps.[2]

Woolf's mother, and Woolf's childhood emotional proximity to her, allowed the author great insight as she created her mother's doppelganger's personality, "Her simplicity fathomed what clever people falsified" and "her singleness of mind...gave her, naturally, this swoop and fall of the spirit upon truth."

Mrs. Ramsay is a mirror to others, reflecting what they give her. She is manipulative by remaining silent behind her beauty and pleasing affect and never hinting at the thoughts and responses she harbors within herself,

> Mrs. Ramsay seemed to fold herself together, one petal
> closed in another, and the whole fabric fell in exhaustion
> upon itself, so that she had only strength enough to move
> her finger...Mrs. Ramsay felt not only exhausted in body
> (afterwards, not at the same time, she always felt this) but
> also there tinged her physical fatigue some faintly disagree-
> able sensation with another origin...[3]

The other protagonist, Lily Briscoe, twenty years younger than Mrs. Ramsay, is unmarried, in love with the whole family and the summer place, and particularly drawn to Mrs. Ramsay, whom she admires greatly. Our first glance at Lily is through Mrs. Ramsay's eyes. Here we gain insight into Mrs. Ramsay's manipulativeness mentioned above,

> Suddenly a loud cry, as of a sleepwalker, half roused, some-
> thing about sang out with the utmost intensity in her ear,
> made her turn apprehensively to see if anyone heard him.
> Only Lily Briscoe, she was glad to find out; and that did
> not matter. But the sight of the girl standing on the edge of
> the lawn, painting, reminded her; she was supposed to be
> keeping her head as much in the same position as possible
> for Lily's picture. Lily's picture! Mrs. Ramsay smiled. With
> her little Chinese eyes and her puckered up face, she would
> never marry; one could not take her painting seriously;

she was an independent little creature, and Mrs. Ramsay
liked her for it; so, remembering her promise, she bent her
head.[4]

Lily Briscoe is frustrated. Her artwork inspires and infuriates her.
As she paints, she muses about art, love, life, family, and marriage. She
sees that beneath the colors on her canvas, there are shapes. Lily seeks
to attain eternity in creating perfect visions with paint. She will capture
a moment and render it eternal. She visualizes it all clearly, but when
she reaches for her brush, the vision changes. The passage of her work
from conception to canvas is a struggle to keep her courage, and she
says to herself,

"This what I see; this is what I see!" Yet when she turns
to her easel, the mounds of green and blue on the palette
seem to her like blobs, and she scrapes them off to begin
anew. Each time she starts over, she is filled with conviction
that she can inspire the paint "to move, flow, and do her
bidding."[5]

Presently, Lily focuses on painting a portrait of Mrs. Ramsay sitting at the drawing-room window overlooking the wide swath of lawn
and the bay beyond, while on the floor at her feet, six-year-old James,
her youngest child, cuts pictures from a magazine. The green hedge and
blue sea and sky form the background for the painting.

If the novel has a mildly antagonistic character, Mr. Ramsay serves
Woolf well. She modeled him on her father and described his remote
crabbiness with a gentle touch. Many years older than his wife, an aging
philosopher and academic, he struggles to fulfill his life's ambitions by
formulating logical proofs. Crotchety and aloof, he relies on his wife to
arrange his life and provide resonance for his emotions. He has at best
an uneasy relationship with all his children but is particularly harsh

on his youngest, James. Jealous of Mrs. Ramsay's attention to James' needs. Mr. Ramsay relies on his wife to smooth the edges of all his relationships, not only with his children,

> If he put implicit faith in her, nothing should hurt him;
> however deep he buried himself or climbed high, not for
> a second should he find himself without her. So boasting
> of her capacity to surround and protect, there was scarcely
> a shell of herself left for her to know herself by; all was so
> lavished and spent; and James, as he stood stiff between
> her knees, felt her rise in a rosy-flowered fruit tree laid with
> leaves and dancing boughs into which the beak of brass,
> the arid scimitar of his father, the egotistical man, plunged
> and smote, demanding sympathy.[6]

Woolf, either intentionally or unintentionally, planted a malodorous Oedipal whiff in the above quote.

Mr. Ramsay understands he lives in the rarified atmosphere of the mind, where he believes he breathes cleaner air. He takes brisk walks across the lawn or on the beach mulling logic puzzles. He envisions his musings as letters in the alphabet, but he is stuck at Q. Q he is sure he can prove. But how can he ever reach R? Why is his mind stuck at the letter Q and his realization that the letter Q spells "Doom"?

Mr. Ramsay resides in his mind,

> It was a splendid mind. For if thought is like the key-
> board of the piano, divided into so many notes, or like the
> alphabet is ranged into twenty-six letters all in order, then
> his splendid mind had no sort of difficulty in running over
> those letters one by one, firmly and accurately, until it had
> reached, say, the letter Q. He reached Q. Very few people
> in the whole of England ever reach Q. Here, stopping for

one moment by the stone urn which held the geraniums,
he saw, but now far, far away, like children picking up
shells, divinely innocent and occupied with little trifles
at their feet somehow entirely defenceless against a doom
which he perceived, his wife, and son, together in the
window. They needed his protection; he gave it to them.
But after Q? What comes next?"[7]

As he strides across the lawn, Mr. Ramsay ponders eternity. He projects the illusion of appearing sparer and barer as he walks into the misty distance, but he never loses his intense focus of thought. Standing on his little ledge, Q, "…facing the dark of human ignorance, how we know nothing and the sea eats away the ground we stand on—that was his fate, his gift."[8]

Mr. Ramsay accepts impermanence that implies decay and erosion—and not eternity.

Six-year old James, the youngest of the eight Ramsay children, clings to his mother's lap and knees with territorial possessiveness. His father frightens him and he knows his mother will shield him.

James continuously nags his father for a promised boat ride to the local lighthouse "the next morning," but day-by-day, his father persistently frustrates his wishes. Mrs. Ramsay seesaws in the tussle, not wanting to see James' desires thwarted or contradict her husband's abrupt and persistent refusal to oblige the boy,

"No going to the Lighthouse, James," he said, as he stood
by the window, speaking awkwardly but trying in deference
to Mrs. Ramsay to soften his voice into some semblance of
geniality at least. …

Odious little man, thought Mrs. Ramsay, why go on
saying that?

"Perhaps you will wake up and find the sun shining and
the birds singing," she said compassionately, smoothing
the little boy's hair, for her husband, with his caustic saying
that it would not be fine tomorrow, had dashed his spirits
she could see. This going to the Lighthouse was a passion
of his...[9]

A constant presence in the novel is the lighthouse, and not only for
James. Mrs. Ramsay feels an affinity for the all-pervasive, rhythmic
strobe light of the lighthouse itself. The light is ever-present, pushing
back the darkness with everyday dependability, warning of dangers,
and never wavering. Mutely it records all it lights up—day-by-day,
year-by-year. For all who live within its radius, their lives are recorded
in discontinuous moments by the rhythmic nature of the lighthouse
beam—now lighting up the shore, now moving over the ocean.

Moments of self-clarity arise in Mrs. Ramsay's mind structure
amid the light of the stroking beams. Sitting at the window and knitting in the dusk she thinks of the little things each of us do every day,
when she has a sudden insight,

Beneath it is all dark, it is spreading, it is unfathomably
deep; but now and then we rise to the surface and that is
what you see us by. ...There was freedom, there was peace,
there was, most welcome of all, a summoning together, a
resting on a platform of stability. Not as oneself did one
find rest ever, in her experience (she accomplished here
something dexterous with her needles) but as a wedge of
darkness. Losing personality, one lost the fret, the hurry,
the stir; and there rose to her lips always some exclamation
of triumph over life when things came together in this
peace, this rest, this eternity; and pausing there she looked

out to meet that stroke of the Lighthouse, the long steady
stroke, the last of the three, which was her stroke, for
watching them in this mood always at this hour one could
not help attaching oneself to one thing especially of the
things one saw; and this thing, the long steady stroke, was
her stroke.[10]

Here and in the quotes below taken from the same passage, Woolf
begins to build the symbolic association of Mrs. Ramsay with the lighthouse. Mrs. Ramsay acknowledges her union with the light, searching,
probing, interrogating,

… She looked up over her knitting and met the third
stroke and it seemed to her like her own eyes meeting her
own eyes, searching as she alone could search into her
mind and her heart, purifying out of existence that lie, any
lie. She praised herself in praising the light, without vanity,
for she was stern, she was searching, she was beautiful like
that light. …[11]

Her musings take a fanciful direction as to what her mind perceives,

There rose, and she looked and looked with her needles
suspended, there curled up off the floor of the mind, rose
from the lake of one's being, a mist, a bride to meet her
lover.

…[12]

In the latter lines there is an obvious implication as to the
sexual nature of the "stroking" light, and Mrs. Ramsay's union with
the lighthouse.

The passage continues,

... She saw the light again. With some irony in her interrogation, for when woke at all, one's relations changed, she looked at the steady light, the pitiless, the remorseless, which was so much her, yet so little her, which had her at its beck and call (she woke in the night and saw it bent across their bed, stroking the floor), but for all that she thought, watching it with fascination, hypnotized, as if it were stroking with its silver fingers some sealed vessel in her brain whose bursting would flood her with delight, she had known happiness, exquisite happiness, intense happiness, and it silvered the rough waves a little more brightly, as daylight faded, and the blue went out of the sea and it rolled in waves of pure lemon which curved and swelled and broke upon the beach and the ecstasy burst in her eyes and waves of pure delight raced over the floor of her mind and she felt, It is enough! It is enough![13]

This complex symbol of the stroking light initially pulls Mrs. Ramsay from the darkness in "the floor of her mind" that lies below her daily "busy-ness" into a sense of unity, of peace, of rest. She emerges with the light from this place like a mist rising, "...a bride to meet her lover." Ultimately, the light's silver fingers release something sealed in her mind into an orgasmic burst of feeling that floods her with intense satisfaction, and she feels that reaching these epiphanies of touching eternity are "enough."

The climactic scene of this section, the dinner party—portrays the triumphant success of the French entree, Bœuf et Daube, and the companionable and civilized conversation—and explores deeper ramifications of Mrs. Ramsay's psyche. In the quote below, we see further intimations of Mrs. Ramsay's association with the lighthouse and its "immunity from change", as well as the nature of the endurance of memory, "the thing is made that endures",

> It partook, she felt…of eternity; as if she had already felt something different about the afternoon; there is a coherence in things, a stability; something she meant, is immune from change, and shines out (she glanced at the window with its ripple of reflected lights) in the face of the flowing, of the fleeting, the spectral, like a ruby; so that again tonight she had the feeling she had had once today, already, of peace, of rest. Of such moments, she thought, the thing is made that endures.[14]

Unlike her husband, Mrs. Ramsay sees eternity in precious moments of clarity retained by memory.

Several pages later, Mrs. Ramsay, as she leaves the dinner party, looks over her shoulder (like the lighthouse beam rotating into darkness) moving away from the past, while in the present, and into the future,

> But dinner was over. It was time to go. …She looked at the window in which the candle flames burnt brighter now that the panes were black, and looking at the outside the voices came to her very strangely, as if they were voices at a service in a cathedral, for she did not listen to the words…
>
> It was necessary now to carry everything a step further. With her foot on the threshold she waited a moment longer in a scene which was vanishing even as she looked, and left the room, it changed, it shaped itself differently; it had become, she knew, giving one last look at it over her shoulder, already the past.[15]

The lighthouse serves as a structural framework throughout the novel. In the middle section, 'Time Passes' for family and friends. The years it covers shutter them from the symbolic presence of the lighthouse.

Woolf describes the decay to the summer house during this period in an elegiac prose-poem that can stands alone in style and tone from the other two sections of the novel. In this section, Woolf may be alluding to the sequence of events in her family history. Indeed, one winter, her mother, Julia Stephen, died in London, away from the lighthouse. Family deaths are treated cursorily (these are Woolf's parentheses),

[Mr. Ramsay, stumbling along a passage one dark morning, stretched his arms out, but Mrs. Ramsay having died rather suddenly the night before, his arms, though stretched out, remained empty.][16]

[Prue Ramsay died that summer in some illness connected with childbirth, which was indeed a tragedy, people said, everything they said, had promised so well.]

And on the next page during the First World War the cursory report of Andrew's death.

[A shell exploded. Twenty or thirty young men were blown up in France, among them Andrew Ramsay, whose death, mercifully, was instantaneous.][17]

The house, too, is dying of neglect,

Only the Lighthouse beam entered the rooms for a moment, sent its sudden stare over the bed and wall in the darkness of winter, looked with equanimity at the thistle and the swallow, the rat, and the straw. Nothing now withstood them; nothing said no to them. Let the wind blow;

let the poppy seed itself and the carnation mate with the cabbage. Let the swallow build in the drawing room, and the thistle thrust aside the tiles, and the butterfly sun itself on the faded chintz of the armchairs. Let the broken glass and china lie out on the lawn and be tangled over with grass and wild berries.[18]

When Mrs. Ramsay is not present to imbue the lighthouse strokes with her associative empathy, the light is merely light, an objective presence.

In the third section, 'The Lighthouse,' after the ten-year hiatus, Woolf returns Mr. Ramsay to the house, along with his remaining children, Lily Briscoe, and other guests, who appeared in 'The Window.' Mr. Ramsay and his now teenage children, including sixteen-year-old James, finally set sail for the lighthouse. On the way there, and while at the lighthouse, they reach a reconciliation of family tensions and differences.

The final scene of this third section (and the novel) portrays Lily Briscoe attempting to complete her painting of Mrs. Ramsay and James she began ten summers earlier. But the empty drawing-room steps into the garden, flood her with free-associating memories of her emotional response to Mrs. Ramsay. Lily dwells on what she has lost, and in so doing, she retrieves the redeemable from the irredeemable. Woolf brilliantly evokes the power of memory to act in this way and universalizes deep feeling in Lily's free-associating thoughts around the loss of a beloved other,

But one only woke people if one knew what one wanted to say to them. And she wanted to say not one thing, but everything. Little words that broke up the thought and dismembered it said nothing. 'About life, about death; about Mrs. Ramsay'—no, she thought, one could say nothing to nobody. The urgency of the moment always missed its mark. Words fluttered sideways and struck the object inches too low. Then one gave it up; then the idea sunk back again; then, one became like most middle-aged people, cautious, furtive, with wrinkles between the eyes and a look of perpetual apprehension. For how could one express in words these emotions of the body? express the emptiness there? (She was looking at the drawing-room steps; they looked extraordinarily empty.) It was one's body feeling, not one's mind. The physical sensations that went with the bare look of the steps had become suddenly extremely unpleasant. To want and not to have sent all up her body, a hardness, a hollowness, a strain. And then to want and want and not to have—to want and want—how that wrung the heart, and wrung it again and again! Oh, Mrs. Ramsay![19]

Lily acknowledges with aching heart and mind that Mrs. Ramsey is gone. Yet simultaneously she begins to accept her emanation as if that of a ghost, "Ghost, air, nothingness", a new mind structure of Mrs. Ramsey forms,

She called out silently, to that essence which sat by the boat, the abstract one made of her, that woman in grey, as if to abuse her for having gone, and then having gone, come back again. It had seemed so safe, thinking of her. Ghost, air, nothingness, a thing you could play with easily and safely at any time of the day or night, she had been that, and then suddenly she put her hand out and wrung the heart thus. Suddenly, the empty drawing-room steps, the frill of the chair inside, the puppy tumbling on the terrace, the whole wave and whisper of the garden became like the curves and arabesques flourishing round a centre of complete emptiness.[20]

Later in this section, Woolf merges the narrative of the novel with philosophical questions on creativity and the nature and function of art, basically a discussion on what constitutes the composition and functioning of a creative mind structure. This may be a nod to Woolf's younger sister, Vanessa Bell, a well-reputed artist. Woolf may be writing her semi-autobiographical self-portrait into Lily's musing and mind structure. She tries to fathom why she cannot move on with her painting—and, indeed, for Woolf, there are echoes of her struggles with her writing process. Lily's aesthetic musings begin,

What was the problem then? She must try to get hold of something that evaded her. It evaded her when she thought of Mrs. Ramsay; it evaded her now when she thought of her picture. Phrases came. Visions came. Beautiful phrases. But what she wished to get hold of was that very jar on the nerves, the thing itself before it has been made anything. Get that and start afresh; get that and start afresh; she said desperately, pitching herself firmly before her easel. It was a miserable machine, an inefficient machine, she thought, the human apparatus for painting or for feeling; it always broke down at the critical moment; heroically, one must force it on. She stared, frowning. There was the hedge, sure enough. But one got nothing by soliciting urgently. One got only a glare in the eye from looking at the line of the wall, or from thinking—she wore a gray hat. She was astonishingly beautiful. Let it come, she thought, if it will come. For there are moments when one can neither think nor feel. And if one can neither think nor feel, she thought, where is one?[21]

In further passages in the text, Lily argues convincingly for non-representational but emotive art and displays her convictions in her painting in which mother and child are reduced to two shapes with a line separating them. Ultimately, the painting of Mrs. Ramsay and James, and the novel, achieve elegant abstract structures.

Aside from the novel's evocative power to retrieve losses through memory, such losses generally thought of as irretrievable, lost in the ravages of time, another significant feature is how Woolf splinters narrative continuity into the tripartite structure of the novel. In this, she is influenced by author-philosopher Henri-Louis Bergson, as mentioned in the conclusion of Chapter Three, who explored the nature of ontology (metaphysical reality) in several famous books. His books expounded on the nature of moment-by-moment intuition and experience.

Unlike mechanical time, in Bergsonian or psychological-intuitive time, a day can live longer in the memory than ten years passing. For instance, in section one, James nags about sailing to the lighthouse; in section two, he disappears; in section three, he voyages to the lighthouse on the first day back. Ten years is a short interlude in discontinuous time or psychological time, whereas fulfilling a childhood passion looms larger and larger. Ostensibly, one can argue, James *does* sail to the lighthouse on the next morning.

In August 1925, on a new page in her writing notebook, Woolf wrote *To The Lighthouse*. Underneath, she drew a diagram of the letter "H" and wrote, "two blocks joined by a corridor, which would make up the structure of the novel—the longer 'Window' and 'Lighthouse' joined by 'Time Passes.'"[22] The time sequences outlined above involving James can be seen as an "H".

Additionally, the novel's structure resembles a literal "H". The first section is one vertical arm of the letter, 'The Window' (set over one day and at one hundred and twenty pages the most extended section). The novel's middle section (at scarcely twenty pages, the shortest section, but set over ten years), 'Time Passes,' covers the time between the family's visits to the house. This is an example of how Woolf breaks from mechanical or continuous-time measurements. Ten years of desolation are glossed over, personal history is described minimally and set amid family death, and the impersonal, historical First World War. However, the decay and neglect of the house is described in precise detail. This section is the horizontal bar in the middle of the "H", a nod to the discontinuous nature of associative memory.

The third and final section is the other vertical arm of the "H" (sixty pages and covering two nights and a day); Woolf returns Mr. Ramsay to the house, along with his remaining children, Lily Briscoe, and other guests who appeared in 'The Window'.

But there is much more to the "H" figure than the structural foundation of the novel. The two vertical strokes joined by the horizontal bar form the substructures as well. Among those already mentioned are the polarities of Mrs. and Mr. Ramsay joined by marriage and children; James, the youngest child and the Oedipal struggle between him and his father for Mrs. Ramsay's attention; and, the polarity of Mrs. Ramsay and Lily Briscoe. Mrs. Ramsay embodies Victorian mores of marriage and women's roles. Lily is emotionally and psychologically torn. Admiring, even loving, Mrs. Ramsay, despising and hating her for what she stands for. Lily constantly crosses between these negative responses,

Such was the complexity of things. For what happened to

her, especially staying with the Ramsays, was to be made to feel violently two opposite things at the same time; that's what you feel was one; that's what I feel, was the other, and then they fought together in her mind as now. It is beautiful, so exciting this love...also it is the stupidest, the most barbaric of human passion...and if you asked nine people out of ten they would say they wanted nothing but this love; while women, judging from her own experience, would all the time be feeling, This is not what we want; there is nothing more tedious, puerile, and inhumane than this; yet it is also beautiful and necessary.[23]

Another substructure of the novel is described in the middle section 'Time Passes'. This section, the bar in the "H" is distinguished more by way of the prose-poem on the private and personal—family death, house decaying back to nature—as well as the psycho-sociological—societal mind structures on time, eternal moments, retrievable and irretrievable memories, and beginnings and endings. Personal family history and historical events are joined by the bar of time passing. This "essay" is acknowledged as a masterpiece of Modernist writing.

In the opening paragraph, Woolf writes,

One by one, the lamps were all extinguished...the moon sunk, and a thin rain drumming on the roof a downpouring of immense darkness began. Nothing it seemed could survive the flood, the profusion of darkness...[24]

Woolf announces the symbolic darkness that falls over the house for the following ten years—and the darkness that befalls the family when Mrs. Ramsay dies. In the following description of the house returning to nature as time passes, Woolf, with poetic and original effect, personifies the "certain airs" and lets us peek into the private life of the house, devoid of the family that brings it to life,

> Nothing stirred in the drawing-room or the dining-room or on the staircase. Only through the rusty hinges and swollen and sea-moistened woodwork certain airs, detached from the body of the wind (the house was ramshackle after all) crept around corners and ventured indoors. Almost one might imagine them, as they entered the drawing-room questioning and wondering, toying with the flap of hanging wall-paper, asking would it hang much longer, when would it fall? Then smoothly brushing the walls, they passed on musingly as if by asking the red and yellow roses on the wall-paper whether they would fade, and questioning (gently, for there was time at their disposal) the torn letters in the waste-paper basket, the flowers, the books, all of which were now open to them and asking. Were they allies? Were they enemies? How long would they endure?[25]

The lighthouse with its probing light remains, constant,

> ...Some random light directing them with its pale footfall upon the stair and mat, from some uncovered star, of wandering ship, or the Lighthouse even, the little airs mounted the staircase and nosed around bedroom doors. But here, surely, they must cease. Whatever else may perish and disappear, what lies here is steadfast.[26]

But for Woolf, historical events seep into the lives of even those who seek to avoid being stained by them,

At that season those who had gone down to pace the beach
and ask of the sea and sky what message they reported or
what vision they affirmed had to consider among the usual
tokens of divine bounty—the sunset on the sea, the pallor
of dawn, the moon rising, fishing-boats against the moon,
and children making mud-pies or pelting each other with
handfuls of grass, something out of harmony with this
jocundity and this serenity. There was the silent apparition
of an ashen-coloured ship for instance, come, gone; there
was a purplish stain upon the bland surface of the sea as
if something had boiled and bled, invisibly, beneath. This
intrusion into the scene calculated to stir the most sublime
reflections and lead to the most comfortable conclusions
stayed their pacing. It was difficult blandly to overlook
them; to abolish their significance in the landscape; to
continue, as one walked by the sea to marvel how beauty
outside mirrored beauty within.[27]

Woolf poses an important existential dilemma: is humankind in
all its complexity able to live symbiotically with Nature?

Did Nature supplement that man advances? Did she
compete with what he began? With equal complacence she
saw his misery, his meanness and his torture, that dream,
of sharing, completing, of finding in solitude on the beach
an answer, was then but a reflection in a mirror, and the
mirror itself was but the surface glassiness which forms the
quiescence when the nobler powers sleep beneath? Impa-
tient, despairing yet loth to go (for beauty offers her lures,
has her consolations), to pace the beach was impossible;
contemplation was unendurable; the mirror was broken.[28]

In the above passage, Woolf widens her lens to share her perspective on how historical events, as time passes, impinge on the consolation we seek in Nature. No-one, nowhere, maintains Woolf, is exempt from the stain of war. Darkened with pessimism about human endeavors, she describes Nature as an inconstant presence, unlike time. Time is omnipresent. Nature is a mirror that reflects the observer what they want to see. But this process cannot occur if the mirror is sharded. History and warfare shatter personal mind structures, however tenuously, we try to cling to what is familiar.

This section ends, when ten years later, Lily Briscoe, one evening, is among the first guests to return to the summer house. She falls asleep in the darkness but awakens,

> …she clutched at her blankets as a faller clutches at the turf
> on the edge of a cliff. Her eyes opened wide. Here she was
> again, she thought, sitting bolt upright in her bed. Awake.[29]

"Awake" carries the symbolic meaning of 'to be open' and aware on a more complex and conceptual plane than that of the daily drudge. Those are the final words of 'Time Passes.'

The succeeding and final section, 'The Lighthouse,' describes the first day back, mainly from Lily's point of view, for the family and their guests. Woolf delves ever more deeply into how one can retrieve, from seemingly irretrievable loss, the past in the present.

The opening sentence of the third section reads,

> What does it mean then, what can it all mean? Lily Briscoe
> asked herself. …For really what did she feel, come back
> after all these years and Mrs. Ramsay dead? Nothing, noth-
> ing—nothing that she could express at all.[30]

If Lily truly believes she cannot express any feelings, this quote foreshadows Lily's struggles with artistic expression.

My main concentration here (by cherry-picking and sharing a selection of quotes) is on how Woolf constructs Lily's consciousness (mind structure) from within while using memory to rescue what T.S. Eliot termed the "irredeemable" from passages of time. Woolf agrees with Eliot that this is possible.

Two strands emerge; Lily Briscoe's thoughts on time, memory and art; and, the family's, particularly James' reaction to reaching the lighthouse.

James, now sixteen years old, his father, and several siblings are in a boat crossing the bay on their way to the lighthouse. James recalls ten years earlier,

"It will rain," he remembered his father saying. "You won't be able to go to the Lighthouse."

> The Lighthouse was then a silvery, misty-looking tower with a yellow eye that opened suddenly, and softly in the evening.[31]

> James looked at the Lighthouse. He could see the white-washed rocks; the tower; stark and straight; he could see windows in it; he could even see washing spread on the rocks to dry. So that was the Lighthouse, was it?

> No, the other was the Lighthouse. For nothing was simply one thing. The other Lighthouse was true too. It was sometimes hardly to be seen across the bay. In the evening one looked up and saw the eye opening and shutting and the light seemed to reach them in that airy sunny garden where they sat. ...[32]

Objects need not have only singular worth but may consist of several values. For James the lighthouse sparks reminisces and memories that enflame his mind; of his mother and her reaction to his father. Of how as when he was six-years-old, of how afraid he had been of his father. In the quote below, Woolf adeptly interweaves James' memories *then* with his feelings *now*. His mother was,

> ...a person to whom one could say what comes into one's head. But all the time he thought of her, he was conscious of his father following his thought, surveying it, making it shiver and falter. At last he ceased to think. ...[33]

On the boat, James, hand on the tiller, stares at the still distant but looming lighthouse, and tries to "flick away the grains of his misery."[34] Then the boat's sails fill and the craft begins to move more quickly,

> The relief was extraordinary. They all seemed to fall away from each other again and to be at ease and the fishing lines slanted taut across the side of the boat. But his father did not rouse himself. He only raised his right hand mysteriously in the air, and let it fall upon his knee again as if he were conducting a secret symphony.
>
> ...So it was like that, James thought, the Lighthouse one had seen across the bay all those years; it was a stark tower on a bare rock. It satisfied him. It confirmed some obscure feeling of his about his own character. ... but as a matter of fact, James thought, looking at the Lighthouse stood there on its rock, it's like that.[35]

This quote suggests that James, when he regards the lighthouse, achieves satisfaction of understanding akin to that peace his mother felt in the lighthouse beams. Whereas she ecstatically engaged with the probing light that carried her to new understandings, he is equally satisfied by a more prosaic, literal understanding of the brick-and-mortar permanency of the sturdy structure.

Suddenly, Woolf shifts the point of view from those in the boat to Lily Briscoe, standing on land, in the garden staring at the vessel, a dot on the ocean crawling its way across the bay to the lighthouse. By making Lily conscious of and actively engaged in watching the boat's progress to the lighthouse, Woolf begins to lay other strands of past and present to be able to enjoin them at the conclusion.

As the boat inches to the lighthouse, earlier in this section Lily stands before an easel set in the garden and prepares to paint, as she had done most days ten years earlier. She remembers one of the other guests saying then, "…women cannot write, cannot paint" and she was,

> … as if caught up in one of those habitual currents in
> which after a certain time experience forms in the mind,
> so that one repeats words without being aware any longer
> who originally spoke them.
>
> "Can't paint, can't write", she murmured monotonously,
> anxiously considering what her plan of attack should be.
> … Then as if some juice necessary for the lubrication
> of her faculties were spontaneously squirted, she began
> precariously dipping her brush hither and thither, but it
> was now heavier and went slower, as if it had fallen in some
> rhythm which was dictated to her (she kept looking at the
> hedge, at the canvas) by what she saw, so that while her
> hand quivered with life, this rhythm was strong enough to
> bear her along with it on its current.[36]

If the third stroke of the lighthouse rays brought Mrs. Ramsay to ecstatic release into an exquisite sense of unity, the act of painting does the same for Lily. Once more, this release is described in sexual terms with words like "lubrication," "squirted," "fallen in some rhythm." You may ask if Woolf's use of explicitly sexual vocabulary and imagery in both instances are deeply unconscious or deliberate. Woolf herself never commented on this matter. Her sister, artist Vanessa Bell, certainly was aware of the sexual undertones and displayed them in her original, phallic cover design for the novel.

While Lily continues to dab at the canvas in bold blobs of green and blue,

> ... her mind kept throwing up from its depths, scenes, and
> names, and sayings, and memories and ideas like a foun-
> tain spurting over that glaring, hideously difficult white
> space, while she modeled it with greens and blues.[37]

"Like a work of art," she repeated, looking from her canvas to the drawing-room steps and back again.[38]

Ten years earlier, Mrs. Ramsay and James, sitting in the drawing room near the steps, modeled for Lily. Her thoughts continue,

> What is the meaning of life? That was all—a simple
> question; one that tended to close in on one with years.
> The great revelation had never come. The great revelation
> perhaps never did come. Instead there were little daily
> miracles, illuminations, matches struck unexpectedly in
> the dark; here was one. This, that and the other; herself
> and Charles Tansley and the breaking wave; Mrs. Ramsay
> bringing them together; Mrs. Ramsay saying, "Life stand
> still here"; Mrs. Ramsay making of the moment something
> permanent (as in another sphere Lily herself tried to make

of the moment something permanent)—this was of the nature of a revelation. In the middle of chaos there was shape; this eternal passing and flowing (she looked at the clouds going and the leaves shaking) was struck into stability. Life stand still here, Mrs. Ramsay said. "Mrs. Ramsay! Mrs. Ramsay!" she repeated. She owed it all to her.[39]

Lily's "great revelation," her epiphany, manifests when she acknowledges the powerful light Mrs. Ramsay shone on her life,

And this, Lily thought, taking the green paint on her brush, this making up scenes about them is what we call 'knowing people,' 'thinking' of them, 'being fond of them'! Not a word was true; she had made it up, but it was what she knew of them by all the same. She went on tunneling her way into her picture, into the past.[40]

Glancing again at the sea and the boat, Lily anticipates the group in the boat will be at the lighthouse by lunchtime. But she noted the wind had changed the sea slightly and blown a trail of smoke across her vision. Before the scene looked fixed, now the changes upset her,

The disproportion there seemed to upset some harmony in her own mind. She felt an obscure distress. It was confirmed when she turned to her picture. She had been wasting her morning. For whatever reason she could not achieve that razor edge of balance between two opposite forces; Mr. Ramsay (in the boat)[41] and the picture; which was necessary. There was something perhaps wrong with the design? Was it, she wondered, that the line of the wall wanted breaking, was it that the mass of the tress was too heavy? She smiled ironically; for had she not thought, when she began, that she had solved the problem?[42]

Lily's free-associating memories of Mrs. Ramsey continue. As her thoughts unfold, we become more and more aware of how deeply Mrs. Ramsay affected Lily. Lily loved her; indeed, she may have been in love with her and fought against any instinct to tell her, "I love you!",

"What was the problem then? She must try to get hold of something that evaded her. It evaded her when she thought of Mrs. Ramsay; it evaded her when she thought of her picture. Phrases came. Visions came. Beautiful pictures. Beautiful phrases. But what she wished to get hold of was that very jar on the nerves, the thing itself before it had been made anything. Get that and start afresh; get that and start afresh; she said desperately, pitching herself firmly again before her easel. It was a miserable machine, an inefficient machine, she thought, the human apparatus for painting or for feeling; it always broke down at the critical moment; heroically, one must force it on. She stared, frowning. There was the hedge, sure enough. But one got nothing by solicitating urgently. One got only a glare in the eye from looking at the line if the wall, or from thinking—she wore a grey hat. She was astonishingly beautiful. Let it come she thought, if it will come. For there are moments when one can neither think nor feel. And if one can neither think nor feel, she thought, where is one?[43]

Woolf's obsession with her mother, according to her diaries and journals, lasted a lifetime. In many ways, Mrs. Ramsay (like Julia Stephen) was a withholding woman with so many intimate family members demanding her love and attention. Woolf felt the lack of that maternal love in her mind structure throughout her life. And it scarred her relationships with people closest to her. Lily experienced that lack, too.

Her thoughts on Mrs. Ramsay continue to flow freely,

There must have been people who disliked her very much,
Lily thought (Yes; but she realized that the drawing room
step was empty, but it had no effect on her whatever. She
did not want Mrs. Ramsay now.) –People who thought
her too sure, too drastic. Also her beauty offended people
probably. How monotonous, they would say, and the same
always! They preferred another type—the dark, the viva-
cious. Then she was weak with her husband. She let him
make those scenes. Then she was reserved. Nobody knew
exactly what had happened to her. And one could not
imagine Mrs. Ramsay standing painting, lying reading, a
whole morning on the lawn. It was unthinkable. Without
saying a word, the only token of her errand a basket on
her arm, she went off to the town, to the poor, to sit in
some stuffy little bedroom. ... Her going was a reproach to
them, gave a different twist to the world, so that they were
led to protest, seeing their own prepossessions disappear,
and clutch at them vanishing.[44]

Lily's stream of consciousness is interrupted when someone enters
the drawing-room she has been staring at. 'For Heaven's sake', she
prayed, 'let them sit still there and not come floundering out to talk
to her.'[45] The person settles inside, and so doing throws an odd-shaped
triangular shadow over the step.

This was Lily's breakthrough moment with her painting,

It altered, the composition of the picture a little. It was
interesting. It might be useful. Her mood was coming back
to her. One must keep on looking without for a second
relaxing the intensity of emotion, the determination not

to be put off, not to be bamboozled. One must hold the
scene—so—in a vise and let nothing come in and spoil it.
One wanted, she thought, dipping her brush deliberately,
to be on a level with ordinary experience, to feel, simply
that's a chair, that's a table, and yet at the same time, it's
a miracle, it's an ecstasy. The problem might be solved
after all.[46]

Finally, Lily can express her thoughts in terms of "intensity of
emotion" and "to experience, to feel" and, "it's a miracle, an ecstasy".
By inference she can feel free *to express in her painting* the hidden, for-
bidden words to Mrs. Ramsay, "I love you." Her thoughts race after
one another,

Ah, but that what had happened? Some wave of white
went over the windowpane. The air must have stirred a
flounce in the room. Her heart leaped at her and seized her
and tortured her.

"Mrs. Ramsay! Mrs. Ramsay!" she cried, feeling the
old horror come back—to want and want and not to
have. Could she inflict that still? And then, quietly, as if
she refrained, that too became part of the ordinary experience, was on a level with the chair, with the table. Mrs.
Ramsay—it was part of her perfect goodness—sat there
quite simply, in the chair, flicked her needles to and fro,
knitted her reddish-brown stocking, cast her shadow on
the step. There she sat.[47]

Here, Woolf succeeds in uniting memory and present moment in
one brilliant flourish. She shows that time is never lost in the past but
always carried alive in memory. There, events and emotions burn as
brightly as they did in their original manifestation.

197

A random thought intercedes as Lily asks an abrupt question to herself, "Where was the boat now?" This rhetorical question breaks Lily's mood and returns her (and us) to the present. However, the boat, too, is traveling into the past, into that summer when James first nagged for this boat ride, the summer when Mrs. Ramsay, a beacon of beauty and efficiency, lit the entire household with her inner light,

> "He must have reached it," said Lily Briscoe aloud, feeling suddenly completely tired out. For the lighthouse had become almost invisible, had melted away into a blue haze, and the effort of looking at it and the effort of thinking of him landing there, which both seemed to be one and the same effort, had stretched her body and mind to the utmost. ...
>
> "He has landed," she said aloud. "It is finished."...
>
> Quickly, as if she were recalled by something over there, she turned to her canvas. There it was—her picture. Yes, with all its greens and blues, its lines running up and across, its attempt at something. It would be hung in the attic, she thought; it would be destroyed. But what did that matter? she asked herself, taking up her brush again. She looked at the steps; they were empty; she looked at her canvas; it was blurred. With a sudden intensity, as if she saw it clear for a second, she drew a line there, in the centre. It was done; it was finished. Yes, she thought, laying down her brush in extreme fatigue, I have had my vision.[48]

So too, Virginia Woolf manifested her vision—*To The Lighthouse* is a novel, as she writes in her notebook, "not a view of the world" but, like Lily's painting, it is also an abstract creation of forms from associated memories.

* * *

In the following chapter, a far cry from the previous two chapters on concepts and imaginings of such philosophical terrain as time, Plato's *The Republic* sets forth a model of societal governance. The model in *The Republic* is posited on an educational system that indoctrinates individuals into a mind structure of how to govern the self. Individual self-governance is extrapolated into a mind structure on a societal scale; governance for The Good of everyone. This idealized form of government has intrigued Plato's supporters and detractors for millennia.

7

EXPLORE THE FORMATION OF MANY WESTERN MIND STRUCTURES IN BOTH THE INDIVIDUAL AND THEIR SOCIETIES

Among ancient Greek philosophers two thousand years ago, lived the most famous: Socrates, Plato and Aristotle. They taught in the agora, the marketplace, in the ancient port city of Athens and created ancient Greek drama, epic storytelling, imaginary societies, among other literary and philosophical endeavors. We relate to their work, as we do to the characters in ancient dramas of Sophocles and Euripides, and the epic grandeur of Homer's *The Iliad*. These characters resonate with us as quickly as do the archetypal portrayals of good and evil in John Milton's epic *Paradise Lost* and George Lucas' *Star Wars* movie series. A remarkable truism is that our experiences may change but the human condition never does.

A development that helped stoke this Golden Age ferment of creativity in Socrates' Athens occurred about five hundred years earlier when Buddhism, essentially reformed and reconstituted Hinduism but without the gods, flourished in northern India. Eventually the Buddha's teachings spread over the sub-continent, and to Nepal, Tibet, China, Japan and Mongolia. Like seeds borne on ocean currents and wind, ideas were likewise carried far, but on trade routes. Over scores of years Buddhism spread on the Great Spice Road and the Great Silk Road as both provided passages from India and Asia to the countries on the eastern Mediterranean.

In this chapter, we learn of the creation of a Western utopia. However, in Plato's *The Republic*[1] we find echoes of Buddhist emphasis on inner discipline and mind training. Plato, in his utopia, exhorted Athenian citizens to embody and uphold The Good. His ideas of self-governance are still omnipresent, fundamental building blocks for the governance of the state.

Inevitably Buddhist ideas penetrated the city-state of Athens, the maritime and mercantile epicenter of that era. Hundreds of years after the Buddha first taught in northern India, Socrates wandered the streets of Athens. One of my insights into the material in this chapter suggests that some of Socrates' ideas complement Buddhism. Perhaps Socrates used those ideas without knowing their origin and therefore stated them as if his own. Without laws protecting intellectual property right, such as we have today, ideas garnered in the marketplace become common knowledge.

The oldest of three famous Golden Age Greek philosophers, Socrates was fearless in pursuing his ideas, regarding the proto-democratic governance of Athens as corrupt and striving to foster in his pupils the desire for social and political change. Young men from elite and wealthy Athenian families gathered in their scores to listen to Socrates teach at his famous Academy in the agora. Socrates did not write or read his talks. Like the ancient sages in India, those that Buddhist monk, Matthieu Ricard (Chapter Three) admires, Socrates spoke extemporaneously, disseminating oral tradition teachings.

The ruling elite of Athens, fearful that Socrates' teachings would corrupt their sons, cause societal upheaval and end their power, eventually had him arrested and charged with heresy and treason. Rather than recant his beliefs, Socrates, sentenced to execution, chose death by drinking hemlock.

All Socrates' followers were men. Girls and women were not allowed to learn anything scholarly or move unaccompanied on the streets of Athens. Let alone to vote. Athenian society did not allow slaves or their children, male or female, any scholarly enterprise, or, unsurprisingly, to be enfranchised, despite the fact that Athens was built and maintained by slave labor. While Socrates entranced his male students at the Academy with stirring words on justice, living a just life, and on the aspiration of all human beings to be just—his wife along with their slaves, ran his household. In Socrates' Athens, the only people regarded as full citizens were Athenian-born males. Hence, ancient city-state Athens was not a democracy but a proto-democracy.[2]

Herein lies a paradox that has bothered Plato scholars and admirers for centuries. Yet, we still have slaves today. We have sex-slave trades and other slave trades related to human and drug trafficking. Many countries have histories of slavery: slaves, slave traders, and slave owners. The human condition never changes.

Of Socrates' most able and famous students, we know chiefly the names of Plato and Aristotle. His star pupil, Plato, an Athenian by birth, inherited Socrates' Academy. The much younger Aristotle was a student of Plato at the Academy from ages seventeen to thirty-seven. He founded his Lyceum in Athens but collaborated with Plato, although the two disagreed on several key Platonic philosophical ideas. A famed scholar in his own right, Aristotle's most famous works include the

Nicomachean Ethics, a treatise on those behaviors and judgments that constitute "good" living. His book *Poetics* is still used to understand dramatic theory. His work on metaphysics is an integral part of Christian theology, and his ideas on logic, the basis of modern logic.

Aristotle was an "outsider" born in Chalcis, Macedonia. He was summoned from Athens by King Philip II of Macedon and tutored Philip's son, Alexander, who later became famous as Alexander the Great. Aristotle returned to Athens. After Alexander died in distant Persia, Aristotle deemed it unsafe for himself or his family in Athens and returned the household permanently to Chalcis.

Even after two millennia, the studies, thoughts, interactions, and writings of these three men remain the bedrock of both Western philosophy and Western mind structures. Plato embarked on projects to recall Socrates' teachings from memory. Many such endeavors exist, and in this chapter, we engage with one such touchstone, the classic, *The Republic.* This idealized discourse on societal governance contains ideas on how to become both an enlightened ruler (governance of the state) and master of the inner self. Plato's proposals and practices advocate aspirations toward a perfected society.

The Republic by Plato

In *The Republic,* Plato seized the momentum of the dying days of Athenian "democracy" to propel his ideas for a utopian ideal. The dialog is a petri dish of Socrates' ideas and possibly some of Plato's. (We have no idea where Socrates' teachings end and Plato's begin.)

In this discussion, I refer to Plato as the author unless a quote evokes Socrates' name. If I comment on that quote, I'm referring to Socrates as a character.

In the dialog, Plato has the character Socrates pose questions to his fellow Athenian philosophers and pupils and formulate answers. In turn, Socrates responds to their answers and, through this dialectic process, helps them refine their ideas, all the while leading them to what he, Socrates, believes. Plato adopted this methodology, now called Socratic dialog, as a literary device. He may have used this form partly to pay homage to his teacher but also to protect himself by deflecting his more controversial ideas onto the recently executed Socrates.

Socrates' dialogs are structured as dialectical (thesis=argument, antithesis=response; thesis=argument, antithesis=response) like a tennis game with the ball flying rhythmically back and forth over the net. But Plato adds to the dialectic thesis/antithesis structure a further step—from the thesis and antithesis emerges a trialectic form—thesis, antithesis, synthesis—this new thesis arising from the previous refining process. Dialog becomes a continual triangular configuration.

Process that the trialectic form demonstrates

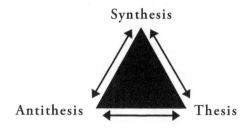

Synthesis

Antithesis   **Thesis**

This configuration features in the larger schema of *The Republic* as well. Books One, Two, and part of Book Three form the thesis. A vigorous dialectal debate on definitions of justice, injustice, and just-ness ensues in the latter part of Book Two and Book Three. We are treated to exposition on how a just society can overcome many challenges. These books state the argument, the thesis.

The end of Book Three through Book Five constitute the antithesis, as Plato's character, Socrates, floats ideas arising from his utopian (no place) republic.

Books Five through Seven describe the synthesis of the trialectic form in which he unites his thesis and antithesis. His synthesis contains revolutionary propositions.

In Books Six and Seven, Plato draws on several literary devices to further synthesize his ideas and help the populace understand that narrow-mindedness and self-serving actions are not to their advantage.

Books Eight through Ten bring us full circle in a finale or addendum of sorts. Plato draws conclusions and highlights ideas from his previous synthesis in Books Five through Seven. In Book Ten, *The Republic* ends unexpectedly, almost abruptly, as Plato rethought some of his earlier ideas. He decries that predictably successful governments such as his vision of a republic based on just-ness and balance (The Good) become victims of their own success. Inevitably selfish individuals and societal greed and corruption win over harmony and balance, both from within the republic and outside. Surrounding city-states become jealous of their successful neighbor and strive to undermine that state's smooth functioning and wealth.

(Before we continue, some words on the context of *The Republic*. The appellation "Utopian ideal" is often used to describe Plato's text. The term "utopia" arises from the work of Sir Thomas More, an English theologian, and philosopher. In his book *Utopia* published in 1516 and written in Latin, he coined the word Utopia meaning "no place," from the ancient Greek word "ou-topos," no place or nowhere. In ancient Greek, "ou" is pronounced "eu" and Thomas More created a pun from the pronunciation, thus "U".

Plato's *Republic*, unlike Sir Thomas More's *Utopia*, is not a place but a visionary ideal where philosopher kings, "just" men of the highest order, rule a population of similarly minded citizens upholding human values of justice or just-ness: key among these values are wisdom, courage, and moderation. His society arises from a universal education system that inculcates an adherence to that principle of just-ness or what he calls the Good.)

Despite the promise of such an idealistic functioning state, Plato's ideas infer that no political system is static but swings like a pendulum over decades from progress to dissolution and back again. Therefore, no realization of a perfect society is possible. However, we can keep striving toward that aspiration.

In a particularly insightful article, British-American political commenter Andrew Sullivan wrote an essay published in *New York* magazine. These excerpts highlight some of Plato's tenets and his, albeit reluctant, realizations on the nature of the political pendulum. The essay written during the 2016 Presidential election cycle exemplifies the universal relevance and truths in *The Republic*,

> As this dystopian election campaign has unfolded, my
> mind keeps being tugged by a passage in Plato's *Republic*.
> It has unsettled — even surprised — me from the moment
> I first read it in graduate school. The passage is from the
> part of the dialogue where Socrates and his friends are
> talking about the nature of different political systems, how
> they change over time, and how one can slowly evolve into
> another. And Socrates seemed pretty clear on one sobering
> point: that "tyranny is probably established out of no other
> regime than democracy." What did Plato mean by that?
> Democracy, for him, I discovered, was a political system
> of maximal freedom and equality, where every lifestyle is
> allowed and public offices are filled by a lottery. And the
> longer a democracy lasted, Plato argued, the more demo-
> cratic it would become. Its freedoms would multiply; its
> equality spread. Deference to any sort of authority would

wither; tolerance of any kind of inequality would come under intense threat; and multiculturalism and sexual freedom would create a city or a country like 'a many-colored cloak decorated in all hues.'

This rainbow-flag polity, Plato argues, is, for many people, the fairest of regimes. The freedom in that democracy has to be experienced to be believed — with shame and privilege in particular emerging over time as anathema. But it is inherently unstable. As the authority of elites fades, as Establishment values cede to popular ones, views and identities can become so magnificently diverse as to be mutually uncomprehending. And when all the barriers to equality, formal and informal, have been removed; when everyone is equal; when elites are despised, and full license is established to do "whatever one wants," you arrive at what might be called late-stage democracy. There is no kowtowing to authority here, let alone to political experience or expertise.

The very rich come under attack as inequality becomes increasingly intolerable. Patriarchy is also dismantled: "We almost forgot to mention the extent of the law of equality and of freedom in the relations of women with men and men with women." Family hierarchies are inverted: 'A father habituates himself to be like his child and fear his sons, and a son habituates himself to be like his father and to have no shame before or fear of his parents.' In classrooms, 'as the teacher ... is frightened of the pupils and fawns on them, so the students make light of their teachers.' Animals are regarded as equal to humans; the rich mingle freely with the poor in the streets and try to blend in. The foreigner is equal to the citizen.

And it is when a democracy has ripened as fully as this, Plato argues, that a would-be tyrant will often seize his moment.[3]

Tyranny and authoritarianism may result. Plato discusses the various types of dictatorships: a timocracy= rule honoring militaristic codes of conduct; an oligarchy=rule by the wealthiest elite; a democracy= majority rule prevails eventually to the detriment of minorities. Another form of tyranny rose to prominence in the post-colonial, latter part of the 20th century, kleptocracy=societies where dictators and occasionally elected leaders steal from the treasury coffers of their people.

If Sullivan is correct that Plato, when he wrote *The Republic,* realized the preternatural ability of his teacher, Socrates' political clairvoyance, then we remain grateful. *The Republic* stands as the seminal work of political philosophy that tackles governance and tracks the movement as governments inevitably swing—sometimes over decades, sometimes over centuries—from democracy to authoritarianism and back again.[4]

In recent times, as Europe tries to cope with wave after wave of Islamic refugees (fleeing disastrous dictatorships in their own Middle Eastern and North African countries), German democracy also shows signs (still in their infancy) of swinging back—to rightwing autocracy. Indeed, this shift to conservatism, nativism, protectionism, and militarism can be seen throughout Europe, Britain, and the United States.

In the United States, the rise of demagoguery and demands of the populace challenge, even threaten, the increasingly liberal and "majority-minority" of American citizens living together and adhering to democratic and constitutional processes. This demagogic movement was perceivable with the advent of the Tea Party in the 2000s that folded into the Republican Party. The movement spiked during the 2016 primary elections for the GOP presidential candidate, reached critical momentum during the first term of the candidate who narrowly won that election. He lost the next election and spawned a horrendous and blatantly false "Big Lie" that the election was stolen. Later in the chapter I refer to Plato's explanation of the (Ig)Noble Lie.

To understand the essential ideas in *The Republic*, we need to grapple with Plato's definitions and ideas on the umbrella concept of The Good or justice or use interchangeably "just-ness" or "the just man". The rubric of the Good umbrella covers concepts of happiness, the value of education, and the role of the guardians.

Central to the discussion in the early books of *The Republic* looms the question of what Socrates means by the term "justice." He bats definitions and refutations back and forth among his listeners, many of whom are well-known philosophers, Sophists versed in the art of rhetoric or persuasion through argument. Socrates gently leads them to his definition of "justice" (The Good) by first discussing and helping to dismantle their ideas around "injustice." Eventually he offers the statement, "Justice is The Good that the happy man loves."[5] This statement begs the question of who is a "happy man" and what is "happiness."

In Buddhist practices, "happiness" is defined as an inner balance that negates anger, hate, and greed. Attaining "happiness" is the dominant wish fulfillment of all Buddhists. By following the Eight-Fold path as set out by the Buddha, this balance can be achieved through meditation and mindful awareness. Likewise, Plato emphasizes happiness as an inner state of balance and is achieved through an education system that teaches in individuals—wisdom (developing conceptual and rational thinking), temperament (through controlling negative emotions), and moderation (curbing selfish desire and unbridled, instinctive reactivity.)

Socrates highlights these thoughts metaphorically, evoking a charioteer (the individual) standing atop a three-horse-drawn vehicle. If one steed steps out of synch, the chariot will not ride smoothly. Socrates explains that these horses symbolize the three parts of the soul—the tripartite soul—where reason, temperament, instinct intermingle. He maintains that we need to balance all three to function as healthy, just beings. Present in every individual, these three elements are also present in the state—*reason* in rulers, orderly *temperament* in professionals, and desire or physical *instincts* in laborers. If we lose self-control of these centers, we lose our individual freedom to be "just" citizens, and society loses a sense of "just-ness." We no longer possess the ease of living in a smoothly functioning society and create dis-ease not only within ourselves but also in our body politic.

As the Irish poet, W. B. Yeats, wrote in his poem *The Second Coming:*

Things fall apart; the centre cannot hold;
Mere anarchy is loosed upon the world,
The blood-dimmed tide is loosed, and everywhere
The ceremony of innocence is drowned.
The best lack all conviction, while the worst
Are full of passionate intensity.[6]

Plato offers another definition, "Justice is... the Good that the happy man loves both for its own sake and for the effects it produces."

Now that we understand what the term "happiness" entails for Plato, we can more readily accept that a "happy man loves" justice "for its own sake" and for being "The Good." In the quote below, Socrates reiterates one of his fundamental principles "as for the individual so for the city".

Socrates lays out his definition of justice in the individual and in the city,

> The reality is that justice is not a matter of external behavior but the way a man privately and truly governs his inner self. The just man does not permit the various parts of his soul to interfere with one another or usurp each other's functions. He has set his own life in order. He is his own master and his own law. He has become a friend to himself. He will have brought into tune the three parts of the soul: high, middle, and low, like the three major notes of a musical scale, and all the intervals between. When he has brought all this together in temperance and harmony, he will have made himself one man instead of many.
>
> Only then will he be ready to do whatever he does in society: making money, training the body, involving himself in politics and in business transactions. In all the public activities in which he is engaged he will call just and beautiful only that conduct which harmonizes with and preserves his own inner order which we have just described. And the knowledge that understands the meaning and importance of such conduct he will call wisdom.[7]

Table of The Good as an Amalgam of its Parts

THE GOOD =	FOUR VIRTUES	CITY	INDIVIDUAL– TRIPARTITE SOUL	CODE OF METALS
	wisdom	= wisdom of rulers	= rational, sagacious decisions	= gold (head)
	courage	= bravery of the guardians; expertise of professionals	= spirited implementation of laws and decisions	=silver (heart)
THE GOOD = (all the elements working together)				
	moderation	= self-control	= appetitive or controlled, living with self restraint	= bronze (body)
	JUSTICE	= harmony arises from everyone Fulfilling their role; no leeching over into each other's societal function	= inner state of just-ness, ease and balance	
	(INJUSTICE)	= result of disharmony; no balance	= inner state of discord; dis-ease	

© Janet Levine, 2014

Plato believes that to establish his republic, the prime function and responsibility of the state must be an education system that serves all the people of the city and imbues all elements of The Good.

He argues that the root cause of social injustice is an unjust education system.

Plato's enduring influence can be found in many mind structure ideas explicit or implicit in writings and speeches of America's Founding Fathers. The Founding Fathers in the United States knew their Plato. Many of their words about public responsibility for education and other matters of polity, attest to Plato's influence on their thinking.

Brad Desnoyer, a law professor wrote,[8]

Two of the greatest Founding Fathers, John Adams and Thomas Jefferson, were political adversaries. But in the first years of our nation, these rivals — with vastly different backgrounds and disparate political views — shared common ground. They both believed in the importance of funding public education.

The whole people must take upon themselves the education of the whole people and be willing to bear the expenses of it, wrote Adams. There should not be a district of one-mile square, without a school in it, not founded by a charitable individual, but maintained at the public expense of the people themselves...

Jefferson wrote,

[T]he tax which will be paid for this purpose [education] is not more than the thousandth part of what will be paid to kings, priests and nobles who will rise up among us if we leave the people in ignorance.

The Founding Fathers argued further that education in the public domain is better handled at the state level. The "equal protection clause" of the 14th Amendment (ratified in 1868) implies that when a state establishes a public school system, no child living in that state may be denied equal access to schooling.

This is the argument made before the Supreme Court in 1954. The Court ruled in favor of *Brown vs. Board of Education* that separate does not mean equal and ushered in the desegregation of education.

The Founding Fathers also adhered to the Platonic ideal that their republic, "a city on a hill" can only be achieved by having an informed and educated electorate. Along with Plato, they believed explicitly that an unjust education system causes social injustice.

For his republic, Plato designed a plan to achieve a just educational system tailored for the city's needs and a fit for each individual. His principle concern centers on choosing the most appropriate rulers and formulating how they are to be educated. Socrates states they will be chosen from an elite group of citizens educated for leadership called "the guardians."

His educational plan threads into his overall schema; everyone receives the same education until age twenty, when those few who show aptitude to become guardians are singled out. At age thirty, even fewer from their ranks are identified as possessing the propensity to be philosophers, "lovers of wisdom." But first, they must spend fifteen years, as Buddhists say, in "the marketplace of life." At age fifty, these men mature into ideal guardians and qualify to study advanced philosophy and take their turn as rulers, "philosopher kings."

The Buddha's teachings are somewhat similar. He taught that the four stages of life are: the first stage, tender years, second the playful childhood, third, physical, sensual pursuits, and the fourth and final stage, the spiritual seeker on a quest through meditation (the inner life) for happiness, peace, and joy.

It is interesting to note that both Plato and the Buddha follow the same pattern of development in their assessment of the stages of life. The first three stages involve the physical or outer senses, but the developmental emphasis is centered on the psycho-spiritual in the final step.

Arising even earlier than the Buddha's teachings, Hindu understanding is similar: baby and youth, householder, retiree, and ascetic.

However, fifteen hundred years later, William Shakespeare's famous speech on the seven stages of a man's life in *As You Like It* denotes only the physical progression of life: infant, schoolboy, lover, soldier, justice, old age, and imminent death.

As pointed to in previous chapters, following the Golden Age of Greek philosophy, Western philosophers and artists largely eschewed or ignored ontological experiences and expressions of these, whether in words, paint or marble. As did Shakespeare in the above example.

Plato expresses at length the role of guardians once they undergo the training described above. He expounds on the four virtues of the city—wisdom, courage, temperance, and justice. And maintains that guardians must also have these virtues held together by justice.

Plato reasons that if a city is to have these four virtues, then it must be comprised of citizens who are educated into valuing and exhibiting these virtues. The guardians who show the highest degree of embodiment of these virtues became guardians in the fullest sense of the word—not only of the city—but of themselves and all the people they lead.

Socrates warns,

> Unless philosophers become kings in our cities, or unless those who are now kings and rulers become true philoso-phers, so that political power and philosophic intelligence converge, and unless those of lesser natures who run after one without the other are excluded from governing, I believe there can be no end of troubles in our cities and for all mankind.[9]

By "philosophic intelligence," Plato outlines he means if physical or instinctual desire are tempered and balanced with both reason and willpower, these three elements of mind structures can bring freedom and joy to benefit the individual, as well as society. This equilibrium constitutes "philosophic intelligence."

In Book Five, Plato, in preparation for his radical proposition that a philosopher king (man of reason and wisdom) lead his republic—a man who will serve a limited term before another philosopher replaces him—Plato floats several red herring arguments hoping that people will find those ideas so excessive they will not balk at the proposal that a philosopher-king rule the republic. But the scheme fails. People hail Plato's ideas of equality for men and women, abolishing marriage and private ownership of property among rulers. However, his final proposal to unite political power with wisdom inherent in philosophers elicits widespread contempt. All reject the notion that their self-interest is better served by harmonious just-ness and a wise leader.

Another idea Plato utilized in education (and for manipulation of the citizenry in general) is the concept of the Noble Lie. Fundamentally, this is a myth or false belief constructed by rulers but "sold" with the conviction that it serves the city's greater good. In reality, it is often a device of "the means justify the ends" that serves the rulers.

Politicians throughout the ages have used these words "I shall try to persuade them …" and "We shall tell them …" as they create noble and, more often, ignoble lies for their supporters and followers.

One glaring modern example of a Noble Lie (decidedly ignoble and self-serving) is President George W. Bush's administration in 2002 insisting to the United Nations and the world that the Iraqi dictator Saddam Hussein held hidden caches of Weapons of Mass Destruction in Iraq. This was the Bush Administration's not so noble pretext for invading the country and deposing Saddam Hussein. Another is the forty-sixth President of the USA and his enablers, insistence on "alternative facts" and "fake news" to counter the media that hold him accountable for words and actions.

There can be no doubt about the power and impact of philosophical ideas and values an educational system promotes. Some philosophers and educators label educational systems as mass brainwashing operations perpetrating vast Noble Lies to preserve the values and mores of the status quo and even nationhood.

In our country, examples of educational systems vary from a

secular, liberal education based on a humanistic agenda to a conservative education based on a fundamental Christian agenda. In other countries, we may have education systems based on different religious precepts or nationalistic and patriotic intent directed at preserving dictatorships.

Educational philosophies are a significant influence on "mind structures." A simplistic example is two babies born in the same nursing home who are misidentified and are reared not by their birth parents but another set of parents. The baby from a humanistic, liberal home may be raised and educated as a diehard conservative, Christian fundamentalist, and the baby from a fundamentalist Christian home may be raised as a liberal humanist. In some instances, the same can be said about adoption, such as Chinese or Russian-born babies removed from their familial and cultural milieu and raised in American homes. The babies in these generalized examples, now grown to adulthood, do not doubt their upbringing as reality. A more specific example might be that children educated in, for example, North Korea embody the belief system that their dictator is a god. In contrast, children educated in, for example, most European countries generally believe in secular humanism.

Child rearing and education are indoctrination and brainwashing. Plato postulated correctly that all education is a dream and not reality. There are so many realities. As we grow older, hopefully, if we feel the need to do so, we can adapt and change, outgrow and question our inherited childhood values and mind structure.

As Ralph Waldo Emerson, the American philosopher, said, humankind's greatest gift is the ability to change one's mind.

Brainwashing may be overcome through developing critical thinking skills, practicing open-mindedness, accepting the illusionary nature of mind structures, and questioning the nature of reality. (In

Hamlet, Chapter Four of this book, there is a thorough investigation on reality and illusion and the nature of mind structures.)

The Republic is replete with literary devices that illustrate Plato's concepts, such as myths, parables, allegories, and models, to enrich his text and illustrate how mind structures are formed. One famous example of a myth is the so-called "myth of the metals." Socrates conceives this social myth, to bolster his idea of the nature of the tripartite soul. *Gold* forms the head—rational, sagacious, and able to reach decisions through reason; *silver*, the heart—spirited with the willpower to implement laws and decisions; *bronze*, the body—desire controlled by a balanced lifestyle, living with self-restraint and an inner state of just-ness, ease and balance.

Socrates illustrates this myth with a code that deciphers its meaning. Earlier I have detailed this myth. Socrates evokes a charioteer and his chariot (the ruler of the state or the state of the individual) standing, holding the reins of a three-horse-drawn vehicle. He maintains that we need to balance all three to function as healthy, just beings.

Socrates hedged his explanation of why he concocted the myth of the metal, clearly, it is an example of a Noble Lie,

> All right I shall speak, but I hardly know where to find
> the words or the audacity to utter them. I shall try to
> persuade first the rulers, then the soldiers, and then the
> rest of the people that all the training and education they
> have received from us are actually products of their own
> imaginations, just the way it is with a dream. In reality,
> they were the whole time deep within the earth being given
> form and feature, and the same with their weapons and
> all other accouterments. When the process was complete,
> they were all delivered up to the surface by their mother

earth, whence it comes that they care for their land as if it were mother and nurse and feel bound to defend it from any attack. Likewise do they regard their fellow citizens as brothers born of the same soil.[10]

…We shall tell them that although they are all brothers, god differentiated those qualified to rule by mixing in gold at their birth. Hence, they are most honored. The auxiliaries he compounded with silver, and the craftsmen and farmers with iron and brass. So, endowed each will usually beget his own kind."[11]

Despite his explanation of the code of the metals, Plato is often represented or misrepresented as positing an authoritarian and elitist culture. Whether or not this was his intention, we do not know. However, by his own rather shame-faced admission that this myth is a Noble Lie to justify to each individual his position in society to help the republic function smoothly and to further the public good, at the very least, he was equivocal about promoting it.

In Book Two, Socrates condemned and banished poets from his republic because they fabricated fables and created myths (or their own Noble Lies) about the gods that present negative role models for humans. Plato understood that by encouraging obeisance to these gods, robs individuals of self-reliance and leans on the (false) certainty that whims of the gods ordain their lives. Socrates speaks,

"Then our program of education must begin with censorship. The censors will approve the fables and stories they deem good and ban those they consider harmful… if we apply this criterion, most of the stories they tell now will have to be discarded."[12]

"Then let this be one of the laws and principles in our city concerning the gods to which our speakers and poets must conform: a god is not the author of all things but only good things."[13]

Plato believes this poet-induced mind structure is detrimental to human development into "just-ness" or The Good. Many philosophers and literary critics find Plato's attack on poets significant, mainly because with this attitude, Plato's reputation as an advocate of censorship surfaced and has negatively impacted him for centuries.

Plato used parables to illustrate the ideas envisioned in his republic. Three of the most famous are the parable of the ship's captain to show the populace's disastrous rejection of philosopher-kings, the Cave allegory to enlighten us to the philosopher-kings role and interpret the Divided Line. The Divided Line model itself augments our understanding of The Good.

The Parable of the Ship's Captain as told by Socrates,

Now, nothing in all of nature can be found to match the cruelty with which society treats its best men. If I am to plead their cause, I must resort to fiction, combining a multitude of disparate things like painters do when concoct fantastic progeny of stags and goats and the like. Let us imagine, then, a set of events happening aboard many ships or even only one. Imagine first the captain. He is taller and stronger than any of the crew. At the same time, he is a little deaf and somewhat short-sighted. Further, his navigation skills are about on par with his hearing and his vision. The sailors are quarreling with each other about who should take the helm. Each insists he has a right to steer the ship though he has never mastered the art of navigation and cannot say who taught him or when he learned. Pushing the matter further, they will assert that it cannot be taught anyway; anyone who contradicts them will be cut to pieces. Meanwhile, the crowd around the captain, badgering him and clamoring for the tiller. Occasionally some will succeed with their entreaties and get the captain's ear, but they will, in turn, fall victim to those who did not and will be put to death or be cast off the ship. Then, after fettering the worthy shipmaster and putting him into a stupor with narcotic or drink, they take command of the ship. Feasting and drinking, they consume the ship's stores and make a voyage of it as might be expected from such a crew. Further, they will use such terms as a master mariner, navigator, and pilot to flatter the man who has shown most cunning in persuading or forcing the captain to turn over control of the ship. The man who is innocent of such skills they will call useless. They, in turn, are innocent of any understanding that one who is a real captain must concentrate his attention on the year's round, seasons, the sky, wind, stars, and all the arts that make him the true master of the ship. The captain does not believe there is any art or science involved in seizing control of a ship—with or without the consent of others. Nor does he think that the practice and mastery of this alleged art is possible to combine with the science of navigation. With such activities going on, would it surprise you if the sailors running the ship would call the true captain a useless stargazer and lunatic?"[14]

The Cave Allegory as told by Socrates

To further consolidate our understanding of philosopher-kings, and the Divided Line model, Socrates narrates the most famous of his allegories, the Cave Allegory, in dialog format. Socrates speaks first,

> "Allegory may show best how education—or the lack of it—affects nature. Imagine men living in a cave with a long passage way between them and the cave's mouth, where it opens wide to the light. Imagine further that since childhood the cave dwellers are shackled their legs and necks shackled so as to be confined to the same spot. They are further constrained by blinders that prevent them from turning their heads; they can see only directly in front of them. Next, imagine a light from a fire some distance behind them and burning at a higher elevation. Between the prisoners and the fire is path along whose edge there is a low wall like the partition at the front of a puppet stage. The wall conceals the puppeteers while they manipulate their puppets above it."

> "So far I can visualize it."

> "Imagine further, men behind the wall carrying all sorts of objects along its length and holding them above it. The objects include human and animal images made of stone and wood and all other material. Presumably, those who carry them sometimes speak and are sometimes silent."

> "You describe a strange prison and strange prisoners."[15]

Plato's cave inhabitants lived in semi-darkness and interacted with shadows until they gained insight illuminated by imbuing tenets of the Good. This is akin to Buddhist practices whose aim is to gain "insight" or "inner sight" through meditation. When the cave dwellers saw the light creating the shadows, they understood that the world they accepted as accurate was merely a shadow cast by that light,

> "Imagine now how their liberation from bondage and error would come about if something like the following happened. One prisoner is freed from his shackles. He is suddenly compelled to stand up, turn around, walk, and look toward the light. He suffers pain and distress from the glare of the light. So dazzled is he that he cannot even discern the very objects whose shadows he used to be able to see. Now what do you suppose he would answer if he were told that all he had seen before was illusion but that now he was nearer reality, observing real things and there-fore seeing more truly? What if someone pointed to the objects being carried above the wall, questioning him as to what each one is? Would he not be at a loss? Would he not regard those things he saw formerly as more real than the things now being shown him?"

> "He would."

> "Again, let him be compelled to look directly at the light. Would his eyes not feel pain? Would he not flee, turning back to those things he was able to discern before con-vinced that they are in every truth clearer and more exact than anything he has seen since?"[16]

They had gained insight. Plato's cognitive model explicitly states that insight lights the "intelligible" (conceptual) world just as the sun does the sensory world,

> "Then let him be dragged away by force up the rough and steep incline of the cave's passageway, held fast until he

is hauled out into the light of the sun. Would not such a rough passage be painful? Would he not resent the experience? And when he came out into the sunlight, would he not be dazzled once again and unable to see what he calls realities?"

"He could not see even one of them, at least not immediately."

"Habituation, then, is evidently required in order to see things higher up. In the beginning he would most easily see shadows; next, reflections in the water of men and other objects. Then he would see the objects themselves. From there he would go on to behold the heavens and the heavenly phenomena—more easily the moon and stars by night than the sun by day."

"Yes."

"Finally, I suppose, he would be able to look on the sun itself, not in reflections in the water or in fleeting images in some alien setting. He would look at the sun as it is, in its own domain, and so be able to see what it is really like."[17]

The cave allegory resonates through the ages and many cultures and societal mind structures. One modern example of its enduring influence is by a renowned the 20th century Hindu teacher, Swami Parahansa Yogananda (1893 – 1952),

"This earth is nothing but movies to me. Just like the beam of a motion picture.

So is everything made of shadow and light. That's what we are. Light and shadows of the Lord. Nothing else than that. There's one purpose. To get to the beam."[18]

The Divided Line[19] template is one of Plato's most ambitious literary devices. He hopes that he can explain why the training of those guardians selected to be rulers is so important to this model. In doing so, additionally, he explains The Good.

Socrates speaks,

> "The Good, then, is what every man wants. For its sake he
> will do all that he does. He intuits what the Good is, but
> at the same time he is baffled, for the nature of the Good is
> something he comprehends inadequately. Nor is he able to
> invest in it the same sure confidence that he does in other
> things. For this very reason, the benefits these other things
> might yield are lost. Now, in a matter of this kind and
> importance, I ask you whether we can permit such blind-
> ness and ignorance in those best of men we want to govern
> the city?"[20]

> ...

> "Recall, then, we were speaking of two entities. One is
> the good, governor of the intelligible order. The other is the
> sun, governing the world of things seen."

The Divided Line
The Four Stages of <u>Cognition</u>

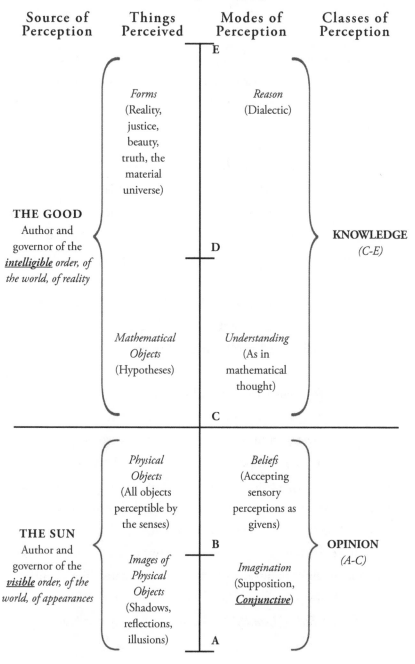

Source of Perception	Things Perceived	Modes of Perception	Classes of Perception

E

Forms
(Reality, justice, beauty, truth, the material universe)

Reason
(Dialectic)

THE GOOD
Author and governor of the <u>intelligible</u> order, of the world, of reality

D

KNOWLEDGE
(C-E)

Mathematical Objects
(Hypotheses)

Understanding
(As in mathematical thought)

C

Physical Objects
(All objects perceptible by the senses)

Beliefs
(Accepting sensory perceptions as givens)

THE SUN
Author and governor of the <u>visible</u> order, of the world, of appearances

B

OPINION
(A-C)

Images of Physical Objects
(Shadows, reflections, illusions)

Imagination
(Supposition, <u>Conjunctive</u>)

A

Plato's cave inhabitants lived in semi-darkness and interacted with shadows. When they saw the light creating the shadows, they understood that what they accepted as real and accurate was merely a shadow cast by that light.

This cognitive model underscores how insight leads to changes in mind structures. The cave dwellers previous mind structure perceptions of "reality" were shattered by "insight." They had to reformulate their perceptual reality.

The Death of Ivan Ilyich by Leo Tolstoy

Leo Tolstoy's novella, *The Death of Ivan Ilyich,*[21] adds a fictional dimension to Plato's concept of the Divided Line. In the character of Ivan Ilyich, the novella portrays a life lived entirely below the line in Plato's realm of opinion and, seemingly without any avenue to access the upper reaches of the realm of conceptual knowledge.

Tolstoy, a Russian master author of the late 1800s, having penned such perennially acclaimed novels as *War and Peace* and *Anna Karenina,* among many other works, created this literary gem, *The Death of Ivan Ilyich,* in 1886.

Death frightened Tolstoy. He lost three children and many other relatives who lived with him, and each time it rendered him more afraid of his death. In many ways, to become an expert on death—to enter that territory—helped him understand and accept the inevitable. Consequently, Tolstoy developed spiritual beliefs as an antidote to what he observed—the finality of death: the almost inconceivable fact that one nana second separates life and death.

The terrifying state of dying for him was to observe someone with an intact intellect in a wasted body. What fascinated him mainly was how the brain processed pain in full consciousness. This is the terrain of *The Death of Ivan Ilyich.* The novella is aptly titled, and Tolstoy opens his work with Ivan Ilyich's funeral. Only a master storyteller can kill off his title character on the first page. We assume then that the main character is not Ivan Ilyich but Death.

An uneasy landowner in pre-Marxist Russia, Tolstoy founded a proto-commune on his land, engaging many serfs whose families lived there for generations. The experimental land use arrangement became a possible utopia—at least for a while—until financial and economic realities, coupled with clashes between Tolstoy's heirs and some of the more radical peasants caused the settlement to collapse.

Tolstoy was a "death watcher"; thanatology fascinated him. The process of dying and the aftermath of death absorbed him. After asking for their agreement, he spent hours and days with the serfs on his lands, watching the death process of aged or ill family members. He under-stood that treating illness was the domain of the medical specialists, but the moment of death, watching that last breath, seeing the flicker of life extinguished, belonged to the family. The family prepared the body for burial according to age-old rites and rituals.

In our contemporary world, we confine the dying to hospitals, nursing homes, and managed care facilities. Not many of us are present when elderly grandparents or other relatives or friends die. In Tolstoy's day and up until the Second World War, death, like birth—was an everyday occurrence in domestic homes. The old grandmother at the hearth knitting socks for the family or the mother giving birth did so in her marriage bed.

Every religious tradition had established rituals for honoring the dead. This eased the immediate pain of the passing and established semantics for death and dying: condolences, respect, murmured words of comfort, and understanding of loss.

In the Jewish religion, everyone is buried in a simple wooden coffin or wrapped in a prayer shawl and placed in a grave. Hindus burn their dead on a funeral pyre, collect the ashes and release them into the nearest river that flows into an ever-greater river and eventually, the ocean, where all the waters of the earth unite. This is a symbolic journey into universal consciousness.

In Tolstoy's novella, Ivan Ilyich is a man whose mind structure is consumed with projecting a successful self-image. He can never examine his decisions in the light of reason and morality but acts like a hamster on a wheel seeking socially acceptable wealth, prestige, and a self-satisfied, smug sense of wellbeing.

(As an aside to this summary, Socrates said famously, "An unexamined life is not worth living." This is an absolute statement. He did not say there might be other significant ways to live, or this may be only one of several ways to experience existence. He states with certainty that examining your life is the only way to reach your human potential. Now that we have studied salient ideas in *The Republic*, we know Socrates believed striving to encompass ever deeper comprehension of what he called our "true nature"—studying and embodying aspects and ramifications of The Good—questioning our beliefs, upholding justice [and all that those concepts entail]; these are the hallmarks of an examined life.)

Ivan Ilyich became a successful lawyer, married not for love but wealth and certain prestige in society, fathered two children, rose to the position of judge, and played cards with a circle of friends. He never questioned his rise on the social and professional ladder; never questioned his loveless marriage or absentee parenting; never questioned the backstabbing and gossip of his "friends" and colleagues; and never felt or shared emotions more superficial than those skin-deep. His sin was omission rather than commission. He lived a conveyor belt life.

The only person he had a vague, warm interaction with was young

Gerasim, one of his servants. Gerasim, arising from the peasant background that we know Tolstoy admired, plays the truth-teller in this tale, his, the voice we can trust. He was never afraid to tell his master the truth of how he perceived situations.

Having achieved all his material goals, Ilyich set about building (what today we would call a Mac-Mansion). He slightly injured himself on one side of his body while hanging curtains,

> It was like the homes of all people who are not really rich
> but who want to look rich, and therefore end up looking
> like one another: it had damasks, ebony, plants, carpets
> and bronzes, everything dark and gleaming—all the effects
> a certain class of people produce, so as to look like people
> of a certain class. And his place looked so much like the
> others that it would never have been noticed, though it all
> seemed exceptional to him.[22]

Several months later, with the pain increasing in his side he sought medical attention and underwent treatment. While playing cards with friends, the omniscient narrator tells us,

> They could see that he was in pain and said: "We can stop
> if you're tired. Rest for a while." Rest? Why, he wasn't
> the least bit tired, they'd finish the rubber. They were all
> gloomy and silent. Ivan Ilyich knew he was responsible
> for the gloom that had descended but could do nothing
> to dispel it. After supper his friends went home, leaving
> Ivan Ilyich alone with the knowledge that his life had been
> poisoned and was poisoning the lives of others, and that far
> from diminishing, that poison was penetrating deeper and
> deeper into his entire being.

And with this knowledge and the physical pain and the horror, he had to go to bed; often to be kept awake by pain the greater part of the night. And the next morning, he had to get up again, dress, go to court, talk and write, or if he did not go, put in those twenty-four hours at home, every one of them torture. And he had to go on living like this, on the brink of disaster, without a single person to understand and pity him.[23]

No remedy helped, and eventually, he was confined to bed. The doctor shared with Ivan Ilyich's wife that he had cancer of the "caecum" (the bowel), and death approached.

Ivan Ilyich, on his deathbed, expressed more emotion than in his entire life. He screamed at, mocked, and did not want his wife near him. Mirroring his past indifference, his daughter was unaffected by his suffering, but his young son tried to approach him. They had a stiff rapprochement. Only Gerasim was allowed to tend to him.

As he lay in bed wrestling with his pain, for the first time, Ivan Ilyich, aware of his mortality and reflecting on his life, realized the damage he had wrought so selfishly on his family. When relief from pain allowed him, he thought about his life. This pre-death stage continued for weeks. In between the pain, Ivan Ilyich drove himself and those around him through a tempest of ill humor, raving about their lack of caring if he lived or died, and he experienced deep disenchantment and anguish. He loathed the agony of pain and called for more and more morphine.

(Tolstoy's writing in these final chapters reads so heartbreakingly honest, as if he was present at scenes such as these many times—as indeed he had been.)

Ivan Ilyich's first epiphany arose when he reflected on his life and realized that perhaps the life he regarded as so successful had been a lie.

He could barely cope with the disappointment as the veil lifted, and he acknowledged the trivial and superficial nature of what he had thought of as reality. With the veil gone, epiphany followed epiphany,

> This lie, a lie perpetrated on the eve of his death, a lie
> that was bound to degrade the awesome, solemn act of
> his dying at the level of their social calls, their draperies,
> and the sturgeon they ate for dinner, was an excruciating
> torture for Ivan Ilyich.
>
> ...
>
> Nothing did so much to poison the last days of Ivan Ily-
> ich's life as this falseness in himself and those around him.[24]
>
> ...
>
> "Perhaps I did not live as I should have," it suddenly
> occurred to him. "But how could that be when I did every-
> thing one is supposed to."[25]

After the doctor's final visit when Ivan Ilyich refused more treatment, the physician told Ivan Ilyich's wife,

> "...His physical agony was dreadful, and that was true;
> but even more dreadful was his moral agony, and it was
> this that tormented him most. ...What had induced his
> moral agony was that during the night, as he gazed at Ger-
> asim's broad-boned sleepy, good-natured face, he suddenly
> asked himself: What if my entire life, my entire conscious
> life, simply *was not the real thing?*[26]
>
> ...
>
> Suddenly some force struck him in the chest and the side
> and made his breathing even more constricted: he plunged

into the hole and there at the bottom, something was shining. What had happened to him was what one frequently experiences in a railway car when one thinks one is going forward but is actually moving backward, and suddenly becomes aware of the actual direction.

"Yes, all of it was simply *not the real thing.* But no matter. I can still make it *the real thing*—I can. But what *is* the real thing?" Ivan Ilyich asked himself and suddenly grew quiet.[27]

...

At that very moment Ivan Ilyich fell through and saw a light, and it was revealed to him that his life had not been what it should have but that he could still rectify the situation. "But what *is* the real thing?" he asked himself and grew quiet, listening. Just then he felt someone kissing his hand. He opened his eyes and looked at his son. He grieved for him. His wife came in and went up to him. He looked at her. She gazed at him with an open mouth and with unwiped tears on her nose and cheeks, with a look of despair on her face. He grieved for her.

Yes, I'm torturing them, he thought. They feel sorry for me, but it will be better for them when I die.[28]

...

And suddenly it became clear to him that what had been oppressing him and would not leave him suddenly was vanishing all at once—two sides, ten sides, all sides. He felt sorry for them, he had to do something to keep them from this suffering. How good and how simple! he thought.

"And the pain?" he asked himself. "Where has it gone? Now, then pain, where are you?"

He waited for it attentively, "Ah, there it is. Well, what of it? Let it be." "And death? Where is it?"

He searched for his accustomed fear of death and could not find it. Where was death? What death? There was no fear because there was no death.

Instead of death there was light.

"So that's it!" he exclaimed. "What bliss!"

All this happened in a single moment, but the significance of that moment was lasting. For those present, his agony continued for another two hours. Something rattled in his chest; his emaciated body twitched. Then the rattling and wheezing gradually diminished.

"It is all over," said someone standing beside him.

He heard these words and repeated them in his soul.

"Death is over," he said to himself. "There is no more death."

He drew in a breath, broke off in the middle of it, stretched himself out, and died.[29]

Tolstoy's tale, especially Ivan Ilyich his dying moments and death, leaves us with many questions to ponder, but a central question arises: Do several small epiphanies and one great moment of clear-sightedness, redress the existence of an unexamined life?

Or as Plato may ask: Does the light at death[30] provide the illumination for Ivan Ilyich to have attained, if even for a brief moment, the highest level of cognition at the top of the Divided Line?

* * *

The following chapter, Chapter Eight, provides us with what appears as unassailable physical reality, the very spaces around us. However, as the chapter examines a sense of place in three extracts from longer works, we realize that associative thoughts invariably color descriptions of the reality of places.

Additionally, the chapter introduces yet another variation on the reality/illusion conundrum, the idea of magical realism illustrated by Columbian author, Gabriel García Márquez. First fashioned by this Nobel prize-winning novelist, the genre is now used universally by other fiction writers.

8

A SENSE OF PLACE AND A SENSE OF MYSTERIOUS REALITY

In all circumstances of our lives—not only in eras of turmoil and uncertainty—the ideas in *Reading Matters* provide a rudder to help us navigate our outer and inner circumstances and move forward; even though our worldview, our mind structure, may be wildly buffeted by winds of change. If to be human is to experience change, what then in our lives is unchangeable.

There is one mind structure that may be real, reliable, solid—a sense of place. A place is real, at least in the physical sense; we can see a place, touch a place, taste substances from a place, smell the scents of a place, and hear the sounds of a place. And we can carry those senses of place with us across years and far distances.

The literature in this chapter comprises short excerpts from Margery Stoneman Douglas *The Everglades: River of Grass*; Jill Ker Conway *The Road from Coorain;* and Janet Levine, *Inside Apartheid.*

The Everglades: River of Grass

Born in Minneapolis in 1890, Marjory Stoneman Douglas followed her father to southern Florida in 1915, where she became society editor for the newspaper, <u>*Miami Herald*</u>, owned by him. The growing threat of destruction of the nearby Everglades, the River of Grass, as the result of over drainage, captured Douglas' attention. She joined the efforts of Ernest Coe, a landscape architect, Harold Bailey, an ornithologist, and the <u>Miami Herald</u>, to halt the destruction. Together with other local activists, they promoted the establishment of a national park in the Everglades. Congress established the Everglades as a National Park in 1934. The Park is designated as an International Biosphere Reserve, a Wetland of International Importance, and a World Heritage site.

Five years in the writing, *The Everglades: River of Grass*[1] was published in 1947 in celebration of the dedication of the Park by President Harry Truman. Stoneman died in 1998 at age 108. She is celebrated by environmentalists internationally for her pioneering conservation efforts. Nonetheless, the Everglades is still in danger of disappearing as water flow, and land use issues continue to haunt its existence.

Margery Stoneman Douglas, in the opening chapter of her book, *The Everglades: River of Grass*, writes of this unique environment in terms so powerful, they leave an indelible impression on the reader. Along with Douglas's pioneering environmental efforts, this book saved what was left of this unique and mesmerizing eco-system. Environmental groups are actively engaging with legislative bodies to restore the Everglades to their natural state. Some initiatives are succeeding, but much more persistence and perseverance are required to reach that goal. The Everglades attracts about one million visitors every year.

Douglas's depiction of her sense of place is real, I can attest to every word, but it is shot through with glimpses into a single-issue mind structure about this place—conservation.

These are the opening paragraphs of the opening chapter of *The Everglades: River of Grass* named "The Nature of the Everglades."

There are no other Everglades in the world.

They have always been one of the unique regions of the earth, remote, never wholly known. Nothing else is like them: their vast glittering openness, wider than the enormous visible round of the horizon, the racing free saltness, and sweetness of their massive winds, under the dazzling blue heights of space. They are also unique in the simplicity, diversity, and related harmony of the forms of life they enclose. The miracle of the light pours over the green and brown expanse of saw grass and water, shining and slow-moving below, the grass and water that is the meaning and central fact of the Everglades of Florida. It is a river of grass.

The great pointed paw of the state of Florida, familiar as the map of North America itself, of which it is the most noticeable appendage, thrusts south, further south than any other part of the mainland of the United States. Between the shining aquamarine waters of the Gulf of Mexico and the roaring deep-blue waters of the north-surging Gulf stream, the shaped land points towards Cuba and the Caribbean. It points toward and touches within one degree of the tropics.[2]

Douglas gives us a sweepingly broad airplane view at several thousand feet of the Everglades,

More than halfway down that thrusting sea-bound peninsula, nearly everyone knows the lake that is like a great hole in that pawing shape. Lake Okeechobee, the second largest body of fresh water, it is always said, "within the confines of the United States." Below that lie the Everglades.

They have been called "the mysterious Everglades" so long that the phrase is a meaningless platitude. For four hundred years after the discovery, they seemed more like a fantasy than a simple geographic and historic fact. Even the men who in the later years saw them more clearly could hardly make up their minds what the Everglades were or how they could be described, or what use could be made of them. They were mysterious then. They are mysterious still to everyone by whom their fundamental nature is not understood.

Off and on for those four hundred years the region now called "The Everglades" was described as a vast, miasmic swamps, poisonous lagoons, huge dismal marshes without outlet, a rotting, shallow, inland sea, or labyrinths of dark trees hung and looped about with snakes and dripping mosses, malignant with tropical fevers and malarias, evil to the white man.[3]

Douglas writes several more pages that outline the advent of white men into the Everglades in the eighteenth century. She compares their heavy footprint to that of the Native American people who lived in the Everglades for thousands of years and left scarcely a trace of their existence,

So it is with the Everglades, which have that quality of long existence in their own nature. They were changeless. They are changed.

They were complete before man came to them, and for centuries afterward, when he was the only one of those forms which shared, in a finely balanced harmony, the forces and the ancient nature of the place.

Then, when the Everglades were most truly themselves, is the time to begin with them.

The Everglades begin at Lake Okeechobee.

That is the name the Indians gave the lake, a name almost as recent as the word "Everglades." It means "Big Water." Everybody knows it.

Yet few have any idea of those pale, seemingly illimitable waters. Over the shallows, often less than a foot deep but seven hundred and fifty or so square miles in actual area, the winds in one gray swift moment can shatter the reflections of sky and cloud whiteness standing still in that shining, polished, shimmering expanse. A boat can push for hours in a day of white sun through the short, crisp lake waves and there will be nothing to be seen anywhere but the brightness where the color of the water and the color of the sky become one.[4]

…Saw grass reaches up both sides of the lake in great enclosing arms, so that it is correct to say that the Everglades are there also.

At the edges of the Glades and towards those southern and southwesternmost reaches where the great estuary or delta of the Glades river takes another form entirely, the saw grass is shorter and more sparse, and the springy, porous muck deposit under it is shallower and thinner. But where the saw grass grows tallest in the deepest muck, there goes the channel of the Glades.[5]

Douglas continues in this vein until the reader feels as if she can reach out from her kayak, touch the mangroves' neatly patterned walking roots, feel the burnished sun on top of her head, and marvel at the vast expanse of the sawgrass, edged with palm trees, majestic, magnificent,

> The water moves. The saw grass, pale green to deep-brown ripeness, stand rigid. It is moved only in sluggish rollings by the vast push of the winds across it. Over its endless acres here and there the shadows of the dazzling clouds quicken and slide, purple-brown, plum-brown, mauve-brown, bronze. The bristling, blossoming tops do not bend easily like standing grain. They do not even in their own growth curve all one way but stand in edged clumps, curving against each other, all the massed curving blades making millions of fine arching lines that at a little distance merge to a huge expanse of brown wires and bristles or, farther beyond to the deep-piled plush. At the horizon they become velvet. The line they make is an edge of velvet against the infinite blue, the blue-and-white. The clear fine primrose yellow, the burning brass and crimson, the molten silver, the deepening hyacinth sky.
>
> The clear burning light of the sun pours of the sun pours daylong into the saw grass and is lost there, soaked up, never given back. Only the water flashes and glints. The grass yields nothing.[6]

The Everglades and Douglas's book are two of the reasons I live in the furthest southern reaches of the eastern United States seaboard—I live between the warm Gulf of Mexico and the cold Atlantic Ocean. When I read and reread this opening chapter of the *River of Grass*, Douglas's words evoke every experience I've had in the Everglades, every photo I've taken or seen hanging in a gallery, every painting of the Everglades.

Douglas's detailed descriptions recollect hundreds of visits into the Everglades. But Douglas adds scientific data—the geological, the hydrological, the demographic—and this input makes the book a classic. A must-read even today in the environmental struggle to save this unique ecosystem.

Simply stated, Douglas loved the Everglades, and I love the Everglades.

But her depiction, precise and lovingly detailed like a petit point tapestry, has a purpose. Even in these early pages, present the polemical nature of why she wrote it: she wants to protect the Glades' existence.

The Road from Coorain

Jill Ker Conway, an Australian writer and academic who moved to the United States in her early twenties, grew up on a vast sheep farm in the Australian outback in the center of the continent. She rose to become the first woman president of Smith College in Massachusetts in 1975 and served in that capacity for ten years. When she retired, she wrote a compelling autobiography about her childhood, *The Road from Coorain*.[7] The outback remained her sense of place all her life.

The book opens with her descriptions of the well-remembered and deeply internalized landscape around the childhood farm. Conway boarded at high school, attended university in Sydney, graduate school in the USA, and lived the academic life in Toronto and Massachusetts but always returned to the farm until the family sold it.

After decades of living in the United States, Conway's memories are rendered into word pictures as precise and evocative as actual paintings. These are the opening paragraphs of *The Road from Coorain*,

The Western Plains of New South Wales are grasslands.
Their vast expanse flows for many hundreds of miles
beyond the Lachlan and Murrumbidgee rivers until the
desert takes over and sweeps inland to the dead heart of
the continent. In a good season, if the eyes are turned to
the earth on those plains, they see a tapestry of delicate
life—not the luxuriant design of a book of hours by any
means, but a tapestry nonetheless, designed by a spare
modern artist. What grows there hugs the earth firmly with
its extended system of roots above which the plant life is
delicate but determined. After rain there is an explosion
of growth. Nut-flavored green grass puts up the thinnest
of green spears. Wild grains appear, grains which develop
bleached gold ears as they ripen. Purple desert peas weave
through the green and gold, and bright yellow bachelor's
buttons cover acres at a time, like fields planted with mus-
tard. Closest to the earth is trefoil clover, whose tiny, vivid
green leaves and bright flowers creep along the ground in
spring, to be replaced by a harvest of seed-filled burrs in
autumn—burrs which store within them the energy of the
sun as concentrated protein. At the edges of pans of clay,
where the topsoil has eroded, live waxy succulents bearing
bright pink and purple blooms, spreading like splashes of
paint dropped in widening circles on the earth.[8]

In the above passage Conway evokes the sense of sight remembered, and possibly embellished by memory. She continues with similar descriptions,

Above the plants that creep across the ground are the
bushes, which grow wherever an indentation in the earth,

scarcely visible, allows for the concentration of more
moisture from the dew and the reluctant rain. There is the
ever-present-round mound of prickly weed, which begins
its life an intense acid green with hints of yellow. As it ages,
its root system weakens so that on windy days the wind
will pick it out of the earth like whirling suns in a Van
Gogh painting. Where the soil contains limestone, stronger
bushes grow, sometimes two to three feet high, with the
delicate narrow-leaved foliage of arid climates, bluish-green
and dusty grey, perfectly adapted to resist the drying sun.
Where the soil is less porous, and water will lie for a while
after rain, comes the annual saltbush, a miraculous sil-
ver-grey plant that stores its water in small balloon-like
round leaves and thrives lone after the rains have vanished.
Its sterner perennial cousin, which resembles sagebrush,
rises on woody branches and rides out the strongest wind.[9]

Note the systematic way Conway layers her descriptions of
the vegetation, like a scientist classifying species, bringing order to a
natural sprawl,

Very occasionally, where a submerged watercourse rises a
little nearer the surface of the earth, a group of eucalyptus
trees will cluster. Worn and gnarled by wind and lack of
moisture, they rise up on the horizon so dramatically they
appear like an assemblage of local deities. Because heat
and mirages make them float in the air, they seem from
the distance like surfers endlessly riding the plains above a
silvery wave. The ocean they ride is blue-grey, silver, green,
yellow, scarlet, and bleached gold, highlighting the red clay
tones of the earth to provide a rich palette illuminated by

brilliant sunshine, or on a grey day a subdued blending of tones like those observed on a calm sea.[10]

Conway is now adding an associative process to her landscape memories. The eucalyptus trees take on dreamlike qualities,

> The creatures that inhabit this earth carry its colors in their feathers, furs, or scales. Among the largest denizens are emus, six-foot-high flightless birds with dun-grey feathers and tiny wings, and kangaroos. Kangaroos, like emus, are silent creatures, two to eight feet tall, and ranging in color from the gentlest dove-grey to a rich red brown. Both species blend with their native earth so well that one can be almost upon them before recognizing the familiar shape. The fur of wild dogs has the familiar yellow of sunbaked clay, and the reptiles, snakes, snakes and goannas, look like the earth in shadow. All tread on the fragile habitat with padded paws and claws which leave the roots of the grass intact.[11]

She reminisces on how the animals that surrounded her blended so precisely through natural camouflage into her overall sense of place,

> On the plains, the earth meets the sky in a sharp black line so regular that it seems as though drawn by a creator interested more in geometry than the hills and valleys of the Old Testament. Human purposes are dwarfed by such a blank horizon. When we see it from an island in a vast ocean we know we are resting in shelter. On the plains, the horizon is always with us and there is no retreating from it. Its blankness travels with our every step and waits for us at every point of the compass. Because we have very few

reference points on the spare earth, we seem to creep over it, one tiny point of consciousness between the empty earth and the overarching sky. Because of the flatness, contrasts are in a strange scale.[12]

As you read, you may wonder at the almost detached way Conway conveys her sense of place. And you are correct to wonder. Coorain is both a place of awe for Conway as she revels in the stark, natural beauty, but it appears also as a place of deep pain,

> A scarlet sunset will highlight grey-yellow tussocks of grass as though they were trees. Thunderclouds will mount thousands of feet above one stunted tree in the foreground. A horseback rider on the horizon will seem to rise up and emerge from the clouds. While the patterns of the earth are in small scale, akin to complex needlepoint on a vast tapestry, the sky is all drama. Cumulus clouds pile up over the center of vast continental spaces, and the wind moves them at dramatic pace along the horizon or over our heads. The ever-present red dust of a dry earth hangs in the air and turns all the colors from yellow through orange and red to purple on and off as the clouds bend and refract the light. Sunrise and sunset make up in drama for the fact there are so few songbirds in that part of the bush. At sunrise, great shafts of gold precede the baroque sunburst. At sunset, the cumulus ranges through the shades of a Turner seascape before the sun dives below the earth leaving no afterglow, but at the horizon, tongues of fire.[13]

As William Wordsworth observed in the preface to *The Lyrical Ballads* a sense of place is, "emotions recollected in tranquility." This is as true of Conway's observations, as of so many other authors writing of their childhood *milieus.*

Conway was an isolated child. At nine years old, she was expected to work with her two older brothers and father on the sheep farm. She never had a 'normal' childhood, for as soon as she could handle simple tasks, she had responsibilities around the farmhouse. Conway was soon baked into a lonely, shy girl, a shyness and reserve, as she confesses late in the book, she always carried with her.

After years of drought in the outback with the farm on the verge of bankruptcy, Conway's disappointed and desperate father committed suicide. Her beloved oldest brother died in a racing car accident. Her mother's behavior became more and more erratic.

The mind structure of Conway's sense of place is fretted with sadness and a sense of loss. The place exists, it is real, but her depiction is a mélange of associative thoughts. Invariably her mind structure of *Coorain* is not in and of itself, real.

Inside Apartheid: One Woman's Struggle in South Africa

In 1986 I began writing my political memoir *Inside Apartheid*[14]. Like Conway and Douglas, I, too, felt compelled to write of the places of my heart. Both to ease my loss of my motherland—and to counterpoint the dark political struggle I was writing about—with a sense of the eternal beauty of the country. This was my mind structure as I wrote this chapter. But my sense of place is as fresh for me now as it was then. Here are several short excerpts,

> "But Your Country Is Beautiful."
>
> Many people who visit South Africa make this comment about the striking landscapes; it is almost as if they utter these words in compensation for having been

condemnatory of the racial policies of the apartheid
regime. Indeed, it is a magnificently beautiful country,
and the physical beauty of the land resonated somewhere
deep within me, striking the core of my being. If I dig
deep enough, something essential, powerfully meaningful,
beneath and beyond sensory perceptions.[15]

...

Africa lost Africa. The fish eagle swooping for bream,
the vast sea of floating green papyrus grass, the white-red,
bejeweled, fingernail-sized tree frogs clinging to the reeds
with tiny, five-fingered hands outstretched, the thousand-
bird-wing-rush at dawn, the glowing fireflies at dusk, the
musk-scented flagrant-crimson flowers, the sun, filtered
through the haze of wood smoke, dark grey-green mist
wrapping the tall, unmoving Livingstone palms, lilac and
pink water lilies, soft in the pools, mirrored and mirroring—watery land, land of water.

The fish eagle cries from the tall lightning-struck tree at
the water's edge, stridently emblematic of a place I love, the
Okavango Swamps in northern Botswana.[16]

...

Another African sunset became the backdrop for another quintes-
sentially African scene, this one in Londolozi Game Reserve, about 40
miles west of Kruger National Park.

Dusk—an almost cloudless sky, a cool breeze in the late
autumn air, the open plain in front of us. In the middle
distance a herd of wildebeest rested near a water hole. Five
male sentinels stood guard dotted around the periphery

of the herd. The younger animals were ensconced amid the others.

"Shall we have our drinks here?" asked Pete, the young blond game ranger.

It would be majestic to watch the sunset from there. Already the far rim of hills was a black silhouette. The grasses, waving gently in the breeze, tossed back at us the pink glow of sunset on their feathered plumes.

Iconic—a primeval African plain at sunset.

Lucas, the Black tracker, went to the back of the Jeep to take out the cooler bag with the drinks. In a low, urgent voice he muttered to Pete, our ranger guide, in his native Shangaan.

Pete turned slowly in his seat and then started the engine. Lucas assumed his station on the hood, his legs resting over the grille of the front fender.

"Cheetah!" said Pete, "Over there…they're stalking."

My heart raced faster. Cheetah were the rarest and the most sought-after game to view. I had seen them before, but only in the distance, in Wankie, in Kruger, but not like this, from an open Jeep in a private game park.

My young sons, Roger and Tony, were rigid with excitement. They were both passionate about cheetah, whose poster pictures festooned their bedrooms. A favorite fantasy game of theirs, when they were preschoolers, was to spend hours stalking around the house on all fours, communicating with high-pitched squeaks and whistles. 'Cheet,' Tony would call lovingly to Roger. 'Come here, cheet.' They had not seen a cheetah in the wild.

"There he is," breathed Pete, having turned the Jeep in a half-circle.

We followed his pointing finger but saw nothing, then I caught the movement of a flickering ear above the tall grasses. Pete drove the Jeep closer to a young male. He was sitting on his haunches, his forelegs stiff on the ground. He watched the wildebeest with a frozen stare.

Lucas muttered to Pete again. Binoculars up, I followed the general direction of his pointing arm. Far around to our right was another cheetah, inching its way forward on its belly. The sun, a fiery orb across the plain, shone into its eyes. Behind us, the eastern horizon was a pink glow. The sun had not yet reached the distant western hills.

Lucas pointed again: yet a third cheetah was away to our left. It was trotting closer to the herd, its movement scarcely discernible in the darkening, lengthening shadows.

Our cheetah began to move, too, trotting slowly in line with its companion to the left. They were upwind from the wildebeest, who, although they could not smell the cheetah, were becoming restless. We could hear the guards snorting, the herd shuffling in the grasses.

In the fading light we watched through the binoculars the now slithering cheetah away to our right. It was obvious that he was going to charge the herd and try to turn it toward his two companions.

Taut with tension we drove on about thirty feet behind our steadily trotting cheetah. We followed him around thorn trees, over rocks and anthills, down small *dongas* (eroded gullies) and up the other side.

Still dusk but dark enough around us for Lucas, now perched at the back of the Jeep to have taken out two huge spotlights. But he did not turn them on yet. The cheetah was a moving shadow ahead, the herd of wildebeest a blackening stain in the sea of grass. Stars pricked their way through the darkening sky behind us. A band of gold played on the horizon where the sun had set, the glory of its blood-red leaving still reflected in the few wispy clouds over the western horizon.

Suddenly, wheeling as one, the heard galloped off to the west, the one direction where no cheetah lay in wait. In seconds our cheetah was running at full speed, sixty miles an hour. Lucas fleetingly held the spotlight on his streaking figure, but we would not be able to catch him, for he moved with a fluidity that seemed to deny that he was moving at all. The air was filled with the sound of galloping hoofs, and we were thrown around in the Jeep while Pete tried to follow Lucas's directions to bring us after the cheetah. The Jeep hit a rock, and we were thrown forward in an almighty jolt.

"Don't you think..." I began, but Pete was not about to listen to my reservations about our safety. His job was to take us to the cheetah. I did not know whether to be relieved or sorry when the Jeep's gears were crashed into reverse and we were off again. "Hold tight, you two!"

My anxious voice admonished the boys. "Oh, Mom!" Derision was the tone of their response. We stopped on a grassy knoll.

In the spotlight I saw the herd standing still, grazing peacefully. Before I could ask a puzzled question of Pete, Lucas's hand-held spotlight picked out three pairs of eyes on the ground a short distance from the herd. The cheetah were already feeding on a young wildebeest.

We watched them for a while.

The surrounding hills were a dark rim at the periphery of the earth. The moon was rising, three-quarters full, and beginning to cast night shadows among the thorn bushes.

"Well, I guess that's it, then?" Pete, his job done, was inhaling on a Camel, his feet relaxed on the front of the Jeep. I nodded.

Almost sedately we regained the sandy road and, under the inverted bowl of the eternal African night sky, finally had that drink.[17]

There are many more impressions of the natural beauty of South Africa that I carry within me. Several more follow,

I have stood at the edge of the world and seen an ocean of cloud two thousand feet below me. It is difficult to find words to describe the beauty of the Drakensberg Mountains of South Africa. For be it Injusti in the Royal Natal National Park, or camps in Giant's Castle, there is a splendor to the earth there, where mountaintop meets the aery light of the African sky.

Like a discover full of wonder, I want to recount what I have seen living on inside me. The colors of the Drakensberg stretch away in front of me, five layers of mountaintops, dark green-gold in the foreground, grey-purple, then purple-black, a lighter blue-grey and, towering in the far distance, light blue jagged peaks.

The red-orange and orange-yellow of ericas and aloes, the pink-red of sugar bush proteas, the various shades of everlasting daisies. Blue agapanthus, salmon-pink watsonias, green alpine grasses carpeting the lower slopes dotted with tiny ground-hugging yellow and blue wildflowers and grasses.

I have also seen baboons, rock rabbits, small buck, and the magnificent lammergeyer riding on air currents; Bushmen paintings, too, of eland, rhino, and strange men in ritual headdresses at Giant's Castle.

The wind rising against the escarpment can blow a waterfall back up the mountain and send plumes of clouds of water vapor streaming through chasms and ravines hundreds of feet into the air.

And at sunrise, at the edge of a precipice, at the edge of the world, layered bands of dark clouds catch the rays of the sun, turning crimson, orange, then gold as the sunlight transforms the cloud ocean below into a solid plane of shifting color.

In the cool of the late afternoon, sitting at an ice-cold rushing stream, you can watch the magnificent white thunderheads build and build behind the mountain ramparts, while at night, if you stand in the cold stillness of the brooding mountain quiet and see the stars, I mean really see the stars, the night sky will dazzle you with its remote alien beauty, for as John Buchan wrote, "the southern constellations blaze in a profound sky."

Come, walk with me along any of the mountain paths, through the mountain forests, and grasslands, for this six-hundred-mile mountain range is wild and beautiful, is Africa, is the county to which I belong and which I love.[18]

You may have noticed in these excerpts from three writers, two similarities emerge, one, the fact that they describe a sense of place that is *south*: Australia in the southern hemisphere; the Everglades: on the east coast the southernmost part of North America, and South Africa on the southern tip of the African continent. The other similarity is that in these places, the sun is vibrant, stunningly bright, burnishing the landscape both the land and the mind structure of the beholder.

In an equatorial place, the Caribbean, a sense of place equally seared by sunlight, is likewise present. This is the milieu of celebrated, 1982 Nobel Prize winner for Literature, Gabriel García Márquez. Márquez was born in 1927 in Columbia. He died in 2014 having lived most of his life in Mexico City, in political exile for his activism in Colombia. A journalist by training, he wrote novels, short stories, and non-fiction.[19] He is acknowledged as one of the great literary figures of the 20th century.

Márquez created the literary genre of 'magical realism' in which he mingled magical elements among real places and events, embedding them in ordinary, realistic situations. This literary construct becomes the third element that comprises a sense of place—memories, associative processes, and magical realism. The two words 'magical' and 'realism' together are not an oxymoron, but rather a breakthrough, syntactical literary device.

Perhaps, in creating this genre, Gabriel García Márquez stumbled upon the essential nature of mind structures—those individual and societal mores both real and unreal. Perhaps what he is saying is that each of us clings to our belief system not realizing it is ever-changing, as well as to the socio-political-spiritually evolving matrix of ideas swirling around us, in which—at any one time—we believe or do not believe.

CONCLUSION

A classic chicken and egg conundrum—our mind structures are partially shaped by the paradigms of literature and literature created through the lens of writers' mind structures.

As I suggest in the Introduction, perhaps after reading the extracts from these texts and the ideas merged within them, we can see possibilities to broaden and even shift our mind structures and thus aspects of our worldviews. Hopefully, the book suggests ways for you to accommodate to this groundbreaking awareness of how our consciousness operates when creativity and great ideas in literature amalgamate.

This book is innovative in how it approaches integrating literature and socio-political ideas into a coherent understanding of mind structures. Maybe some of these ideas unsettle, puzzle or intrigue you. While others you easily dismiss. Many such responses arise from your mind structure. Great literature can trigger "ah-ha" moments or shift your mind structure over time. As we read, we may be moved by visceral reactions to the writer's intellect, emotions, and psycho-spiritual creativity but seldom do you pause to say, "My mind structure is changing." We may say, "this blew my mind," and weeks or months later realize we are contemplating aspects of our consciousness with shifted insights; much like Plato's cave dwellers moving from a world of shadows into a world lit by awareness of newly acquired inner mind structure modifications.

Let us revisit some of the "caves" in which we dwell, seen now in light of reading this book. The sins of omission or commission—experiences in a Nazi concentration camp—with Jean Meyer and Primo Levi. Explorations into the complex relationship dynamic of Michael or Hanna or both in the aftermath of Nazi Germany's holocaust. David Lurie's redemptive journey in post-apartheid South Africa entwined with the changing circumstances of Lucy's or Petrus' lives.

Buddhist philosophy and practices add insight into our mind structures—as we follow Siddhartha—and learn of his malleable, changing mind structure that enables him to learn (or not) from the wisdom embedded in his own and others' teaching.

Hamlet, our touchstone to Western individualism, in his struggles to free himself from hierarchical and paternalistic bonds of the societal mind structure into which he was born.

Shafts of light that shine into the nature of reality and illusion.

Our place in the universe (or multi-verses) as we try to grasp concepts of time through Lightman's futuristic visions, T.S. Eliot's conceptual schemas and Woolf's eternal moments.

Plato's *The Republic* arousal of echoes of our current twenty-first century perilous dynamics of governance. Plato's metaphor of the pendulum swing of political ideologies—swinging now left and now right—and the rise and collapse of states and empires have historical validity for us in the present moment. Ideas like the "myth of the metals" and the "noble lie" may enlighten our mind structure to understand ignoble lies such as misnomers' "fake news" or "alternative facts." Our understanding of excerpts from *The Republic* may preclude your mind structure or belief system from further adherence to any political system knowing of the impermanence of all political ideologies.

The emphasis on a sense of place and mystery highlights the power of associative thinking in our mind structures.

Reading Matters is a foray into mind structures and literary creativity to evoke responses to enquiries posed by merging great literature with your mind structure. Responses and questions perhaps unwittingly posed by the writers we have read, who may have had little idea of what they were creating beyond using their talent to express their artistry and elements of their individual and collective mind structure.

I trust your adventures with these great writers have been enlightening and enjoyable.

ACKNOWLEDGMENTS

I am deeply indebted to everyone who helped with this book, whether you are mentioned here or not, whether you know you helped or not. Thank you. Special thanks and deep appreciation to my agent Mary-ann Karinch of The Rudy Agency for her unwavering support, belief in and passionate advocacy for the book. Special thanks to the entire team at Armin Lear Press, so reassuring to have your expertise and experience behind the book. Special thanks to my beloved teacher, mentor and friend from when I was a child, the late June Wilson, who opened the treasure chest of literature for me. Special thanks to Lama Surya Das, Dr. John Makransky, and the many past Dzogchen masters whose words inspire my insights into Buddhist psychology. Thanks to Mark and Carolyn for professional advice. Thanks to friends AnnaMae, Barbara, Bernice, Caddy, Carolyn F, Deval, Helaina, Katie, Leila, Margery, Merri, Milt, Nan, Rose, Tom, and Tze, and to so many colleagues in several walks of life and to my students, likewise encountered in so many settings. Last, but not least, thanks to my wonderfully supportive and caring sons, Roger, and Antony. My heartfelt and sincerest thanks and appreciation to my greatest supporter and cheerleader in the writing of this book, my friend, Franklin (Sandy) Levine, for his painstaking editorial scrutiny, patience, compassion for my wrestles with the manuscript, and for putting up with all those panicked late night phone calls.

ABOUT THE AUTHOR

JANET LEVINE was born in Johannesburg, South Africa. Levine is an author, educator, and non-profit entrepreneur. She has lived in the USA since 1984, both in Boston and in southwest Florida. Levine has decades of published writing experience both as a book author and a freelance journalist. She is the author of four published works. *Know Your Parenting Personality* (Wiley 2004); *The Enneagram Intelligences* (Greenwood Publishing Group 1999) nominated for the 2002 Grawemeyer Education Award; *Inside Apartheid* (Contemporary Books 1988); *Leela's Gift* (Lulu, 2010) and available in several editions. These books reviewed in <u>The New York Times Book Review</u>, <u>The New York Review of Books</u>, <u>The Yale Review</u>, and many other publications both paper and electronic. Her books are translated into several languages. Levine has published prolifically in magazines and professional journals as a writer both in her native South Africa and the United States. She is a book reviewer for the online <u>New York Journal of Books</u>. Her work has appeared in <u>The New York Times Sunday Magazine</u>, <u>The Sowetan</u> (in South Africa, the only white journalist to have a column in a black newspaper, 1978-1981.) <u>Boston Globe</u>, <u>Boston Phoenix,</u> and many online journals and magazines. She was interviewed by Terri Gross on *Fresh Air* and has appeared on all major TV outlets.

Levine has many years of experience as an educator and presenter. From 1986-2014 she taught in the English department at Milton Academy in Massachusetts. In 2014, she retired from her teaching career to concentrate on writing. Levine leads talks, workshops, and programs internationally on the Enneagram, reading and writing, and, occasionally, current events in South Africa. An anti-apartheid activist, she is an expert on South Africa and South African politics (see *Inside Apartheid*).

Levine was twice elected (1977 and 1982) to the Johannesburg City Council to represent the Progressive Federal Party. She was a member of many anti-apartheid organizations. Levine is the founder and leader of several successful non-profit organizations both in South Africa and the United States.

ENDNOTES

INTRODUCTION

1   Author's Note: *Reading Matters* (Additional Resources) Research on how literature changes mind structures through reading. Researchers are finding a neurological basis for this mind structure shift. As Maryanne Wolf, director of the UCLA Center for Dyslexia, explains in *Proust and the Squid: The Story and Science of the Reading Brain,* they find that the reading brain literally makes "new connections among its existing structures, a process made possible by the brain's ability to be reshaped by experience." Reading, "unlike watching or listening to media, gives the brain more time to stop, think, process, and imagine." (Thomas Oppong, "Your Brain on Reading," medium.com, May 23, 2018)

http://www.oprah.com/health/how-reading-can-improve-your-memory

https://medium.com/swlh/this-is-your-brain-on-reading-why-your-brain-needs-you-to-read-every-day-a472b04da2e0

https://www.theatlantic.com/education/archive/2014/01/study-reading-a-novel-changes-your-brain/282952/

https://www.psychologytoday.com/us/blog/the-elusive-brain/201810/the-reading-brain

CHAPTER ONE

1   Wood, James, "The Art of Witness" a review essay of an edition of the *Complete Works of Primo Levi*

in the New Yorker magazine. Published September 28, 2015

2   Published in the USA as *Survival in Auschwitz* by Collier Books, 1961

3   First published in Italian by Guilio Einaudi, Torino,1986. Published in translation in the USA as Primo   Levi, *The Drowned and the Saved.* Summit Books, 1988

4   Ibid, p. 11

5   Ibid, p. 14-15

6   Ibid, p. 16

7   Ibid, p. 17

8   Ibid, pp. 36-37

9   Ibid, p. 38

10   Ibid, p. 44

11   Ibid, p. 47

12   Ibid, p. 49

13   Ibid, p. 50

14   Ibid.

15   Ibid, p. 51

16   Ibid, p. 53

17   Ibid, p. 69

18   Schlink, Bernhard, *The Reader*. Copyright © 1995 by Diogenes Verlag AG, Zurich. Translation copyright by Carol Brown Janeway 1997

19   Ibid, p. 7

20   Ibid, p. 54

21   Ibid, p. 92

22   Ibid.

23   Ibid, p. 95

24   Ibid, p. 104

25   Ibid, p. 107

26   Ibid.

27   Ibid, p. 112

28   Ibid.

29   Ibid, p. 116

30   Ibid, p. 158

31   Ibid, p. 134

32   Ibid, pp. 150-151

33   Ibid.

34   Ibid, p. 152

35   Ibid.

36   Arendt, Hannah, *Eichmann in Jerusalem: A Report on the Banality of Evil* (Penguin Classics) Paperback – September 22, 2006. First published by Viking Press, 1963

37   Schlink, Bernhard, *The Reader*. Copyright © 1995 by Diogenes Verlag AG, Zurich. Translation copyright 1997 by Carol Brown Janeway.

Ibid, p. 157

CHAPTER TWO

1 J. M Coetzee, *Disgrace*. Published by Secker and Warburg, London, 1999.

2 Ibid, p. 1

3 Ibid, p. 15

4 Ibid, p. 25

5 Ibid, p. 27

6 Author's Note: After the Fall, Lucifer Became Satan, Angel of Darkness

7 Ibid, p. 32

8 Ibid, p. 38

9 Ibid, p. 59

10 Ibid, p. 61

11 Ibid.

12 Ibid, p. 64

13 Ibid, p. 78

14 Ibid, p. 79

15 Ibid.

16 Ibid, p. 94

17 Ibid, p. 95

18 Ibid, p. 96

19 Ibid, p. 107

20 Ibid, p. 114

21 Ibid, p. 115

22 Ibid, p. 122

23 Ibid, p. 133

24 Ibid, p. 140

25 Ibid.

26 Ibid, pp.140-141

27 Ibid, pp. 142-143

28 Ibid, p. 149

29 Ibid, p. 150

30 Ibid, p. 157

31 Ibid, p. 158

32 Ibid, p. 166

33 Ibid, p. 168

34 Ibid, p. 171

35 Ibid, p. 172

36 Ibid.

37 Ibid.

38 Ibid, p. 173

39 Ibid, p. 176

40 Ibid, p. 180

41 Ibid, p. 182

42 Ibid, p. 183

43 Ibid, p. 184

44 Ibid, p. 203

45 Ibid, p. 205

46 Ibid, p. 212

47 Ibid, p. 214

48 Ibid, p. 216

49 Ibid.

50 Ibid, p. 217

51 Ibid.

52 Ibid, p. 220

CHAPTER THREE

1 Jean-Francois Revel and Matthieu Ricard; *The Monk and the Philosopher*. Schocken Books, New York, 1999

2 Ibid, p. 7

3 Hermann Hesse; *Siddhartha*. Bantam edition, New York, 1971

4 Ibid, p. 3

5 Ibid, p. 4

6 Ibid, p. 5

7 Ibid, p. 7

8   Ibid, pp. 14-15

9   Ibid, p. 20

10   Ibid, p. 28-29

11   Ibid, p. 30

12   Ibid, p. 33

13   Ibid.

14   Ibid, p. 35

15   Ibid.

16   Ibid, p. 47

17   Ibid, p. 49

18   Ibid, p. 71

19   Ibid, p. 72

20   Ibid, p. 73

21   Ibid, p. 83

22   Ibid, p. 84

23   Ibid, p. 87

24   Ibid, p. 89

25   Ibid, p. 95

26   Ibid, p. 100

27   Ibid, p. 107

28   Ibid, p. 119

29   Ibid, p. 132

30   Ibid, pp. 135-136

31   Ibid.

32   Ibid, p. 137

33   Ibid, p. 142

34   Ibid, p. 145

35   Ibid.

36   Ibid, p. 151

37   Ibid, p. 152

38   Chögyam Trungpa. *Shambhala: The Sacred Path of The Warrior.*

Shambhala Press, 1988

39 Ibid, p.13

40 Garnick, Evan. From essay

41 Oursler, Addie. From essay

42 *Hamlet*, Act 1, scene, lines 210-211

43 Ibid.

44 Ibid, Act 2, scene 2, lines 68-70

CHAPTER FOUR

1   William Shakespeare. *Hamlet.* Washington Square Press, New York.
    Copyright Folger Shakespeare Library, 1992

2   Ibid.

3   Ibid.

4   Ibid.

5   John-Paul Sartre. *Being and Nothingness* (first published 1943 in French
    by Éditions Gallimard); Washington Square Press. 1993, New York

6   John Milton. *Paradise Lost.*

7   William Shakespeare. *Hamlet.* Washington Square Press, New York.
    Copyright Folger Shakespeare Library, 1992

8   Ibid.

9   Ibid.

10 Ibid.

11 Ibid.

12 Authors note: Dovetailing with the play's central theme of revenge
    cycles

13 Ibid.

14 Ibid.

15 Ibid.

16 Ibid.

17 Ibid.

18 Ibid.

19 Ibid.

20 Ibid.

21   Ibid.

22   Ibid.

23   Ibid.

24   Ibid.

25   Ibid.

26   Ibid.

27   Ibid.

28   Ibid.

29   Ibid.

30   Ibid.

31   Ibid.

32   Ibid.

33   Ibid.

34   Author's note: An unexpected and extraneous plot device in a play or novel.

35   Author's note: "Disassociation" describes this psychological state as a variety of experiences ranging from mild and temporary detachment from one's familiar surroundings to more severe detachment from physical reality.

36   Ibid.

37   Ibid.

38   Ibid.

39   Ibid.

40   Ibid.

41   Ibid.

42   Ibid.

43   Ibid.

44   Author's note: "Rudimentary" because Shakespeare had no psychological sources to reference.

45   Author's note: In Greek mythology Hyperion was one of the original twelve Titan offspring of the Earth goddess, Gaia. The inference is clear, his father was a Titan among men.

46   Author's note: Niobe: In Greek Mythology, Niobe was so grief-stricken

at the loss of her children

that she could not cease crying and was transformed into a stone from which water continually flowed.

47 Author's note: In Roman mythology Hercules was the Roman name for the Greek hero, Herakles, son of the mighty god Zeus and a mortal woman. Herakles is famous for his strength and adventures.

48 Ibid.

49 Ibid.

50 Ibid.

51 Ibid.

52 Ibid.

53 Ibid.

54 Ibid.

55 Ibid.

56 Ibid.

57 Author's note: Bergson's most famous works are *Time and Free Will* (1889), *Matter and Memory* (1896), *Creative Evolution* (1907) and *The Two Sources of Morality and Religion* (1932)

CHAPTER FIVE

1 Alan Lightman. *Einstein's Dreams,* Warner Books Edition, New York. 1994

2 Ibid, pp. 3-4

3 Kern, Stephen: *The Culture of Time and Space*, Harvard University Press (2003)

4 *Einstein's Dreams*, Ibid, pp. 3-4

5 Ibid, p. 8

6 Ibid, p. 9

7 Ibid.

8 Ibid, p. 8

9 Ibid, pp. 10-11

10 Ibid, p. 11

11 Ibid.

12 Ibid, p. 12

13 Ibid, p. 13

14 Ibid, p. 14

15 Ibid, p. 16

16 Ibid, p. 33

17 Ibid, p. 34

18 Ibid, p. 35

19 Ibid, p. 37

20 Ibid, p. 68

21 Ibid.

22 Ibid, p. 130

23 Ibid, pp. 130-131

24 Ibid, pp. 178-179

25 T.S. Eliot. *The Four Quartets*. Faber & Faber Limited, London. 1968. This edition copyright Valerie Eliot 1968

26 Sartre's built his existentialist theories on the nihilistic philosophy of 19th century German philosopher, Friedrich Nietzsche. Nietzsche famously affirmed the centrality of human existence declaring the death of God. He also affirmed that political struggles are a clash of human wills and the group with the greatest will to power succeeds. In his work *Übermensch* he laid out many precepts that influenced Hitler's Nazism.

27 T.S. Eliot. *The Four Quartets*.

Ibid, p. 11

28 Ibid.

29 Ibid, p. 13

30 Ibid.

31 From "Among School Children" in *Collected Poems* of W. B. Yeats: A New Edition edited by Richard Finneran. MacMillan Publishing in 1933.

32 Shakespeare William, *The Tempest*, Folger Shakespeare Library, 2009

33 T.S. Eliot. *The Four Quartets*.

Ibid, p. p.14

34 Ibid, p. 21

35 Ibid.

36 Ibid, p. 22

37 Ibid, pp. 22-23

38 Ibid, p. 36

39 Ibid, p. 37

40 Nietzsche, Friedrich. 'On the Advantage and Disadvantage of History for Us," an essay written in 1874.

41 Ibid.

42 T.S. Eliot. *The Four Quartets*

    Ibid, p. 37

    Ibid.

43 Author's Note: This line may reference that of Percy Bysshe Shelley, another English poet: "Wild Spirit, which art moving everywhere;/ Destroyer and preserver; hear, oh hear!" "Ode to the West Wind" by Percy Bysshe Shelley (written in 1819). Published in a collection of his poems *Prometheus Unbound* by Charles and Edmund Ollier, London, 1820.

44 T.S. Eliot. *The Four Quartets*.

    Ibid, p. 46

45 Ibid.

46 Author's Note: Many spiritual traditions abide by this tradition of humbling yourself through prostration, kneeling, or even lying prone on the floor or ground, arms stretched in front of you. One exception is Judaism.

47 Ibid, p. 46-47

48 Ibid, p. 47

49 Ibid, p. 54

50 Ibid.

51 Ibid.

52 Ibid.

53 Author's Note: Symbolism of the rose. Some critics trace this symbol to the works of Dante's *Inferno* and Tennyson's *Maud* both of which Eliot knew well.

54 Ibid.

55 Ibid, p. 55

56 Ibid.

CHAPTER SIX

1 Woolf, Virginia. *To The Lighthouse*, first published by Hogarth Press, 1927. Virginia and her husband, Harold Woolf, owned and operated the press in their home. Edition used here first published under by Harcourt copyright 1927.

2 Ibid, pp. 28-29

3 Ibid, pp. 38-39

4 Ibid, pp. 16-17

5 Ibid, p. 49

6 Ibid, p. 38

7 Ibid, pp. 33-34

8 Ibid, p. 44

9 Ibid, pp. 14-15

10 Ibid, pp. 62-63

11 Ibid.

12 Ibid, p. 64

13 Ibid, pp. 64-65

14 Ibid, p. 105

15 Ibid, pp. 109-111

16 Ibid, p. 128

17 Ibid, p. 133

18 Ibid, p. 138

19 Ibid, p. 178

20 Ibid, pp. 178-179

21 Ibid, pp. 193-194

22 Virginia Woolf: *Holograph Draft: To The Lighthouse* first published 1983.

23 Ibid, p. 102

24 Ibid, pp. 125-126

25 Ibid, p. 126

26 Ibid.

27 Ibid, pp. 133-134

28 Ibid, p. 134

29 Ibid, p. 143

30 Ibid, p. 145

31 Ibid, p. Author's Note: Another penile reference

32 Ibid, p. 186

33 Ibid, p. 187

34 Ibid.

35 Ibid, p. 203

36 Ibid, p. 159

37 Ibid

38 Ibid, p. 161

39 Ibid.

40 Ibid, p. 173

41 Author's Note: My parenthesis

42 Ibid, p. 193

43 Ibid, pp. 193-194

44 Ibid, pp. 195-196

45 Ibid, p. 201

46 Ibid, pp. 201-202

47 Ibid, p. 202

48 Ibid, pp. 208-209

CHAPTER SEVEN

1 Plato. *The Republic.* Richard W. Sterling and William C. Scott, translators, Plato: The Republic, Norton Paperback edition, 1996.

2 Author's note: I use the term proto-democracy because there was no universal suffrage in Athens. In South Africa when I was growing up, the apartheid government also governed a proto or partial democracy (whites-only electorate) until 1960 when it pivoted away from democracy to a militarized police state.

3 Andrew Sullivan, "Democracies End When They Are Too Democratic", (New York Magazine: May 2, 2016)

4 Author's Note: It is interesting to note that Aristotle's *Nicomachean Ethics* argues the same pendulum swing of political movements.

5   Plato. *The Republic.*

    Ibid, p. 53

6   W. B. Yeats "The Second Coming" written in 1919. First published by *The Dial* in 1920.

7   Plato. *The Republic.*

    Ibid, p. 137

8   Brad Desnoyer is a law professor at the University of Missouri Law School. This excerpt from an article "Founding Fathers Agreed: Funding public education is not a debate." Published in St. Louis-Dispatch, March 3, 2014

9   Plato. *The Republic*

    Ibid, p. 165

10 Ibid, p. 113

11 Ibid.

12 Ibid, p. 73

13 Ibid, p. 77

14 Ibid, p. 178

15 Ibid, p. 209

16 Ibid, p. 210

17 Ibid.

18 Author's Note: Common knowledge

19 Ibid, p. 204. A Diagrammatic Rendering.

    (The Divided Line: The Four Stages of Cognition according to Plato's prescriptions pp. 196-199)

20 Ibid, p. 195

21 Leo Tolstoy. *The Death of Ivan Ilyich.* Translation copyright Bantam Books, 1981. (Translated by Lynn Solotaroff). Published by Bantam Classics, New York, 1981.

22 Ibid, p. 66

23 Ibid, p. 83

24 Ibid, pp. 103-105

25 Ibid, p.120

26 Ibid, p. 126

27   Ibid, p. 132

28   Ibid.

29   Ibid, pp. 133-134

30   Author's Note: Not only Tolstoy but many medical and care professionals report evidence of this death light, as do many who have recorded near death experiences.

CHAPTER EIGHT

1   Douglas, Marjory Stoneman. *Everglades River of Grass*. Published by Rinehart & Company, New York, 1947

2   Ibid, pp. 5-6

3   Ibid, p. 6

4   Ibid, pp. 8-9

5   Ibid.

6   Ibid, pp. 12-13

7   Ker Conway, Jill. *The Road from Coorain*. Published by Alfred A. Knopf, Inc, New York, 1989

8   Ibid, p. 3

9   Ibid.

10   Ibid.

11   Ibid, pp. 4-5

12   Ibid.

13   Ibid.

14   Levine, Janet. *Inside Apartheid*. Published by Contemporary Books, Chicago, 1988

15   Ibid, p. 95

16   Ibid, p. 102

17   Ibid, pp. 106-108

18   Ibid, pp. 108-109

19   Author's Note: Two of Márquez's most famous works are the novels, *One Hundred Years of Solitude* and *Love in the Time of Cholera*